THE
SEMINARIAN

THE
SEMINARIAN

Martin Luther King Jr.
Comes of Age

PATRICK PARR

Lawrence Hill Books
Chicago

Copyright © 2018 by Patrick Parr
All rights reserved
Published by Lawrence Hill Books
an imprint of Chicago Review Press Incorporated
814 North Franklin Street
Chicago, Illinois 60610
978-0-915864-12-6

Library of Congress Cataloging-in-Publication Data
Is available from the Library of Congress.

Sketch artwork: Wayne Watson
Typesetting: Nord Compo

Printed in the United States of America
5 4 3 2 1

For Norma Frank and 後藤 由紀

Contents

Year III: Revelation

Appendixes

Foreword

by David J. Garrow

PATRICK PARR'S *The Seminarian: Martin Luther King Jr. Comes of Age* is without question the most original and important book about King's life to appear in more than a quarter century, since Keith D. Miller's *Voice of Deliverance: The Language of Martin Luther King, Jr., and Its Sources* was published in 1992.

The depth and thoroughness of Parr's research is nothing short of astounding. To take the most striking example, over thirty years ago I discreetly published the name of King's Crozer Seminary girlfriend, Betty Moitz, in an endnote,[1] but the people-search technologies of the early 1980s afforded a young historian few options for finding someone whose marital surname was unknown, and King's life from 1955 onward, not his seminary experience, was my primary focus.

Three decades later, not only did Parr find his way to Moitz and coax her to talk frankly to him about her long-ago romance, but he also carried out the difficult legwork that is the real meat of historical research: carefully reviewing the seminary's local newspaper, the *Chester Times*, for all its stories about life at Crozer and its mentions of King, and mining the seminary's own old academic records for the light they could shed on the content and progression of King's coursework. In so doing, Parr has gone well beyond all prior scholars, and he offers what

without doubt will always remain the utterly definitive account of Martin
Luther King Jr.'s life from 1948 to 1951.

Not only is this a book of exceptional and unparalleled historical richness, it is also most approachably and felicitously written. One need not
be a King scholar, or a student of Protestant theology, to understand and
appreciate the compelling and insightful narrative that Parr offers chapter
after chapter. His detailed reconstruction of King's academic coursework
will impress the most demanding of scholars, but his always empathetic
and persuasive interpretations of King's development, personal as well as
intellectual, will appeal to all interested readers of whatever background.

In addition to Betty Moitz, Parr also brings to the fore a half dozen
or more other influential figures in King's early life whom history should
remember better than it has to date. His portrayal of King's relationship with Martin Luther King Sr. is original and convincing. Chester's
Rev. J. Pius Barbour stood second only to King's father in his paternal
and pastoral influence on the young preacher, and King's fellow African American seminary classmates Walter McCall, Horace Whitaker,
and Marcus Wood all receive their well-deserved due, too. Parr likewise
offers the best portraits to date of King's faculty instructors, particularly
Kenneth L. Smith, and he similarly provides the best existing account
of King's intellectual forays at the nearby University of Pennsylvania.

Yet without question it is Parr's gentle, respectful, and pioneering
analysis of King's intense youthful love for Betty Moitz that will draw the
most attention to this book. Thirty years ago I offered only a one-paragraph
account of that romance,[2] but, unable to find Moitz herself, I did not
accord that indelible life experience more attention. Now Patrick Parr has
done the seemingly impossible, reaching back across more than *sixty-five
years* to record and recount Moitz's own memories of her relationship with
King. It is a powerful and painful story, a deeply personal testament to how
the racial—or *racist*—strictures that so severely limited Americans' lives in
the mid–twentieth century fundamentally altered the life course of even
so well-advantaged a young African American as Martin Luther King Jr.

In short, *The Seminarian* is a work of top-notch scholarship and insightful reflection. It makes a remarkable, landmark contribution to our understanding of Martin Luther King Jr.'s life, and it will forever remain on the
very top shelf of all books that seek to illuminate how King's legacy should
continue to inspire all of us.

Note to the Reader

TWENTY-SIX YEARS and ten months.

That's how old Martin Luther King Jr. was on December 5, 1955, the day Montgomery, Alabama, civic activist Rufus Lewis nominated him to be the president of the newly formed Montgomery Improvement Association. By then, King was a husband and father and a reverend with a doctorate, and Lewis saw in his Dexter Avenue Baptist pastor just the right mix to appeal to the black community, even if King seemed "more like a boy than a man" in appearance.[1]

Lewis's nomination during that afternoon meeting marked a turning point: in the next twelve years King rose from relative obscurity—leading the successful 381-day Montgomery bus boycott, writing the "Letter from a Birmingham Jail," co-orchestrating the March on Washington, receiving the 1964 Nobel Peace Prize, and serving as the driving force behind the Voting Rights Act—to become the legendary figure we now know.

The Seminarian is not about this twelve-year period in Martin Luther King Jr.'s life, about which so much has already been written. Instead, it focuses on a formative time before his rise to prominence—specifically, the three years he spent studying at Crozer Theological Seminary in Chester, Pennsylvania, between 1948 and 1951. Biographers and historians have described these years briefly but never fully. In fact, they have detailed very little about King's day-to-day life pre-Montgomery, so much of this book, laid out chronologically, term by term, will be new information not just to the general reading public but also to researchers eager to learn more about King's life before the boycott. It will explore fully for the first time the contributions of many figures who contributed to King's development as a young man—individuals such as Rev. J. Pius Barbour, Walter McCall, Horace Whitaker, Betty Moitz, Kenneth Smith, and Marcus Wood.

Throughout the book, I refer to King as "ML," the nickname by which his family and most of his friends called him. Though he also went by other names,* I chose to use "ML" because it suggests a more informal and personal perspective on King while also evoking his common appellation "MLK." This is in keeping with my larger goal of showing the connections between the young man he was at the time and the icon he would eventually become.

Some readers may be surprised by exactly *how* young ML was when he entered his first year at Crozer, a college graduate at only nineteen years of age. This is because he skipped the ninth and twelfth grades of high school, due not to incredible academic performance but to fortuitous timing. When the Atlanta Laboratory School closed down in his ninth-grade year, thirteen-year-old ML was allowed to enter Booker T. Washington High School as a tenth-grader. And by the time he finished the eleventh grade, World War II had caused such a downturn in college enrollment that the president of Morehouse College, Benjamin E. Mays, decided to take advantage of a recent Georgia state law and accept promising high school juniors. King passed the admissions test and became an undergraduate at Morehouse at the age of fifteen, while still living at home. He graduated at nineteen, and the following fall he began his studies at Crozer Theological Seminary.

---

* King was also called "Martin," of course, especially during the civil rights movement. As a boy he was known as "Little Mike," and several Morehouse College classmates called him "Big Mike." The "Mike" nicknames derived from a mistake made by Dr. Charles Johnson, who delivered King Jr. around noon on January 15, 1929, in the King family home on Auburn Avenue in Atlanta. Dr. Johnson filled in "Michael" on his birth certificate after Martin Luther King Sr. requested his son be named after him. Dr. Johnson was a friend of the family, having also delivered King Jr.'s older sister, Christine, and had always called Daddy King "Mike." Before traveling overseas in 1934, Daddy King saw the mistake while applying for a passport. He had his son's birth certificate corrected, but along Auburn Avenue the nickname stuck.

Prologue
On a Bus in Georgia, April 1944

"It was the angriest I have ever been in my life."

—Martin Luther King Jr.[1]

ON A MONDAY AFTERNOON, April 17, 1944, Martin Luther King Jr. boarded a public bus headed for Dublin, Georgia. He was fifteen years old, and he had prepared a speech as a member of the Booker T. Washington High School debating society. The city of Dublin was hosting an oratorical contest, with the Black Elks as the sponsor, and debate teams from black high schools all over the state would be competing. As ML sat on the bus, running the lines in his head, he harbored hopes of perhaps winning first prize. "It turned out to be a memorable day," he would say two decades later.[2]

ML had little public speaking experience under his belt at the time, but one day earlier he'd edged out nine other speakers at Booker to qualify for this state contest. With him on the bus ride to Dublin was the runner-up, Hiram Kendall, as well as his teacher Miss Sarah Grace Bradley. The title of ML's speech was "The Negro and the Constitution," and with Miss Bradley's help, he had honed the grammar and rhythm of the speech to a fine point, to be complemented by his newly developed baritone voice. Now all he had to do was deliver it with authority and conviction.[3]

ML King Jr. at fifteen years old, after winning a speaking contest at Booker T. Washington High School. *From the Atlanta Daily World*

The 140-mile bus ride to Dublin went smoothly. Hiram and ML made their way into Dublin's historic First Baptist Church, where they joined the other participants—two more young men and four young women—and waited for their turn behind First Baptist's pulpit that night. Although the setting was explicitly Christian, their speeches weren't required to be.[4]

Indeed, the speech ML had prepared was not particularly religious. At this point in his life, he had little desire to follow in the footsteps of his father and grandfather and become a preacher. Still, at an early age ML knew he had a gift for the spoken word, one nurtured by his experiences at Ebenezer Baptist Church, where his father was the pastor and his mother the organist and choir director. From his mother, Alberta "Mama" King, ML inherited a strong singing voice, and any worries he may have had about appearing in front of a large crowd had vanished as he made regular appearances as a boy soloist in her choir. His father, Martin Sr.—"Daddy King"—taught his son by example: week after week after week ML listened to him pound the pulpit with his fist, sermonizing the congregation into a frenzy. In fifteen-year-old ML, these two parental dynamics—harmony and authority—were beginning to synthesize to the benefit of his oratory.[5]

When ML's turn came, he stepped up to the pulpit and started his speech. Twenty-four hours earlier he'd given the same address to a home-town audience, but this crowd was different. Besides Miss Bradley and

Hiram, the rest were strangers, including a timekeeper who would hold him to the predetermined limit.[6] Pushing away any distraction, he started:

> Negroes were first brought to America in 1620 when England legalized slavery both in England and the colonies and America; the institution grew and thrived for about 150 years upon the backs of these black men. The empire of King Cotton was built, and the southland maintained a status of life and hospitality distinctly its own and not anywhere else.
>
> On January 1, 1863, the proclamation emancipating the slaves which had been decreed by President Lincoln in September took effect—millions of Negroes faced a rising sun of a new day begun. Did they have habits of thrift or principles of honesty and integrity? Only a few! For their teachings and duties had been but two activities: love of master—right or wrong, good or bad—and loyalty to work. What was to be the place for such men in the reconstruction of the South?[7]

From his family and friends, from his schoolteachers, from the segregated community in which he grew up, ML had learned well the history of black suffering. The audience in front of him knew it well too. But ML's speech wasn't simply a historical retelling:

> Black America still wears chains. The finest Negro is at the mercy of the meanest white man. Even winners of our highest honors face the class color bar.

ML offered as an example the famous African American singer Marian Anderson, who could sing with tears in her eyes in front of the Lincoln Memorial as "seventy-five thousand people" listened with hope in their hearts, but could not "spend the night in any good hotel in America" or "be served in many of the public restaurants in her home city, even after it has declared her to be its best citizen."[8]

With World War II raging and Americans dying each day in both Europe and the Pacific, ML was careful how he characterized the injustices black Americans faced in their own backyards. He framed it as yet another national paradox: "As we gird ourselves to defend democracy from foreign attack, let us see to it that increasingly at home we give fair play and free opportunity for all people."

ML had absorbed one more crucial lesson from listening to his father and other local preachers: the importance of a strong ending. So as he wrapped up his speech that night in Dublin, he gave it his all:

> My heart throbs anew in the hope that, inspired by the example of Lincoln, imbued with the spirit of Christ, they will cast down the last barrier to perfect freedom. And I with my brother of blackest hue possessing at last my rightful heritage and holding my head erect, may stand beside the Saxon—a Negro, and yet a man![9]

He didn't win. The judges were more impressed by an eleventh-grade female student named Eurls Smith, from Beach High School in Savannah. She took the top prize, while second place went not to ML but to his Booker classmate and former runner-up Hiram Kendall.[10] Still, it was an honor to even participate, and as Hiram, ML, and Miss Bradley boarded a bus to head home, he had to have felt a mixture of satisfaction and disappointment. Had his nerves gotten the best of him? Had he allowed the new environment to shake his confidence? Or had the judges simply preferred the content of other speeches?

As the bus made its way toward Atlanta, it most likely followed US Route 441 north then shifted over to Georgia State Route 57 west. After an hour of driving, the bus stopped in the city of Macon, and a crowd of white passengers started to board. Before this rush, the black passengers were free to sit anywhere, and ML and Hiram had seated themselves toward the front. But as soon as seats became scarce, the white bus driver stared at ML and Hiram and "ordered us to get up and give the whites our seats," King later recalled. At first, ML and Hiram did nothing, ignoring the escalating tension. "We didn't move quickly enough to suit him, so he began cursing us." With white passengers standing in the aisle, the bus driver demanded that ML and Hiram move out of their seats, calling them "niggers" and "black sons of bitches." *Move on out!* he shouted.[11]

Miss Bradley swooped in to resolve the matter. According to ML, "Mrs. Bradley urged me up, saying we had to obey the law." Anger boiled within as he was pressed to capitulate to the racist system he had just railed against in his speech. "I refused to go to the back of the bus," but "the teacher pleaded with me. She said it would be advisable." Eventually, with passengers looking on and the bus ride at a standstill, ML reluctantly gave in.[12]

ML, Hiram, and Miss Bradley walked to the back of the bus and grabbed a handle. "I had to stand all the way to Atlanta," King remembered decades later, his anger still there. As the bus went up the rural highway, ML had nothing to look at but seated white people and the darkness outside. "It was late at night and I was tired, but that wasn't the point. It was the humiliation." For ninety miles, ML barely kept his contained anger at bay. "That night will never leave my memory," he said. "It was the angriest I have ever been in my life." Yes, he'd been angry at Miss Bradley for pushing him to leave his seat, but, far more, he resented the "chains" of America that had shackled him to the back of the bus. "Suddenly I realized you don't count, you're nobody."[13]

The bus ride from Dublin had inspired in ML a passion for social change that could no longer confine itself to well-crafted speeches at oratorical competitions. It was a conviction his own father shared. By using his pulpit as a megaphone, Daddy King had often galvanized local residents into action. Whether boldly walking into city hall alone and using the WHITES-ONLY elevators until the signs were removed, or focusing on voter registration to help with local school funding, Daddy King found a way to be involved in not just church affairs but local politics as well. Young ML saw this intertwining of church and social issues so often that it may have even resembled common sense.

But despite his newfound thirst for social justice, ML was still unsure that a religious path was for him. As he'd been demonstrating in appearances such as the one in Dublin, his experiences at Ebenezer Baptist had taught him how to speak, how to *communicate*. What gave the young man pause was the *way* Daddy King and other preachers communicated. "I had doubts that religion was intellectually respectable," King confessed as an adult. "I revolted against the emotionalism of Negro religion, the shouting and the stomping. I didn't understand it and it embarrassed me."[14]

This early embarrassment led ML to consider career possibilities outside the church, such as law and medicine. But as his mind fluctuated between potential futures, ML and his good friend Larry Williams started paying attention to the newly renovated Wheat Street Baptist Church, a couple blocks away from Ebenezer. For years, Daddy King had no rival when it came to preaching, but when six-foot-tall, muscular Rev. William Holmes Borders arrived on Auburn Avenue to take over Wheat Street, it began a forty-year competition for the hearts and minds of black Atlanta parishioners.

At Ebenezer, you had Daddy King, a preacher who'd come to Atlanta with a sparse educational background. His mother and father could not read or write. He called himself a "backwoods Bible thumper" and scraped his way through Atlanta's Morehouse College, a highly regarded all-male institution known for forging young black students into "Morehouse men" devoted to living purposeful lives through the ideals of integrity, boldness, and spiritual brotherhood. It was with a sense of pride and accomplishment that Daddy King earned a bachelor's in theology from Morehouse in 1930 at age thirty-one. If he could do it, anyone could. And so when Daddy King preached, it was as an everyman figure. He was direct, plain, and to the point. Ornaments were for Christmas only.[15]

Rev. W. H. Borders, on the other hand, believed in empowerment through education. "Being educated," Borders once wrote, "no white man can take that away from you." He fired off nimbly articulated sermons filled with illustrative stories. Within a few years of settling in to Wheat Street Baptist, Borders was asked to deliver weekly sermons on the radio, and his smooth yet rumbling voice was soon heard in thousands of homes. ML and Larry Williams took note; they would secretly listen to Borders's 11:00 PM Sunday radio program, *Seven Minutes at the Mike*. Williams actually wedged himself into the orbit of Rev. Borders, becoming his assistant. ML's father took his young parishioner's move personally. *Stay away from Rev. Borders*, Daddy King advised his son.

ML didn't. He resolved to learn as much as he could about this reverend. He soon discovered that Borders, who'd grown up in Macon,

Georgia, and was also a Morehouse College alum, had spent considerable time in the North. While attempting to pay off his Morehouse debt, Borders had worked in the summer on a tobacco farm near Hartford, Connecticut, and later he attended Garrett Theological Seminary, a divinity school near Chicago. Daddy King, meanwhile, had made only brief visits to the North, never long enough to be transformed by its culture. ML's father didn't need to experience life in the North to know that segregation was an unjust system.

But to fifteen-year-old ML, fresh off his revealing ride from Dublin, such firsthand experience seemed vital. So in June 1944, as he awaited official word on his early admission to Morehouse for the fall, he followed in the footsteps of Rev. Borders and many other Morehouse students and took a train north to Simsbury, Connecticut, northwest of Hartford, to pick shade tobacco for the Cullman Brothers Tobacco Company. It would be his first extended trip away from his family in Atlanta—and an important step on his road toward the ministry and Crozer.

"It was not the Lord but the hot sun of the tobacco fields [in Simsbury] that 'called him' to the ministry."

—Christine King Farris, ML's sister

On his way up to the tobacco farm, ML switched trains in Washington, DC. You could also say he switched cultures. He left behind the segregated passenger cars of the South, and as he continued his trip through New York City, he found himself staring out the window in awe: "[New York City] is the largest place I have ever seen," he wrote to his mother. He saw integrated restaurants, schools, and movie theaters. As they reached Hartford, the "free North" continued to mesmerize. Again, to his mother, ML described his amazement: "I never though[t] that a person of my race could eat [at any location] but we ate in one of the finest restaurants in Har[t]ford."[16]

In Simsbury, ML attended Sunday services at the all-welcoming First Church of Christ. As the choir director of that church recalled, the Morehouse students came to the church "in an old pickup truck with benches mounted in the truck's bed." For ML, worshipping alongside a white congregation was again a surreal experience: "We were the only negroes there. Negroes and whites go to the same church."[17]

After the romanticism of the North wore off, ML had work to do, picking the shade tobacco leaves used to make high-quality cigars. Under the shade tents that veiled the fields, the heat was intense, and to keep the sticky nicotine from coating his forearms, ML harvested the leaves in a long-sleeved shirt. His pay was around five to seven dollars a day on average, and he sent money home to cover his upcoming tuition costs; if his acceptance to Morehouse came through as he expected, he'd owe the school around forty-five dollars per semester. Unfortunately, how much he earned depended on the weather and the amount of overtime he put in: "We were paid by the hour," said a summer coworker of ML's, William G. Pickens, "and when it rained, we were not paid. . . . We did see our pay as very low [and] we did gripe about the loss of pay during inclement weather." During a massive August thunderstorm, ML wrote to his mother about "losing plenty of money because of rain."[18]

ML didn't just write his mother that summer. One June 1944 letter to his father has a dutiful tone to it, as if he was writing because his mother told him to. ML made sure to tell his father what he wanted to hear: "I am the religious leader [and] we have a [b]oys choir here and we are going to sing on the air soon." At the end of the letter, ML assured his father that he wasn't causing any trouble: "I am not doing anything that I would not [be] doing [in] front of you."[19]

It was true that ML sang at integrated churches in Hartford, and he was also selected by his peers (exactly 107 of them, according to ML) to read to them from the Bible each Sunday. ML was able to throw in a few sermons as well, since he'd spent most of his young life listening to preachers such as his father, his father's friend Sandy Ray, W. H. Borders, and Harry Fosdick (on the radio). Though he didn't yet have the core passion to preach, he knew how to capture the *sound* of a powerful sermon. Silas W. Davis, a Simsbury coworker and ML's future Morehouse intramural basketball coach, recalled that King's first dips into sermonizing "were always on a serious note. It was always about helping people, always about elevating people."[20] ML's father would have beamed at the news that his oldest son was practicing the art of preaching on a northern tobacco farm.

ML's 1944 Simsbury, Connecticut, Work Schedule

Times are estimates

6:00 AM	Get out of bed in a two-floor dormitory/bunkhouse
7:00 AM	Breakfast (sausage and grits)
8:00 AM–12:00 PM	Work under the shade tents picking tobacco leaves
12:00 PM–1:00 PM	Lunch; ladle out milk and other drinks to coworkers and hand out bag lunches (a piece of fruit and a bologna, peanut butter, or cheese sandwich)
1:00 PM–5:00 PM	Back to the fields
5:00 PM–6:00 PM	Dinner, a hot meal from wood-fired stoves
10:00 PM	Bedtime/lights out[21]

What Daddy King wouldn't have wanted to hear was how much ML enjoyed living in the integrated North. At lunch, for example, young white women working on farms nearby sometimes sat with the Morehouse group. William Pickens, decades later, remembered how awestruck he and ML were: "It was just an unfamiliar situation, that one could chat with a white person who was a peer. . . . They were workers just like we were, and we could talk to them, briefly, during lunch time, and not get taken to jail for it."[22]

During rain days, when there wasn't much to do except play cards and wait out the storm, ML and other coworkers talked often about the problems back home. Silas Davis remembered the hours of conversation the Morehouse workers would have about changing their social system. ML in particular, Davis recalled, laid out his ambitions as a social reformer. "I think one of the major things that came out of our bull sessions is that he always wanted to do something different." To Davis, ML wanted "to contribute to society in ways that no one else had ever done."[23]

After three months of manual labor under the tobacco tents, ML returned to Atlanta in mid-September. Christine, his sister, saw that the summer away had transformed his character: "My little brother had become a man."[24] Daddy King also noticed his son's newfound sense of responsibility, commenting on how he came home "buzzing with stories about the integrated life of the North, and how different for the Negro such an existence was." Daddy King could tell that his son "had seen . . . a freer society" and would never again be "able to look at segregation . . . without burning with a determination to destroy that system forever. . . . The North wasn't entirely without racial discord, of course, but there was some relief from the presence of laws intended to turn people into things that were less than human."[25]

ML had a more tempered recollection of his return: "It was a bitter feeling going back to segregation. It was hard to understand why I could ride whenever I pleased on the train from New York to Washington, and then had to change to a Jim Crow car at the nation's capital in order to continue the trip to Atlanta." In another account, ML expressed his bitterness more fully, remembering how a waiter moved him to a different seat in the rear of the train and jerked down a dividing curtain. "I felt as though that curtain had dropped on my selfhood."[26]

ML entered Morehouse in the fall as expected. Still reluctant to commit to a career as a preacher, he spent his first few years fluctuating between majors. At only sixteen, he was far more focused on teenage romantic pursuits. ML and his friends Larry Williams and Walter "Mac" McCall often hung out around the Yates and Milton drugstore on the corner of Auburn Avenue and Butler Street in Atlanta, enjoying the view of female passersby. The three young men spent the summer of 1945 chasing local women, dubbing themselves "the wreckers" for their ability to break a woman's heart.

But these youthful adventures did not ease the resentment ML felt toward the injustices of Jim Crow, and he started looking more broadly at the society that empowered such a system. "I was at the point where I was deeply interested in political matters and social ills," ML later said about this time in his life. "I could envision myself playing a part in breaking down the legal barriers to colored people's rights."[27] After two years at Morehouse, he selected a major in keeping with his expanded perspective: sociology.

ML again stayed in the South for the summer of 1946, working for the Atlanta Railway Express Company. That experience ended in anger, however: after being called a "nigger" by a white foreman, ML quit, his tolerance for racism lower after his experiences in the North. That same summer, ML wrote a scathing letter to the *Atlanta Constitution* titled "Kick Up Dust." He did not mention the incident with the foreman, but his anger is obvious. His letter may also have been motivated by a pair of racist crimes: In late July, former Army veteran Maceo Snipes was murdered after being the only African American to vote in his district during a Georgia primary. The next day, two married black couples were killed by a gang of white men on a bridge about sixty miles from ML's home. The murders of these five individuals made the national news.[28]

The *Atlanta Constitution* letter makes it clear that ML, now seventeen years old, was beginning to find his voice. "We want and are entitled to the basic rights and opportunities of American citizens," he wrote. He also criticized a "certain class of people" who are in a "hurry to raise a scarecrow of social mingling and intermarriage." ML wanted to make it clear that black people in general are not "eager to marry white girls, and we would like to have our own girls left alone by both white toughs and white aristocrats." According to Daddy King, ML's angry 185-word letter "received widespread and favorable comment."[29]

The following summer, ML decided against remaining in the South. He returned to the tobacco farms of Simsbury, a few years wiser and less inclined to be amazed by how much freer the North was. As in 1944, ML participated in the choir and sang at churches around the Hartford area, but in 1947 there was a new sense of restlessness about him. He was entering his final year at Morehouse, and he knew he'd soon have to make the difficult decision about his future.[30]

His restlessness manifested itself in a number of ways that summer in Simsbury. For one thing, according to his friend Emmett Proctor, he didn't work as hard. In fact, Proctor and ML were voted the "laziest workers," and instead of picking tobacco they often put up their nets and allowed the rest of the group to go ahead of them. They even fell asleep in the fields and had to walk home in the dark. ML also pulled a few pranks. Once, when a fellow worker was asleep, ML lit a match and slid it between the student's toes. As the flame neared the skin, ML waited eagerly for the student to awaken and burst from his bed, stomping his foot.[31]

During his second Simsbury stint, ML had one of his first brushes with police. Unfortunately, we can never know exactly what occurred, but a few students who were there said it involved quite a bit of "horseplay, rebellion . . . and beer drinking." Whatever transpired, it led to a confrontation between ML and a police officer, but that was the end of it.[32]

By the end of that summer, ML had made a decision about his future plans. After returning home, he officially informed his father that he was going to become a preacher. To some around him, it came as a surprise, but to his old friend Larry Williams, who'd stayed up with ML to listen to Rev. W. H. Borders on the radio, it seemed inevitable: "It was already kind of concluded that he was going in [to the ministry]. It was just a question of when." Still, Williams believed that the incident with the police that summer may have altered the timing of ML's announcement. By offering news Daddy King wanted to hear, ML would have deflected attention from what had happened and thus avoided punishment.[33]

Preachers often speak of receiving some sort of "call" to the ministry. Perhaps a powerful emotional moment fills them with conviction, or perhaps they hear God speak to them in a time of uncertainty. ML's call was not one of these overwhelming moments of catharsis. For most of his young life, he'd chafed against the sense that becoming a minister was an obligation, and recently he'd flirted again with the idea of becoming a lawyer, along with best friend and Morehouse classmate Walter McCall—who would later play a pivotal part in his years at Crozer as well. But both young men finally concluded that the black pulpit, if used correctly, could have a far greater effect on society. In the fall of 1947, ML didn't so much want to be a preacher because of his deep, abiding faith in God. Instead, he saw the ministry as the best way to combat segregation and inspire change.

And in order to do that, he chose to apply to a seminary in the North. He was following the example of Rev. Borders, who had shown him that there was power in education and value in new experiences and self-improvement. ML wanted to continue to improve himself. "Education," he wrote in his final year at Morehouse, "must enable one to sift and weigh evidence, to discern the true from the false, the real from the unreal, and the facts from the fiction."[34]

Mostly likely, ML at least entertained the idea of attending Crozer Theological Seminary in Chester, Pennsylvania, during his earlier Morehouse College days. In fact, the president of Crozer, E. E. Aubrey, had delivered a baccalaureate speech to Morehouse students in 1945, when ML was in his second year. He had also taught ML's Morehouse mentor—the school's president, Benjamin Mays—at the University of Chicago. Aubrey promoted Crozer as a racially integrated, liberal seminary that accepted students from as far away as Greece, China, and Japan.[35]

But a far greater influence on King's decision came from a family friend with a larger-than-life personality: Rev. J. Pius Barbour. Daddy King and Rev. Barbour likely crossed paths frequently at major Baptist conventions, and ML, who was often dragged along to these events from an early age, would have encountered the gregarious "northern" preacher throughout his childhood. In 1936, Rev. Barbour had become the first black seminarian to graduate from Crozer, and he eventually put down roots nearby, at Calvary Baptist Church in Chester. Rev. Barbour not only knew Crozer's course catalog, he also knew each of the professors at the school. Barbour was also a "Morehouse man" (class of 1917), and he understood ML's desire to leave the South to pursue a broader educational perspective.[36]

In February 1948, the same month he was ordained as a minister at Ebenezer Baptist, ML submitted his application to Crozer. In it, he identified the summer of 1944 as a pivotal moment in his journey toward the ministry:

> My call to the ministry was quite different from most explinations [sic] I've heard. This dicision [sic] came about in the summer of 1944 when I felt an inescapable urge to serve society. In short, I felt a sense of responsibility which I could not escape.[37]

The bus ride in Georgia that spring had ignited a fire within the young man, and those idyllic summer days spent with white and black students in Simsbury, Connecticut, had allowed him to believe in the vision of a more integrated society. And now, as ML would recall years later, he was ready to use the church to create the social change he hungered for: "Not until I entered Crozer Theological Seminary did I begin a serious intellectual quest for a method to eliminate social evil."[38] That quest brought him out of the South, to a seminary on a hill.

Year I

Genesis

An aerial view of the Crozer Theological Seminary campus circa the 1940s: 1. Old Main, Crozer's main building, where ML lived in room 52 on the second floor. The central perpendicular section housed the dining hall; the perpendicular section at the bottom was the chapel. 2. Pearl Hall, the campus library built in honor of Margaret Crozer Bucknell, who championed its construction. 3. Arrayed behind Old Main, the three buildings where many of the faculty, staff, and married students lived. 4. Ship Creek Woods, through which ML liked to walk when he had a break from classes in the spring. 5. Commencement Hall, most notable for being the site of Crozer graduation ceremonies. *Courtesy of Colgate Rochester Crozer Divinity School, Rochester, NY*

1

Young and Alone

Term 1, September 14– November 24, 1948

"Each of us is something of a schizophrenic personality. . . . We're split up and divided against ourselves. There is something of a civil war going on within all our lives."

—Martin Luther King Jr.[1]

Room 52 and Lucius Z. Hall: "Martin . . . I'm Gonna Kill You"

Martin Luther King Jr. took in his new accommodations on the second floor of Old Main, Crozer Theological Seminary's main building. Room 52 was a furnished six-by-eight-foot space, featuring a twin bed with covers and a pillow, and opposite it three sets of drawers in which to place his clothes. At the back of the room was a wooden desk with a table lamp and a basic chair. A cushioned lounge chair sat in the corner, and a window overlooked the campus's front lawn lined with maple trees. Though far from a five-star hotel, it would do just fine for a young preacher without any attachments. The shared bathroom would be a constant reminder, however, that he was not completely alone.[2]

The front entrance to Old Main, circa the late 1940s. ML would have seen this photo in the Crozer catalog, which he requested while applying to the school in February 1948. *Courtesy of Colgate Rochester Crozer Divinity School, Rochester, NY*

During the Civil War, Old Main had been a military hospital, and ML's room had been occupied by a wounded Confederate soldier. On the outside of his door was the outline of a hole through which the soldier was given his food. Two stories up, the walls of the fourth-floor cupola still bore the signatures of wounded soldiers from both sides of the conflict.* This history held particular significance for the building's African American residents; as a past black graduate had written, "A soldier fighting to keep my people enslaved had used that very room. Now, it was my room, and I was using it to learn how to harvest enough spiritual energy to achieve our full freedom."[3]

But the Civil War was eight decades ago, and as ML unpacked his neatly folded clothes, he was focused on his future. In September 1948, ML was a nineteen-year-old, five-foot-seven, 150-pound rookie preacher. His time at Crozer meant he'd be away from his family and the seventeen sheltered blocks of "Sweet Auburn," the prosperous African American community around Auburn Avenue in Atlanta where the Kings lived and ministered. By choosing a seminary in the North, ML had decided to come out from beneath the shadow of his father and his Ebenezer Baptist domain. At Crozer, King now had a chance to follow his own path.

In those first days at Crozer, however, the main thing ML wanted to do was fit in with his fellow divinity students, most of whom were older than he was. He could always rely on his best friend, Walter McCall, to help him relax and enjoy himself, but Mac would not join him at Crozer until the next term. So for the time being, at least, ML felt overwhelmed by a certain dread and timidity. "If I were a minute late to class, I was almost morbidly conscious of it and sure that everyone noticed it," he recalled. "I had a tendency to overdress, to keep my room spotless, my shoes perfectly shined and my clothes immaculately pressed." He affected a "grimly serious" demeanor, and made sure not to be the guy who laughed too much or dispensed undeserved compliments.[4]

Though it made him feel self-conscious, ML's anxiety was far from abnormal, especially among his floormates. While the third floor of Old

---

* See appendix C, page 233, for more information on Old Main's history and a photograph of its Civil War signatures.

Main had rooms for older, married students looking to settle down at a church as soon as possible, the second floor was packed with single young men like ML, many of whom struggled to adjust to the newness of an integrated living environment. They would be studying with seminarians from Georgia and from New York, from China and Panama.[5] Some were former soldiers who'd fought in World War II and others were pacifists who chose jail instead of enlisting. Some, like ML, had barely maintained a B average during their college days. And many were looking for a way to differentiate themselves from others. No one wanted to be thought of as the "weak" preacher, the one who could not inspire a congregation, or the one who did not have the proper leadership skills to manage a church. Competition was fierce, and inevitable self-doubt, both general and specific—*Is this my path? Do I have the necessary charisma to increase the membership of the church?*—crept in daily.

His class of incoming students—sixteen men in a student body that at that time hovered around forty students—would produce the largest percentage of black graduates in Crozer's history.[6] Like ML, other southern black preachers had been drawn to the school ever since it graduated Morehouse alum J. Pius Barbour in 1936. King's Crozer classmate Marcus Wood explained decades later that "the trend of blacks then was to get into a white school"—then there was a chance people would say, "He must be something; he went to a white seminary."[7]

In the mornings, ML and other black seminarians marveled at the fact that white maids were cleaning the hallways and each student's room. ML had been raised within the confines of segregation—he'd drunk from segregated water fountains, used elevators specifically for "people like him," and attended only segregated schools. But now a shift had occurred: white maids, white fellow students, and white professors would be a part of his daily Crozer experience.[8]

It didn't take long for the black students to identify one particular white classmate who could be trouble. A few doors down from ML's room 52 lived Lucius Z. Hall, a twenty-five-year-old former soldier from Hartsville, South Carolina. To ML, Lucius's personality was unfortunately familiar: in Lucius sat the preconceived notions of a nineteenth-century southern white man. Lucius had no qualms about calling black students "darkies" or appreciating the history of the Confederate flag.[9]

Lucius walked with a limp and often used a cane. The reason for his handicap was, at least from what he told others, an injury he suffered as an infantry lieutenant during the Battle of the Bulge. Lucius kept a pistol close by and often created mischief among his classmates. As one fellow student said, "He was a great practical joker. He just couldn't take a joke."[10]

Lucius's history of pranks dated back to his college days at Mercer University in Georgia. Once, he wanted to use a public phone but a man was in the phone booth talking to his girlfriend. Lucius grew tired of waiting and decided it would be funny to make a long line of lighter fluid that ended up near the man's feet. As he let the match fall and watched the fire approach the booth, the man dropped the phone and ran out of there in a hurry.[11]

Horace E. Whitaker, or "Whit," a married student who for that first year lived above King on the third floor, remembered Hall clearly: "The thing that perhaps upset him the most was that the southern black was there to challenge his particular views. . . . There was a movement at the time of racial integration, coming slowly as it was, and some just could not deal with it."[12] Like Hall, Whitaker was a war vet; like King, he was a black southerner, hailing from Seaview, Virginia. Whit was one of the men who took ML under his wing that first term. He was eleven years older than ML, and when ML needed perspective he often traveled up the stairs to the third floor to talk to him. ML admired Whit's measured, reasonable nature.

King's own capacity for restraint was put to the test early in his Crozer tenure, in an encounter with Lucius Z. Hall. The details are uncertain; the incident has been described from multiple perspectives by several students who were there, but the man at the center, Hall himself, could not be found, so we are left to piece together the clearest version we can.

During the fall term of 1948, while ML was away from Old Main for a few hours, Hall and several coconspirators placed a water bucket above his door, closing it just enough so that the room didn't appear to be tampered with. When ML returned and pushed open the door, he was doused with ice cold water.[13] All in good fun so far. The truth was that the water bucket prank went up and down that second floor, and even the third. Executing such capers was easy, since Crozer had removed all locks from students' doors to encourage interpersonal trust.

Eventually the novelty of soaking one's classmates wore off, and students attempted to take the pranks to the next level. They started breaking into a target's dorm room and stacking his furniture—desk, chair, shelves—on the bed, or moving it into a pile in the hallway. Some pranksters would take vital pieces of furniture and hide them in random places around Old Main. So it was that ML returned to his room to find he had no mattress to sleep on. He roamed the building, attempting to ignore the smug smiles of Lucius Hall and his fellow pranksters. Eventually, ML found the mattress in the basement—nicknamed the "catacombs"—and had to drag it up three flights of stairs as fellow students looked on.[14]

ML believed it was Lucius who'd hidden his mattress and wanted to retaliate, as did others who'd been water bucket and furniture stacking victims. But ML and the others didn't want to simply redo a prior prank. Instead, they went for something bigger.

One night, Hall left his room, and his fellow second-floor students knew they had a couple of hours to complete their mission. From Hall's dorm room they took the bed, the table, the chairs, the desk. They carefully walked it all down the staircase and out the front door of Old Main. They chose a spot on the front lawn and arranged all of Hall's furniture so that it was in the same configuration as it had been inside.[15]

When wounded war vet Lucius returned, he viewed his new outdoor living arrangements with rage. Here he was, a man in his midtwenties who'd seen the horrors of war, who'd been raised to assume that blacks were inferior, getting a strong dose of his own medicine from a nineteen-year-old black kid who still received a weekly five-dollar allowance from his mother.[16]

Lucius grabbed his pistol and headed to room 52.

ML had been watching Lucius's reaction from a window, and when he saw how angry Hall had become, he picked up a book and pretended to be reading. When Lucius entered his room, ML gave him a quick glance, then went back to staring at his book.

"Martin . . . I'm gonna kill you," Lucius said, his gun pointed and ready. ML remained silent, attached to his book like one would be to a shield.

The confrontation attracted the attention of another black student in ML's class: Marcus Wood, one of the few actively practicing preachers, and older than many of his classmates. (He was nine years older than ML.) Wood entered room 52 and attempted to calm the situation. "Hall . . . don't do that," he said. "It's all fun . . . you don't even know Mike did it."

Rev. Marcus Garvey Wood. *Courtesy of Rev. Marcus G. Wood, Co-pastor, Providence Baptist Church, Baltimore, MD*

By now, students black and white had gathered around the room. As Wood later recalled, "It took another hour of strenuous argument before he finally agreed to put the weapon away." Once Lucius finally calmed down, he went back to his room. The poise ML showed during that hour under threat, and the ability to not panic or fan the flame of Lucius's anger, was enough to earn admiration from the rest of the students.[17]

The next day the dean of Crozer, Charles Batten, arranged a meeting with the seminarians in Old Main and banned the practice of room raids. According to the available records, Lucius Hall would only attend one year at Crozer before moving on.[18]

Classes and Professors: Out with the Old

"I am informed that he is a little above average in scholarship."

—Letter of Recommendation to Crozer from Lucius M. Tobin, Professor of Religion at Morehouse

"You will see from their records that they are not brilliant students, but they both have good minds."

—Letter of Recommendation to Crozer from Benjamin E. Mays, President of Morehouse, discussing both ML and Walter McCall

"The academic record of Martin Luther King Jr. in Morehouse College is short of what may be called 'good.'"

—Letter of Recommendation to Crozer from George D. Kelsey, Director of Morehouse School of Religion[19]

Introduction to the Old Testament

At eight in the morning on Tuesday through Friday,* after an early breakfast in the dining hall in the center of Old Main's first floor, ML headed down the hallway, past the receptionist's room, and into a classroom.

---

* The seminary held no classes on Mondays. Chapter 3, page 76, explains why.

ML's Class Schedule

Year I, Term 1, September 14–November 24, 1948

Time	Tuesday	Wednesday	Thursday	Friday
8:00 AM	Introduction to the Old Testament	Introduction to the Old Testament	Introduction to the Old Testament	Introduction to the Old Testament
9:00 AM				
10:00 AM	Chapel service	Optional service		Devotional pd.
10:30 AM	Orientation for Juniors	Preaching Ministry of the Church	Orientation for Juniors	Preaching Ministry of the Church
11:00 AM				
11:30 AM	Lunch	Lunch	Public Speaking	Lunch
12:00 PM				
12:30 PM				
1:00 PM				
2:00 PM			Choir	
3:00 PM			Church Music	
4:00 PM			Vespers service (4:15 PM)	
5:00 PM				

No classes on Monday | Thanksgiving break: Nov. 25–29
ML's GPA for the term: 2.61

Introduction to the Old Testament
James Bennett Pritchard, BD (Drew), PhD (UPenn)
Course Description: "The general patterns of religion and thought in the ancient Near East, and their influence upon the peoples of the Old Testament; the geography of Palestine; the canon and texts of the Old Testament; and a survey of the literature. A knowledge of the contents of the Old Testament in English is presupposed." (Credit hours: 8; ML's grade: B-)

Orientation for Juniors
Edwin Ewart Aubrey, MA, BD, PhD (Chicago), DD (Bucknell); President of Crozer, 1944–1949
Course Description: "The place of religion in contemporary culture; the role of critical studies in ministerial preparation; bearings of modern knowledge on religious living; the Church at work in the world today. Required." (Credit hours: 2; ML's grade: C-)

Preaching Ministry of the Church
Robert Elwood Keighton, BD, ThM (Crozer)
Course Description: "Purposes of preaching; history of preaching and its relations to the prevailing culture." (Credit hours: 2; ML's grade: B+)

Public Speaking
Robert Elwood Keighton, BD, ThM (Crozer)
Course Description: "Fundamental physical and psychological elements of public speaking." *One-third of a credit.* (Credit hours: ⅓; ML's grade: Pass)

Choir
Ruth B. Grooters, Diploma (Iowa Falls Conservatory of Music)
Course Description: "Choral methods studied. Two choral programs are prepared and presented publicly each year." (Credit hours: ⅓; ML's grade: Pass)

Church Music
Ruth B. Grooters, Diploma (Iowa Falls Conservatory of Music)
Course Description: "This course runs in a three-year cycle, one term each year. A minor credit is given for the three terms. The subjects considered will be Elementary Harmony and Sight Singing." (Credit hours: ⅓; ML's grade: C+)

On Tuesday, Wednesday, and Friday, a half-hour period was set aside at 10:00 AM for services in the chapel. On Tuesdays was a mandatory service led by Crozer president E. E. Aubrey. Wednesday services were optional, generally led by a member of the faculty or an invited pastor from an evangelical institution. The Friday devotional period was run by the students themselves and presided over by the chairman of the Devotions Committee. On Thursday, the 10:00 AM slot was a free period, and a vespers service was held at 4:15 PM. This tightly planned service featured a speaker from a prescheduled list, usually a Crozer professor or a guest speaker from another institution.[20]

For the next two hours, his professor was thirty-nine-year-old Dr. James B. Pritchard, a biblical scholar who had traveled the world researching the actual history behind the stories of the Old Testament. A Methodist at heart, he was at the time busy completing *Ancient Near Eastern Texts Relating to the Old Testament*, a book that would eventually become a definitive text for scholars in the field.[21] He and New Testament scholar Morton S. Enslin, who would instruct ML starting the following semester, represented the "reality check" built into the Crozer curriculum.

During ML's time at Crozer, the seminary was considered, in one student's words, a "scholar's school," with an emphasis on academic inquiry instead of the practical concerns of preaching and evangelism.[22] Yet Crozer students often entered seminary with little background in theological scholarship and with literalist views on biblical truth. Yes, Moses parted the waters of the Red Sea. Yes, Noah's animals went in two by two. Pritchard noted years later that his African American seminarians were particularly prone to this way of thinking: "Enslin and I had all these black students from the Deep South— fundamentalists" who were reluctant to abandon their rigid views and consider their religion from the perspective of, say, a biblical archaeologist.[23]

Dr. Pritchard saw it as his responsibility to knock the fundamentalist ideas out of his students' heads forever. He focused on correcting their view of Moses as a "legendary character" and their "overinflated" sense of the story of Exodus so they could preach the tale with more precision. Later in the year it would be Enslin's turn to eliminate all the glorified myths of Jesus and build him back up from scratch.[24]

There were nine students in Pritchard's "O.T." class, including a few of ML's friends, such as wise counselor Horace Whitaker, room-raid savior Marcus Wood, and a unique but remote black seminarian from Panama, Cyril Pyle, who quickly found a role in the Chester community as a preacher and moderator at the local West Branch YMCA. King sat in the second-to-last row of the classroom, soaking in his professor's pragmatic explanations. ML was quiet and dressed in an unwrinkled white-collared shirt, a black tie, suit coat, and black pants. The nineteen-year-old may have worried about whether he came across as a peer to his older classmates, but while some of them were paralyzed by the very idea of cutting Moses down to size, he enjoyed being challenged to dissect and scrutinize his previous beliefs. ML had always wanted Daddy King to take a more cerebral approach to his preaching. Over the years, he had watched his father deliver his message backed by not much other than plainspoken enthusiasm. It was this primal authority (*Make it plain, son!*) that pushed ML toward the other end of the spectrum.[25]

The first week of O.T. made clear what Crozer expected, and it was exactly what ML was hoping for. This was the intense class he needed to shake himself out of his youthful academic stagnation. In a letter to his mother in October 1948, he wrote, "Some times the professor [Pritchard] comes in class and tells us to read our . . . assignments in Hebrew, and that is really hard."[26]

ML's grades were considerably better than those of the other black students in the class, whose underperformance may reflect their resistance to Pritchard's antifundamentalist approach. Perhaps they felt at first that it was unimportant whether a story was "true" or not. Like Daddy King, they may have surmised that preaching was more about delivery, passion, conviction, and belief. But for Dr. Pritchard, treating myth as truth for the sake of convenience meant short-changing the possibilities of a sermon. It was only with an understanding of historical fact that Old Testament legends could be most powerfully retold.[27]

Introduction to the Old Testament

Dr. James Pritchard, Term 1 Grades, Sept.–Nov. 1948

Robert C. Hill	A-
Robert E. Hopkins	B
Martin Luther King Jr.	B-
Joseph T. Kirkland	D-
Wendall A. Maloch	B
Cyril G. Pyle	D+
George T. Walton	A-
Horace E. Whitaker	D
Marcus G. Wood	D-

Dr. Pritchard: "I was tough in those days."[28]

King may have been quicker to attune himself to his professor's expectations, but at the time his writing skills were far from excellent. His work for Pritchard's Old Testament class provide early examples of the problem documented by the King Papers Project at Stanford University: ML spent years at Crozer and Boston University lifting uncited passages from books and passing them off as his own. It is safe to say that if ML were a literature major at an American university in 2018, he would not be able to get away with such behavior. All a professor would need to do was paste a suspicious passage from ML's paper into a search engine to find the matching source, and ML would be dismissed from school for plagiarism. But this was 1948, at a divinity school not heavily concerned with the rules of proper citation, and ML's actions would go unpunished.[29]

In retrospect, however, the plagiarism is clear. Here are two examples of material ML lifted for an Old Testament paper about the prophet Jeremiah:

"Religion, in a sense, through the prophet, provides for its own advancement, and carries within it the promise of progress and renewed power."	"**Religion, in a sense, through** men like Jeremiah, **provides for its own advancement, and carries within it the promise of progress and renewed power.**"
—**T. Crouther Gordon**, *The Rebel Prophet: Studies in the Personality of Jeremiah* (New York: Harper & Brothers, 1932)	—**King**, "The Significant Contributions of Jeremiah to Religious Thought" (Fall 1948)
"... he perceived that what religion was to him it must be to all men—the response of the heart to the voice of God within."	"**... he perceived that what religion was to him it must be to all men—the response of the heart to the voice of God** ['within" omitted]."
—**John Skinner**, *Prophecy and Religion* (Cambridge: Cambridge University Press, 1940)	—**King**, "The Significant Contributions of Jeremiah to Religious Thought" (Fall 1948)

Tweaking only one or two words of a passage and presenting it as one's own work is not something a student would do by accident. ML would have been fully aware that he was cribbing. And, to Pritchard's credit, the professor did attempt to nudge ML very subtly in the direction of proper citation. In this paper, Pritchard corrected a footnote citation, and even made sure to let ML know about keeping better track of who wrote what: "This is Wellhausen as quoted in Pfeiffer."[30]

Near the end of the paper, ML offered some telling words that were mostly his own: "[Jeremiah] was lightly esteemed in life. He became the supreme example of ... the suffering servant. He was despised and rejected, a man of sorrows and acquainted with grief." Although he had a bit of help from Isaiah in that last line, it's clear that ML had sympathy for Jeremiah, "the suffering servant."

Dr. Pritchard would long remember ML's presence both in and out of his classroom. "I do have, of course, vivid memories of him in my class in Old Testament," he recalled, but he knew ML better as his family babysitter, watching the professor's children for thirty-five cents an hour: "On a more informal level were the numerous occasions when he came to our home on the campus to stay with our two young daughters when we would be out for the evening. They too came to know and appreciate him."[31] The job provided King with one of his early glimpses into white middle-class culture.

Meanwhile, ML was acclimating to the Crozer routine. He didn't have much time to recover from Dr. Pritchard's gauntlet of reality checks and Hebrew language demands, but back then Old Main was its own little world. From the classrooms on the first floor, ML could have headed down the stairs to the kitchen and grabbed a small snack. If he wasn't hungry, he could have gone down the hall in the basement to the recreation room and set up a game of pool, table tennis, or shuffleboard with another seminarian. If he needed to cram for class, he could have perused the student-run bookstore for books related to a class topic. "He was a normal human being, especially in those early years," Horace Whitaker recalled.[32]

Orientation for Juniors

> What are the major problems confronting the Church today?
> What qualities, knowledge, and skills are required of religious leaders?
> What should be the aims of the churches?
>
> —E. E. Aubrey[33]

These three questions sat atop Dr. Edwin Ewart Aubrey's outline for ML's second class of the day on Tuesdays and Thursdays, Orientation for Juniors. (At Crozer, a seminarian's first year was referred to as "junior year," the second year "middle," and third year "senior.") Students considered Aubrey, the president of Crozer at the time, to be "cold," "stern and unyielding," and someone who spoke "above" them. This was demonstrated one night in late September, when Aubrey called together all the new students. As ML, Marcus Wood, Horace Whitaker, and the other juniors took seats in the chapel, Aubrey stood in front of them and declared that they were "the dumbest class the school has ever had."[34]

Dr. E. E. Aubrey, circa the early 1950s. *From the Collections of the University of Pennsylvania Archives*

To the faculty, their president was an "idealist" and a man who refused to "cut corners." He had wanted to keep the academic standards high at Crozer, but the school's trustees leaned on him to increase enrollment, hoping for the swift financial kick many other institutions were then enjoying by expanding their student body. With soldiers returning from the war and looking to continue their studies, and black preachers hoping to follow in the footsteps of J. Pius Barbour, there were plenty of applicants, even if their grades were middling.[35] Aubrey was not impressed by these enthusiastic but average enrollees, not even the full-grown men who'd seen battle. From his perspective, they were *lucky* to be Crozer students. In fact, for his Orientation for Juniors class, one of the first required readings was an article titled "Theological Education in the Post-War World." The author? A British academic by the name of E. E. Aubrey.[36]

Aubrey could sense that his time at Crozer was approaching its end. Not only was he being asked to lower his standards, but midway through the first term he lost a valued ally and friend, renowned Crozer faculty member Maynard Cassady. Professor Cassady died at home on October 24, 1948, and Aubrey, perhaps preoccupied with funeral arrangements, scheduled a test for the Orientation class on October 26.[37] Several weeks later, Aubrey would resign as president of Crozer, choosing instead to head up a new religious department at the University of Pennsylvania. Due perhaps to Aubrey's tumultuous situation but likely also to ML's own timidity, this class resulted in the lowest grade ML would ever receive at Crozer, a C-.[38]

Aubrey shouldn't be dismissed as merely a snooty disciplinarian, however. According to Samuel D. Proctor, a well-respected black preacher who graduated from Crozer two years before ML's arrival, Aubrey was a family man devoted to his wife and two children. Proctor and his own wife, Bessie, lived with the Aubreys as "domestic help" in 1946, and Proctor made a point of highlighting the human side of Crozer's president:

[Aubrey and his wife] loved books, opera, the symphonies and art galleries; they never listened to the radio, never knew which football team was out front, who won the World Series, or which basketball teams made the final four. They could not dance. In nine months of living in the same house with them (we had a private apartment on the third floor), I never saw her without heels, stockings, and makeup; and I never saw him without a collar and tie. Bessie and I studied them as though they were in a museum. I enjoyed talking theology with Dr. Aubrey, and Mrs. Aubrey wanted to teach my wife more about cooking than she would ever need to know.[39]

The Proctors' experience with the Aubreys was similar to ML's with the Pritchards: it provided an extended peek into the lifestyles of upper-middle-class white people who, as Samuel Proctor recalled, "did not have to be concerned with their survival, their identity, or their space and basic rights and freedom." Eventually, Proctor came to see the Aubreys as gracious "stage actors." He appreciated their welcoming spirit, but their souls were "laminated"—shielded, Proctor believed, from actual human suffering.[40]

Preaching Ministry of the Church; Public Speaking

Around the time ML decided to attend Crozer, the professor who would soon be teaching his Preaching Ministry and Public Speaking courses, Robert Keighton, contributed a fiery essay to the *Crozer Quarterly*. Entitled "I Am a Minister," the essay described the devolving cultural status of the preacher, and how vital it was not to succumb to this downhill slide into irrelevance:

> The uncomfortable fact is that the ministry has lost its sense of dignity. The minister has acquiesced in the general conspiracy to rob him of his authority. . . . I have known some ministers who were more concerned to have us know that they had a secretary than that they had a gospel.[41]

Though his essay may have emphasized the importance of biblical truth over empty signifiers, all recorded accounts suggest that Professor Keighton himself was a dramatist at heart,* a frustrated scholar of British

---

* True to this, he was also Crozer's drama club teacher, instructing the students who acted in the annual vespers holiday concert.

Professor Robert Keighton in the early 1950s.
From the book jacket of The Man Who Would Preach, published by Abingdon Press

literature who'd found a way to pay the bills by teaching preachers how to perform. To prove a point in class, nine times out of ten Keighton would quote a literary figure; he chose authors such as Keats, Auden, Virginia Woolf, and Dickens over Matthew, Mark, Luke, and John. Other professors often jabbed him for his lack of scriptural emphasis. *If only you knew your Bible the way you knew Shakespeare!* was a comment Keighton heard frequently.[42] A few professors also described him as "dry," while one future colleague who'd once been Keighton's student refused to mince words: "Arrogant . . . [a] son of a bitch."[43]

Whether pompous or a champion of ministerial high standards, Keighton was Crozer's sole preaching professor, and as such, his impact on ML's education was considerable.* ML would end up taking ten courses from him, and the moment he first walked into Keighton's

---

* It should be noted, however, that King had already studied the fundamentals of preaching at Morehouse College, under George Kelsey.

classroom was the first day of his education in the ways of a white liberal preacher. For over a decade, ML had soaked in the power and bluster of southern black preachers like his father and William Holmes Borders. There was an urgency to these men's voices, a sort of confident desperation. Every Sunday they pushed the message *Things need to change!* Keighton, on the other hand, did not come from the South, nor had he suffered for long periods of time as a "secondary citizen." For Keighton, the act of preaching meant asking the audience *How can we be better?* and *Can we get there with dignity?*[44]

Keighton's vision was that a minister should inspire through confidence, grace, and sophistication; from his perspective, *whooping* had no place in a sermon. One former student recalled that "Keighton did not like the style of black preachers, full of imagery of fire and brimstone. Black students did not do well in his class."[45] ML was an exception, however, earning a B+ in Preaching Ministry. And over ML's years at Crozer, Keighton's ever-present example would help him to understand what many white people of faith wanted to hear, and *how* they wanted it delivered.

By a few accounts, Keighton was mainly indifferent to ML as a student, later calling him a "product of his environment." A day after Dr. King was assassinated in Memphis, Keighton was quoted as saying that ML was "a rather quiet, unassuming, good student who I feel gave very little evidence of the direction or the way he was going to develop."[46]

But, in fact, it was in Keighton's Preaching Ministry class that ML first started to formulate grand ambitions for what he could accomplish as a religious leader. "On the one hand," ML wrote in a handwritten outline of sermon notes, "I must attempt to change the soul of individuals so that their societies may be changed. On the other I must attempt to change the societies so that the individual soul will [have a chance to] change." He asserted "that the minister should possess profundity of conviction. We have [too] many minister[s] in the pulpit who are great spellbounders and [too] few who possess spiritual power. It is my profound conviction that I, as an aspirant for the ministry, should possess these powers."[47] Now *this* was a driven man, and Keighton, the suppressed Shakespearean, would surely have approved.

Choir; Church Music

"To this day [fifty years later] I can picture Mike King standing at the front of our choir group, leading all of us through the soaring passages of his favorite hymn: 'When I Survey the Wondrous Cross.'"

—Marcus Wood[48]

If you entered the tall front doors of Old Main in 1948, took a left, and headed down the hallway until nearly the end, you would find a door on your right that led into the chapel. On Thursday afternoons, ML would pass through this door to spend two hours singing for and learning from Ruth B. Grooters, organist extraordinaire.[49]

With the exception of a professor he would take a class from at the University of Pennsylvania in his middle year, Grooters was the only female instructor ML had during his years at Crozer. Very little has been written about ML's experience with Grooters, but considering he'd spent his childhood singing in the choir at Ebenezer Baptist for Mama King, Grooters's course must have provided at least a small dose of weekly nostalgia. At Ebenezer, King's mother would play the organ as his already smooth voice cranked out "I Want to Be More and More Like Jesus," gospel style. The congregation ate him up, and ministers all around loved to have ML come over to their church to sing, giving them a chance to start a "special collection" in his name. ML's love of music continued at Morehouse College, where he sang in the glee club.[50] So it's unsurprising that he made a positive impression on Ruth Grooters as well. Said Bobbie Hoopes, Ruth's daughter, "She was a very private person, but I remember her mentioning, later in life, that Martin Luther King Jr. had been in her chapel choir, and in class, where he was a good singer and student."[51]

The first hour of Grooters's class was Choir, dedicated to hymnal singing, the men's voices bouncing off the broad walls of the chapel. The second hour, Church Music, was more instructional. Grooters had the students—basses, baritones, and tenors—sit down and work on the basic harmonies within the group. She gave them "sight singing" assignments, passing around new music and having them work out their parts on the fly. The main goal of Grooters's instruction was to make sure the students were ready for the annual candlelight vespers holiday concert, held in the chapel each December. It was open to the public, and almost always locally reported by the *Chester Times*.[52]

Hoopes remembers her mother with love as she describes her educational style: "In her teaching she quietly shared her faith by example, and in interpreting the music of faithful Christians such as Bach, pointing out examples of 'text painting' and other compositional devices which held symbols of deep meaning."[53]

Hoopes adds, "I remember her telling me that in the little town where she was raised, there were no black people. She never met a person of African descent until they moved to Philadelphia around 1937." One might expect a person from such a sheltered background to feel a bit of uncertainty over directing ML, Marcus Wood, and other black students in her choir. But Hoopes is certain her mother had no such issues: "We were taught to respect every person equally, and . . . she held no prejudice in racial (or any other) areas."

With a kind and considerate instructor in a discipline he knew well, the class would have given ML a break from his trio of intense professors. But he earned only a C+ in Church Music despite making a good impression on Grooters, which her daughter believes was due to erratic attendance. Apparently ML needed another respite from Crozer's scholarly climate—a reminder not just of his musical past but of his life along Auburn Avenue more broadly. Thankfully, he found one, in the form of a powerful and enthusiastic preacher whose home was a forty-minute walk from Crozer.[54]

The Gospel of Barbour: "King in Particular Would Challenge Him."

> "The Negro Church has lost influence like ALL CHURCHES, in this money-mad, liquor-drinking gadget-crazy age. But, it still stands as the Hope and Inspiration of a struggling people. And for that position it must thank the Negro Preacher."
>
> —Rev. J. Pius Barbour[55]

Rev. J. Pius Barbour, pastor of Calvary Baptist Church and first black graduate of Crozer Theological Seminary. *Courtesy of Calvary Baptist Church, Chester, PA*

Often when we find ourselves outside our comfort zone, we gravitate back toward the familiar. For ML at Crozer, that elusive link back to his own culture was the man who had led him to Crozer in the first place: Rev. J. Pius Barbour. Whenever ML found himself overwhelmed by this new world—the high-mindedness of Robert Keighton and E. E. Aubrey, or the threatening eyes of Lucius Hall—he knew he could always head over to Rev. Barbour's home in Chester and reconnect with the world he knew best.

"He was like a father to all of us," Horace Whitaker said of Barbour, "and all of us made use of his home and his church. And we gathered rather frequently around his dinner table. . . . He was a very supportive person."[56]

As Rev. Barbour himself recalled, ML "was in and out of my house just like one of my sons." It was normally on the weekends when he would stop by. For instance, one Saturday in his first few months at Crozer, ML entered Barbour's home and smelled a nice home-cooked meal of steak with brown sauce waiting for him at the table. "He could eat more than any little man you ever saw in your life," Barbour's wife, Olee, said. As he ate, usually with Rev. Barbour, Olee, and their three children, he'd push away the stifling stress of Crozer and feel at home for a few hours. In October 1948 he wrote home to his mother that Barbour was "full of fun, and he has one of the best minds of anybody I have ever met."[57]

Following dinner, ML would practice his latest sermon in the mirror as Barbour looked on, feeding him words and phrases that carried with them a symphony of sound, such as "the paralysis of analysis," or reeling off the exotic names of Greek philosophers in order to support an idea: *Well, as Euripides demonstrated* . . . These were the kinds of tips ML could appreciate and absorb immediately. Whereas Keighton emphasized dignity and sophistication, Barbour helped ML retain his black roots by focusing on authority and impact.[58]

And, perhaps most important, there were debates. Barbour could have allowed his young seminarian guests to simply come over for dinner, practice their sermons, and chew the fat. Instead, he insisted on challenging the young men with revolutionary ideas and opinions. Rev. Barbour's grandson saw firsthand what a powerful impact these sessions had on the young men: "He was a pioneer in his time. He would combine politics, economics and theology. He would put you on the spot, and five minutes later you would realize you had grown in some way. He challenged you to a deeper faith, and he challenged you into action."[59]

He and ML "used to argue about violence and nonviolence right in my parlor," Barbour remembered.[60] At times, such debates got greatly heated. "It was an enriching experience," said Whitaker. "King in particular would challenge him, and they would have quite the debate. And I think this was where he likely sharpened his philosophical views in many ways. He had an opportunity to let [his ideas] flow freely, to test them out."[61] ML appreciated that Barbour would never allow him an easy way out of a conversation. He'd continue to play devil's advocate as long as there was still ground to cover.

In particular, these exchanges helped ML test and toughen his nonviolent views, as Barbour often took the side of the issue that was *for* violence. Other Crozer students remembered listening to one debate between King and Barbour about the nonviolent approach used by Mahatma Gandhi (who'd been assassinated the previous January) and whether it could work in America. With his booming voice, Barbour verbally jabbed ML for hours about how America was different from India, how its moral conscience was steeped in hate, and that by taking a nonviolent approach black people would stand defenseless and weak. *Who in this country would listen to that?*[62]

But ML offered a rational, level-headed response: *It's a matter of arithmetic.* It did not make any sense for those in the minority to resort to violence. Fewer people and fewer resources would blunt the impact of any display of force, and risk precious lives in a futile cause. As ML tried to articulate to Barbour, for a minority to improve its status, it must value every life and confront the problem from the perspective of a unified whole that encompasses minority and majority alike. Only then, ML believed, could the majority be turned.[63]

Rev. Barbour's daughter, Almanina, who was around twenty-three at the time, remembered even decades later how electric these conversations had been. ML "was so full of life. I had never known anybody that alive. And . . . he was as turned on about religious ideas and philosophy as people are about prize fights. And the discussions that he and my father would have were just absolutely enthralling. I would just sit and listen."[64]

King, meanwhile, must have been fascinated by Rev. Barbour's lifestyle. In addition to being a husband and father, Barbour was involved in local politics, which helped augment a preacher's salary that never exceeded $6,000 per year. His main political role was as a sort of racial middleman for the city of Chester. Although this was the free North, there was still a mammoth disconnect between white and black residents and officials. Barbour acted as a bridge, reaching local white audiences with commentary in the *Chester Times* newspaper while crafting passionate sermons for his largely black congregation at Calvary Baptist Church.[65]

And, many a time, Barbour relinquished his pulpit for the week and handed it over to an ambitious young preacher from Crozer looking to log a few hours in front of a live congregation. ML would soon be one of those beneficiaries. The congregation didn't mind, but at times it was painfully obvious that a seminarian was fighting upstream to deliver a message. A longtime Calvary churchgoer would nudge a friend's shoulder and mutter, "He's got those students preaching on us."[66]

Rev. Barbour also attempted to provide another service to the young seminarian. As soon as ML arrived at Crozer, the reverend all but advertised ML's bachelor status to the Calvary Baptist congregation. In a letter to his mother, ML wrote, "Since Barbor [*sic*] told the members of his church that my family was rich, the girls are running me down." Not that he needed the help. "Do you know the girl I used to date at Spelman (Gloria Royster)[?]" he asked his mother. "She is in school at Temple and I have been to see her twice. Also I met a fine chick in Phila who has gone wild over the old boy." He hastened to add, "Of course, I dont [sic] ever think about them [since] I am to[o] busy studying."[67]

ML was certainly concerned with academic advancement—particularly since his GPA after term 1 was a modest 2.61—but what continued to preoccupy him was his social standing on campus. Although Rev. Barbour or a former Spelman flame could provide relief from the white-dominated Crozer community, eventually ML needed to return to Old Main, where social events and mingling proved a daunting challenge:

> I remember once at an outing how worried I was when I found they were serving watermelon. I didn't want to be seen eating it because of the association in many peoples' minds between Negroes and watermelon. It was silly, I know, but it shows how white prejudice can affect a Negro.[68]

Charles Turney was a young white man who got to know ML during these early days of solitude. Turney would soon leave for college, but for now he worked as a dishwasher in the Old Main kitchen. He remembered ML trying his best to figure out this strange new interracial culture he'd become a part of. "[During those months], Martin was very much a young, lonely man. He gravitated to those who were simply accepting, and that was what my family was like."[69] Turney was the nephew of Hannah Moitz, Crozer's cook and dietician. Called "Miss Hannah" by students and faculty, Mrs. Moitz was indeed a welcoming soul. Students would walk downstairs and into Miss Hannah's kitchen, hoping for some of her Dutch beef porridge, and she often opened her home on campus to the seminarians. ML volunteered to wash dishes in her kitchen, joining Charles Turney at the sink in the back room.

It was in Miss Hannah's kitchen that ML first noticed a young white woman with brown hair who ventured past the counters and steel pots and pans. She was Betty Moitz, Miss Hannah's twenty-year-old daughter. For the time being, ML's racial anxieties made him reluctant to approach her, but that was about to change. With his gregarious friend Walter McCall slated to join him for Crozer's second term, King would soon break free from his temporary loneliness.

2

Breaking Free

Term 2, November 30, 1948–
February 16, 1949

The Mike and Mac Show: "We Played Pool Until Sometimes Three O'clock in the Morning"

> *"I used to tell Mike . . . he who would do great things must also tighten his hide such that when the criticisms are leveled against him he would never fear them."*

—Walter McCall[1]

In September 1944, fifteen-year-old Morehouse freshman Martin Luther King Jr. needed a haircut. He'd heard about a fellow student who cut hair in the basement of the college's Graves Hall. The barber, named Walter McCall, was a twenty-one-year-old army veteran. ML heard that he was cutting hair for a dime, so he went to him and gave it a try.

After the cut, McCall asked for the dime. ML explained that he didn't have a coin on him but that he'd pay him later. This idea of an IOU system did not sit well with McCall. *You and I both know you have a dime*, he insisted. "Man. I haven't got it now," ML replied. "So there's nothing you can do about it, unless you want to go to the grass." The phrase "go to the grass" was new to McCall, but he knew what it meant: King believed he could take him in a fight.[2] McCall tackled his customer and they wrestled on the floor—a vet fighting a teenager. The pushing and shoving eventually made its way outside onto the lawn, their bout intense enough to attract other students. For those who saw the fight, many expected the older soldier to easily beat up on the smaller, less experienced ML. But for one of the few times in ML's young life, he fought back, and he earned the vet's respect.

From that point on, the two young men were friends. "I always called him 'Mike' and he called me 'Mac,'" said McCall years later. They bonded despite being opposites in almost every way. ML was cautious and reserved, living comfortably in Sweet Auburn as the son of a successful preacher. McCall was bolder and louder, and always struggling to make ends meet. Born August 3, 1923, in Conway, South Carolina, he'd mainly lived in his home state but had bounced around cities such

Walter McCall in 1952. *Courtesy of Fort Valley State University Archives*

as Detroit, Wilmington, and Philadelphia. In a way, each friend had what the other wanted: Mac envied ML's financial situation and parental support, while ML longed for Mac's hard-earned life experience and his knack for livening up any social encounter.[3]

McCall served as a constant reminder to his friend that there was more to experience than classes and church. During their years at Morehouse, they held secret dance parties at ML's home while Daddy and Mama King were out. "One night I remember so well—boy, we had a good time going," said McCall. "The old man [Daddy King] . . . stood at the door to listen to the music and he peeped through the keyhole and we didn't know it. All of a sudden he burst into the house and there we were just swinging away into the night."

The friends also shared a serious interest in social reform. Though their early ambitions to fight for justice by becoming lawyers declined over the years, the fierce discussions about how to best effect social change continued. "We used to sit up oh way into the morning discussing the social issues of the day," Mac recalled. "Particularly, we discussed very seriously at many times the role of leadership in liberating the Negro."

Such pursuits ultimately led both men to Crozer Theological Seminary, though without ML's financial resources, Mac took a while longer to get there. He worked for three months in the Camden, New Jersey, public school system to save up enough money to pay the tuition, missing the first term of junior year.

When McCall entered Crozer after the Thanksgiving holiday, he took note of how ML's seminary experience had already changed him. "He began to take his studies more seriously; he began to take preaching more seriously," McCall remembered. "He began to take what glorious opportunities that his father and mother provided for him more seriously. . . . He would sometimes, if necessary, stay up all night to make certain that he got an idea or pursued an idea to his satisfaction."[4]

Mac remained cognizant of how his friend's "glorious opportunities" contrasted with his own day-to-day financial struggles. Not only was ML drawing a regular allowance from his parents, but Daddy King's reputation up and down the East Coast would mean that potential preaching engagements for his son were just a phone call away.[5] Mac, on the other hand, brought the tools of his trade with him to campus and began cutting hair in his small dorm room next to ML's. "Mac's Barbershop" featured a constant dialogue with other students about his current predicament: *Honestly?* Mac often confessed, *I'm broke, got arthritis . . . I'm as poor as Job's turkey . . . I have to work in spite of my ailments.* Mac's perpetual grumbling that first year earned him the nickname "Job."[6]

Once during their first year, Horace Whitaker later recalled, Mac came back late at night, shouting "The Lord is good to His children!" down the hallway. At first, Whit and others were confused. Had Mac lost it? Nope, he'd found a job. At least temporarily.[7]

Though their economic differences caused some tension, ML and Mac were inseparable, and Mac's presence in Old Main transformed ML's social life. In the first term, ML had been reluctant to put himself into social situations on campus, but soon he and Mac were holding court in the recreation room below the chapel. "We played pool until sometimes three o'clock in the morning," Mac said. They would turn the ceiling into a cloud of cigarette smoke as they played, getting to know the other students who joined in the game. The pair would also play cards until late at night, Mac's choice of background music—like Johnny Mercer's "Ac-cent-tchu-ate the Positive"—helping to alleviate ML's stress.[8]

The two friends had their own special brand of repartee that left a memorable impression on their fellow seminarians. Lloyd Burrus, a Shaw University graduate from Norfolk, Virginia, who was two years ahead of them at Crozer, experienced this "Mike and Mac show" first-hand. In late November 1948, ML's mother came up from Atlanta to check in on him. After seeing ML's shaky term 1 grade report, she told her son that "Buck Benny will stop by to see you later.'"

Burrus had been listening from afar, but the name "Buck Benny" was new to him, so he went over to dig a bit deeper: *Hey . . . who's Buck Benny?*

Next to ML was, of course, McCall, who nearly dropped his jaw at the thought that someone didn't know *the* Buck Benny. Mac couldn't let this one go, and even though the question was directed at ML, Mac had to give Burrus a hard time. "Preacher, you are a senior in one of the country's top divinity schools. Do you mean to tell me that you do not know Buck Benny?"

ML stepped forward. This was their shtick: Mac let loose, and ML calibrated. "Remember, Mac," ML said calmly. "Burrus attended little Shaw University. How is he to know that America's itinerant pastor and the president of Morehouse College, 'Dr. Benjamin Mays' is known and admired by his students as Buck Benny?"[9]

Yes, how *could* Burrus have known such a thing?

The Mike and Mac show most definitely had a center of gravity: women. Ever since their days as self-proclaimed "wreckers" at Morehouse College, ML and Mac used their juxtaposed personalities to the benefit of nabbing dates. Quiet yet sophisticated? Talk to ML. Bombastic yet slightly offbeat? Mac could be your kind of man. And with Mac by his side, never judging, ML found it easier to be bold. So when the two briefly worked together washing dishes in the Old Main kitchen, his friend's presence encouraged him to pursue a possibility he'd previously been too timid to explore . . .

"That's how we met, in the kitchen."

From a young age, Betty Moitz had a family connection to Crozer Theological Seminary. It started with her grandmother Elizabeth, who became Crozer's dietician in 1933. When she retired, Betty's mother, Hannah Moitz, took over the position, and she kept it throughout ML's time there. The family lived in a five-bedroom, three-bathroom home on the Crozer campus, and Betty graduated with honors from Eddystone High School, located only two miles away. Betty spent many days in her youth walking over to the kitchen to check on her mother, lend an extra hand, or just hang around and chat. Her elegant presence would provoke a shift in the male-dominated conversations among seminarians and faculty who stopped by.* "I was a part of Crozer in my small way from age five until twenty-three," Betty says. "I knew most all of the students."[10]

---

* There were very few female seminarians at Crozer during ML's three years. Several were listed as "unclassified," which meant they either had not finished their four-year degrees or were not taking enough credits to be enrolled full time (they included Sarah Anne Corbett; Phyllis J. Snoad, wife of Richard Snoad; and Geneva A. Brooks). There were also several female Chinese students participating in Crozer's "Oriental certificate" program

Despite the constant exposure to their world, Betty had no intention of becoming a divinity student. "I graduated from high school in 1946 and went directly to Moore College of Art. . . . I planned on becoming an interior designer, so this is how I was spending my days."[11]

Betty was still a student at Moore (right across the river from the University of Pennsylvania) when she paid one of her regular visits to her mother in the basement of Old Main and met a well-dressed, ambitious young man out of Atlanta, Georgia. He had a smooth voice and a sly smile. At first, she and ML were just making small talk in Miss Hannah's kitchen, nothing that would cause nearby students to turn their heads. As they spoke on and off over the next few months, Betty learned about ML's background and his tremendous hopes for the future. "Crozer was known as a very radical religious institution," she says, "so I was surprised to hear from ML himself [that he] had more conservative beliefs." It was the enthusiasm with which he spoke on a wide range of topics that first attracted Betty.[12]

ML's own feelings for Betty were something he tried to keep secret. Though he'd even written to his mother about his other recent dating prospects, he would not have been at all eager to inform Mama King that he was interested in a young white woman. Mac knew, of course, but he saw no harm in helping his best friend separate himself even further from racial norms they both believed were outdated. And though a few other students took note of ML and Betty's friendly dialogue—it was, after all, a small world inside Old Main—no one seemed too bothered. Marcus Wood in particular understood some of what spurred ML's attraction: "I supposed he thought that, here I am out of the South now, and not back home . . . out in the open, nothing illegal, a free place, sure I can go over and talk to this white girl."[13]

<hr />

(see page 86), such as Dorothy Lei Hsu. Only one female divinity student was enrolled full time at the seminary during ML's time there. Her name was Irene Easter Lovett, and she would have been in her late thirties at the time. Lovett, who would have encountered King primarily in his first and second years, described him to a *Chester Times* reporter on April 5, 1968, as "a very quiet, meditative individual. As I recall, he didn't stand out in the group, but was a very solid part of it." Rev. Dr. Irene Lovett passed away in 2003 at the age of ninety-two.

ML's Class Schedule

Year I, Term 2, November 30, 1948–February 16, 1949

Time	Tuesday	Wednesday	Thursday	Friday
8:00 AM	History and Literature of the New Testament	History and Literature of the New Testament	History and Literature of the New Testament	History and Literature of the New Testament
9:00 AM				
10:00 AM	Chapel service	Optional service		Devotional pd.
10:30 AM	Preparation of the Sermon		Preparation of the Sermon	
11:00 AM				
11:30 AM			Public Speaking	
12:00 PM				
12:30 PM				
1:00 PM				
2:00 PM				Great Theologians
3:00 PM				
4:00 PM			Vespers service (4:15 PM)	
5:00 PM				

No classes on Monday | Christmas vacation: Dec. 23–Jan. 2 |
Spring vacation: Feb. 17–21
ML's GPA for the term: 3.25

History and Literature of the New Testament
Morton Scott Enslin, BD (Andover Newton), ThD (Harvard), DD (Colby)
Course Description: "Introduction to the study of the New Testament.
The environment and sources of early Christianity; its rise and develop-
ment from 200 B.C. to A.D. 150; origin, canonization, and transmission
of its literature. A competent knowledge of the contents of the English
New Testament is required and will be tested early in the course."
(Credit hours: 8; ML's grade: B)

Preparation of the Sermon
Robert Elwood Keighton, BD, ThM (Crozer)
Course Description: "The sermon as a form of literature; elements of its
composition; sources and selection of material. Prerequisite course 360.
Required." (Credit hours: 2; ML's grade: A)

Public Speaking
Robert Elwood Keighton, BD, ThM (Crozer)
Course Description: "Fundamental physical and psychological elements
of public speaking." (Credit hours: ⅓; ML's grade: C+)

Great Theologians
George Washington Davis, BD, ThM (Colgate-Rochester), PhD (Yale)
Course Description: "Seminar, second term, every alternate year. . . .
Augustine, John of Damascus, Thomas of Aquinas, Duns Scotus, Luther,
Calvin, Schleiermacher, and Karl Barth." (Credit hours: 2; ML's grade: A-)

*On Tuesday, Wednesday, and Friday, a half-hour period was set aside
at 10:00 AM for services in the chapel. On Tuesdays was a mandatory
service led by Crozer president E. E. Aubrey. Wednesday services were
optional, generally led by a member of the faculty or an invited pastor
from an evangelical institution. The Friday devotional period was run by
the students themselves and presided over by the chairman of the Devotions Committee. On Thursday, the 10:00 AM slot was a free period, and
a vespers service was held at 4:15 PM. This tightly planned service featured
a speaker from a prescheduled list, usually a Crozer professor or a guest
speaker from another institution.*[14]

Classes and Professors: In with the New
History and Literature of the New Testament

> *"When I first met and observed Martin both in my class-*
> *room and in my home (he dined in my house several*
> *times), I saw that he was always a perfect gentleman*
> *and knew that he was marked for the sword belt [he was*
> *destined to succeed]; he was going to be someone, not a*
> *private but an officer in the rank. He was a smooth boy*
> *and knew the world was round."*
>
> —Morton S. Enslin[15]

Crozer seminarians knew when Professor Morton Scott Enslin was coming to class. Since Enslin lived near Old Main, his students would look
out their classroom window and see Enslin leave his home with a lit pipe
in his mouth. "He was puffing away," recalls a former student, "march-
ing toward the building as if he was in the army." After Enslin's human
locomotive act, he'd "come into the room very fast."[16]

Having endured Dr. James Pritchard's downsizing of Moses and
the Old Testament in term 1, ML and his classmates were prepared for
Enslin's New Testament course to continue Crozer's program of stripping away biblical myths. They knew that Enslin would try his best to
force his students to rethink how they viewed the life of Jesus Christ,
to consider him as an actual *human being*. Enslin was a good friend of
Pritchard's; the two had planned their multiterm reality check together
as a way of weeding out any students who still clung to a fundamentalist view of the Bible.

Like Pritchard, Enslin was more biblical scholar than preacher.
When Enslin gave a sermon, he never worried about memorization or
eye contact; he just read each sermon word for word. When asked why
he did so, he shrugged. *That's just the way I am.*[17]

By the time ML entered Crozer, Professor Enslin had been at
the seminary for over twenty years. A proud graduate of Harvard
Divinity School, he was serious about his role as editor of the *Crozer
Quarterly*, a widely read academic journal. A family man, Enslin had

a wife and children and stayed in close touch with his parents. But there was an eccentric side to Enslin that after two decades was well known among students and faculty. According to Pritchard, Enslin had no qualms about swearing or drinking and almost always had his pipe within reach. Enslin's handwriting was microscopic in size, and he often allowed his children to run around campus naked as the day they entered the world.* "He was peculiar," said a longtime Crozer trustee.[18]

Through others, ML soon learned that Enslin often retreated alone to Philadelphia to attend church services and prayer meetings. Loyal to routine, Enslin sat in the same exact seat during services and meetings. Enslin believed in this routine so strongly that he would turn down any dinner invitation that interfered with his solo church excursions.[19]

Among the seminarians, the eccentric professor was both a figure of fun and an object of admiration. "[Some of the] Crozer students would talk about him in the cafeteria in jest as 'Saint Morton,'" international student James Beshai recalls, adding that Enslin was "somewhat of a rebel thinker."[20] But Beshai was impressed with Enslin's memory for details: "Dr. Enslin was a typical Harvard man. He was a very disciplined historian, and would not talk off the top of his head. He was always citing references and citing evidence to support every claim he made."[21]

ML himself must have been very aware of Enslin's background as a scholar and an editor, and when he turned in papers, he seemed to work harder to paraphrase than he had in Pritchard's course, perhaps respecting Enslin's ability to sniff out improper citations. One A- paper for Enslin includes the following example of borrowed language—still bad, but less egregiously so:

* Enslin's children also knew about the dumbwaiter used to move food from Old Main's basement kitchen to the first-floor dining hall. They would sneak inside the dumbwaiter after it arrived in the cafeteria and ride it back down.

"In the New Testament from the first page to the last it is either explicitly stated or implicitly understood that a man can only receive the divine forgiveness on condition that he forgives his neighbor."	"In the New Testament, it is understood throughout that one can only receive the divine forgiveness on the condition that he forgives his neighbor."
—R. H. Charles, *The Testaments of the Twelve Patriarchs* (1908)	—**King**, "The Ethics of Late Judaism as Evidenced in the Testaments of the Twelve Patriarchs" (Winter 1948–1949)[22]

Only King knows whether this was an intentional modulation. In any event, Enslin's most lasting impact on ML would be through the ideas to which the professor exposed him. ML would later say of Enslin, "He was one of those precise scholars and superb linguists, who had a rather iconoclastic manner of criticism." Paraphrasing Immanuel Kant's famous description of how David Hume influenced his thinking, King wrote that "[Enslin] knocked me out of my dogmatic slumber."[23]

Professor Enslin would cause ML and the rest of the class to reassess their entire biblical foundation. As they began to doubt their deep-seated beliefs, they found that it affected their ability to preach. Enslin's intent was not to torture his students; his end goal was to build them back up so that they could better serve Christian society.

Seminarians had a habit of checking in on other seminarians as they preached, so once when Marcus Wood was asked to give a sermon in Philadelphia, ML and Mac decided to see if he was practicing what Enslin had been putting down. They snuck into the service and lay down in the balcony so Wood couldn't see them. As their friend spoke, they listened to see how closely he followed Enslin's version of the New Testament. Did Wood fall into any of the traps Enslin cautioned against? Did he summon a Virgin Mary or otherwise mythologize the story of Jesus?

After the service, Wood discovered the two young men. They had critical looks in their eyes, and he knew what they were about to say: "They tore me apart."[24]

Public Speaking; Preparation of the Sermon

> "The greatest need of civilization is not political security;
> the greatest need of civilization is not a multiplicity of
> wealth; the greatest need of civilization is not the superb
> genius of science, as important as it is; the greatest need
> of civilization is moral progress."
>
> —Martin Luther King Jr.[25]

ML also continued to study the practical aspects of preaching under Robert Keighton, pulling in low grades for the second term of Keighton's Public Speaking class. One can only speculate as to why this relatively inconsequential course gave ML such trouble. After all, he had no lack of experience speaking in public; he'd spoken in front of his father's congregation at Ebenezer and to audiences at Morehouse. Perhaps Keighton's aforementioned distaste for the black style of preaching affected his grade. It may have also been a sign that the professor had already lost ML to Rev. J. Pius Barbour's influence.

King did better in Keighton's Preparation of the Sermon course, earning an A and getting exposure to a number of different sermon formats and organizational techniques—some more useful than others. Keighton taught forms such as the gimmicky "jewel" sermon, in which the preacher introduces a single fact (the jewel) and shows it off by exploring it from different perspectives (*One out of every seven people in this city are homeless. Let's think about that for a moment . . .*), and the so-classic-it-became-cliché "three points and a poem" sermon, which is exactly what it sounds like. These fundamental formats had been around long before ML or even Daddy King had started preaching, and ML was resistant to such rigid formulas. He would use them the same way creative writers use writing prompts: simply as random inspiration to kick-start his own imagination.[26]

More directly useful were Keighton's tips on how to organize a sermon via a written outline. ML developed several of his future sermons using the six-part template Keighton taught, including "Facing Life's Inescapables," which he would deliver in March 1949 at Rev. Barbour's

Calvary Baptist Church. At various points in his notes, ML arranged his thoughts according to the elements in Keighton's template, which are collected below:

Title:
Facing Life's Inescapables

Theme:
There are certain great inevitables in life which cannot be escaped.

Purpose:
To show the listeners how to face these inevitables.

Introduction:
One of the tragic tendencies that has characterized man ever
since the dawn of recorded history has been his attempt
to escape his moral responsibilities. Man is forever trying
to escape the realities of life. He is forever trying to make
the false seem true; the evil seem good; the ugly seem beautiful;
and the unjust seem just.

Body:
—First, you cannot escape yourself. You are the one person
from whom you can never get a divorce.
—Second, we cannot escape sacrifice. No one ever accomplishes
anything in this life without sacrificing themselves
for one thing or another.
—Finally we cannot escape Jesus. For 19 centuries we have
tried to escape him. But only to find that every time we
attempt to escape him he stands right before us.

Conclusion:
This is the conclusion of the whole matter. We can't escape
ourselves; we can't escape sacrifice; we can't escape Jesus. We
had better accept these as the great inevitables of life.[27]

Like the sermon formats Keighton taught, the template above was a common way for preachers to organize their material. But it would not take long for ML to break free from such conventions and distinguish himself from all the other aspiring ministers at Crozer.

———————

Meanwhile, ML continued his education at "Barbour University." Rev. Barbour had a grading system that was very different from Keighton's. He would watch ML and other beginning preachers closely as they practiced their sermons in his home, assessing their performance in three categories: content, delivery, and audience reaction. Even decades later, one of Rev. Barbour's "students" remembered the intimidating assessment: "You could get an A in content, but a D in audience response . . . the lesson was that every sermon had to have relevance to the people listening."[28]

At this stage of ML's Crozer journey, earning all As from Rev. Barbour would have been next to impossible. But Barbour's stern guidance would help him find his way, not only at "Barbour University" but back at Crozer as well.

Once more, the reverend served as a middleman, bridging the gap between the culture at Crozer and the world of young black seminarians such as ML. To do so, he drew on his own life experiences. J. Pius Barbour grew up a Texan, near Galveston, where his father preached for nearly four decades. Having watched his father and brother commit their entire beings to the pulpit, Barbour was resistant to following the same path. (His brother would later collapse and die in the middle of a sermon.) Instead, he chose to pursue a law-related track at Morehouse College, got married,* and then landed a job as an English professor at Alabama's Tuskegee Institute. It was while at Tuskegee that he felt a call to the ministry, "mystical" in nature. He chose to study at Crozer, and it was there that he realized how much doubt he actually had about

———————

* Rev. Barbour met his wife, Olee, while attending Morehouse. Olee Littlejohn Barbour had her own stories to share with ML. Not only was she an excellent singer, but she also had been an art student at the Tuskegee Institute under George Washington Carver. Carver showed her how to paint using natural pigments from berries. After gaining experience, Olee Barbour helped sketch many of Carver's new plant findings in the 1920s.

his own faith in Christianity. But his professors encouraged him to strengthen that faith by learning as much as he could about theology. With his background in law and the humanities, Barbour welcomed this intense scrutiny. He went on to earn not just a bachelor's but also a master's in theology from Crozer.

J. Pius Barbour knew Crozer's curriculum, and he knew that anyone coming from a background similar to his would have a tough time finding an authentic experience there. "A course in ministry at Crozer had no relationship to the black church," explained his daughter, Almanina Barbour. "It had no emotion or tension. . . . Furthermore, it did not speak to the conditions of black people, because how you see Christianity depends upon what your reality is." That's why, she added, "there had to be somebody to translate all this, and that is what my father did for all of them."[29]

Great Theologians

> "After the Bible has been stripped of all its mythological and non-historical content, the liberal theologian must be able to answer the question—what then?"
>
> —Martin Luther King Jr.[30]

For two hours every Friday afternoon, ML took a seat in a classroom on the first floor of the main building and listened to a short, kind man named George Washington Davis tell him about the great theologians who had come before him—tales of men such as Karl Barth, Walter Rauschenbusch, Thomas of Aquinas, and his namesake Martin Luther.

ML had dreams of one day joining their ranks, and he wasn't shy in telling his fellow students about them. "More than once," Marcus Wood recalled, "he told us how he hoped to be 'immortalized,' by heeding the fiery prophets of the Eighth Century [BC, such as Amos, Hosea, Isaiah, and Micah]. . . . We simply laughed at him. . . . He had wild, wild dreams of what he would accomplish in society."[31]

ML's mind wandered in class, and he had a habit of writing lines in the gaps of his notebook that at least *sounded* like the words of a great spiritual leader. It was likely in Davis's Great Theologians class that

ML scribbled the following inside the cover of his notebook, a sentence yearning to be spoken with echoes:

> We are experiencing cold and whistling winds of despair in a world sparked by turbulence.[32]

Though young ML may have been fond of grandiose sentiment and larger-than-life ancient figures, Davis's class focused on religiously driven individuals whom ML was able to apprehend on a more human level. Criticizing the Old Testament prophets would be akin to punching a cloud puff. But Martin Luther? That was different. ML's opinion was that although the German theologian was courageous in rebelling against the Catholic Church, he didn't care enough for the common people of his time.[33] And after listening to a sermon by contemporary Swiss theologian Karl Barth for class, ML was appreciative of the views he expressed but far less laudatory of his skills as a preacher, complaining that Barth "left the average mind lost in the fog of theological abstractions. . . . For these reasons I found this sermon very boring."[34] Such examples were just what ML needed in order to anchor his dreams to the ground.

Professor Davis was himself an accepting, nonjudgmental professor with a smooth yet commanding voice. He was seen as a pacifist who "opposed all wars," and one student thought he came across in the classroom as "very serious and a bit distant."[35] Outside of class, Davis opened up, inviting students to his home, located just behind Old Main. Since Davis was also the chairman of the scholarship committee, many of the conversations focused on "the next step," such as earning a doctorate. "He was a marvelous teacher," ML wrote years later, "conversant with the trends of modern culture and yet sincerely religious. He was warm and Christian. It was easy to get close to him."[36]

Off Campus: "This Food Is Good, Man! I Can't Wait on Y'all"

By his second term, with his friend Walter McCall at his side, ML was settling into life at Crozer, both on campus and off. The Crozer grounds themselves were known to many as "the most beautiful spot in Chester." They covered forty acres, lined with silver maple trees that the Crozer family had imported from China in the early 1870s. The trees shaded the students from the daily rigor of Chester, a manufacturing port with a population hovering near seventy-five thousand. For students who didn't have their own car, a local bus stopped in front of Old Main to pick up anyone looking to head into downtown Chester or, more often, to the Chester train station, where they then could make their way to Philadelphia. ML was carless most of his time at seminary, but he usually preferred to rely on friends with cars, including Walter McCall and Horace Whitaker (he loved Whit's Chevy "Power Glide"), to take him to places off campus.[37]

Another classmate who took part in ML's off-campus excursions was a southern white student named Dupree Jordan. Jordan graduated from Mercer University in 1947, the year before pistol-waving Lucius Hall, but the similarities stop there; Dupree and ML became friends early in their first year. Mercer was located in Macon, Georgia, so Dupree and ML at least had local culture to talk about. The chairman of the Crozer student athletics committee, Jordan was active by nature, and he saw ML as introverted by comparison: "He was very studious; he spent a lot more time on his lesson assignments than most of us did."[38]

One day, ML and Dupree decided to travel to downtown Philadelphia to grab a bite to eat. They chose Stouffer's, a sit-down restaurant. Jordan had recently contributed an article to the *Chester Times* after attending Reinhold Niebuhr's December 12 visit to Swarthmore College, located five miles from the Crozer campus. Though ML hadn't yet become too deeply immersed in Niebuhr, he would have been fascinated by Jordan's account of the contemporary theologian's visit.[39] But five minutes passed as they sat at their table at Stouffer's, waiting for a server. No one. Ten minutes . . . still no one.

The restaurant wasn't busy, yet something all too familiar was occurring, and ML must have sensed it. "Finally," said Jordan, "we demanded service, and we got service. . . . Unfortunately, in one or more of his vegetables that he was served, he had sand on his plate."[40]

ML had every right to speak up. This wasn't the South. The restaurant wasn't segregated. All ML wanted was a decent plate of food with a friend. But, Jordan remembered, "he took it rather quietly, and did not want to make demands that would make a scene."[41]

Although far superior to cities in the South, Philadelphia circa 1948 was not exactly a model of civil rights progress. Within its city limits sat a heartbreaking collection of impoverished black neighborhoods. Chester's racial culture was similar, but Crozer Theological Seminary served as an oasis of liberalism and equal rights.

After the sand-in-his-vegetables incident, it must have been clearer to ML how miraculous the Crozer campus was. Perhaps Jordan, after the incident, relayed to ML the words he'd heard from Reinhold Niebuhr at Swarthmore: "The establishment of a successful working community is the only true test of a worthwhile religion . . . but self-righteous pride makes this difficult."[42]

ML's sister, Christine, would have been the only one in ML's family to fully understand the incident at Stouffer's. When it came to their education, ML and Christine were living parallel lives. After graduating from Atlanta's predominantly black, female-only Spelman College in 1948, Christine took a segregated train bound for New York City with her friend Juanita Sellers. They ate their packed meals in the "colored dining car." As Christine recalled, "We were separated from the white passengers by two curtains."[43]

Christine and Juanita ended up at the Emma Ransom YWCA House, located at 175 West 137th Street in Harlem. Christine was there to attend Columbia University Teachers College, hoping to earn a master's degree in education. Her plan was to then return to Atlanta to become a teacher.

While Christine and Juanita lived at Emma Ransom, ML and Mac would often snag a train from the Philadelphia station and head up to NYC to see them. "Juanita and I waited like giddy schoolgirls for their arrival." Although ML was one year younger than Christine, Daddy King wanted ML to keep an eye on her, to protect her from "all the slick boys up North."[44] Christine noticed that even after such a short time away from Atlanta, ML's character had already started to mature. "It was at Crozer that ML became serious about his studies, much more so than he had been at Morehouse. His intellectual curiosity was sharpened, focused, and challenged."[45]

Yes, he'd grown more serious, but he still knew how to have a good time. McCall remembered that during one trip to New York City, he and ML decided to eat at a high-class restaurant. "I can't remember the name," McCall said, "but it was truly a heavenly place in appearance." By then, ML was notorious among family and close friends for his casual eating habits. In a fine NYC restaurant, surrounded by well-mannered customers with sophisticated dining etiquette, ML went the other direction. "Instead of . . . putting on the dog in terms of table manners, he brought his same old country habits of eating there; and we just rolled. We just couldn't help from rolling." When ML grabbed the food with his hands, he shook his head at everyone and said, "This food is good, man! I can't wait on y'all." As King once famously said, "Eating is my great sin." Mac concurred, recalling that ML "ate wherever he could."[46]

Christine and Juanita visited Chester as well, where they stayed at Rev. Barbour's house, since only Crozer students and staff were allowed inside Old Main. Christine, even a half century later, remembered her time there. She and ML "enjoyed frequent dinners at the home of Reverend Dr. J. Pius Barbour. . . . These dinners provided additional mental stimulation [for ML], and allowed for intellectual debate and spirited conversation."[47]

In between his verbal jousts with Rev. Barbour, ML thought about the women around him. Christine's friend Juanita was one of a few Atlanta women whom he considered going with. They had dated on and off in the past, but according to Juanita, ML thought her "too liberated" to be a suitable wife. Dating Juanita would have also meant being reminded of Atlanta and the long shadow of Daddy King, who was apt to scrutinize any potential wife his son might consider.[48]

Besides, ML had this new northern world to consider. In addition to the local girls "running him down," ML had started casually seeing an "almost white" woman at Marcus Wood's church in Woodbury, New Jersey.* And his friendship with Betty Moitz continued to develop as their chats moved out of Miss Hannah's basement kitchen.

Most of their time together was now spent talking innocently around campus, safe from the cold stares that would have come from the residents of downtown Chester. And soon ML was also making the straight five-minute walk from Old Main to visit her at the Moitz home. "He used to go over their house quite often to see her," said Marcus Wood.[49]

ML felt at ease with Betty. "He would talk, and talk and talk," Betty says. More than anything, she enjoyed his rumbling enthusiasm and his sincerity. At first they discussed his time in the South and how different it was from the idealized culture within the seminary. He didn't yet know how but, according to Betty, "one thing ML knew at age nineteen was that he could change the world."[50]

---

* Marcus Wood commuted to his church in Woodbury every weekend, and ML, Horace Whitaker, and Walter McCall would sometimes travel up there as well to surprise their friend. While at Wood's church, the trio would head over to the parsonage and empty out the fridge filled with food that local farmers had brought as a donation to the church—yet another manifestation of ML's ravenous appetite. (Wood, *And Grace Will Lead Me Home*, 50; Wood, notes from interview by Branch.)

3

Finding a Voice
Term 3, February 22–
May 6, 1949

Calvary Baptist Church: "You Cannot Escape Yourself"

Just months into his education at Crozer, ML was putting what he'd learned into practice in front of congregations in Chester and the surrounding area. Although some members of Rev. Barbour's Calvary Baptist Church recall hearing King preach in the fall of 1948, his first documented appearance at a local church came on February 27, 1949, when he delivered a sermon at Prospect Hill Baptist Church, a four-mile drive from campus.* The service had been publicized in the *Chester Times* as open to

---

* Though this is ML's earliest documented appearance in front of an area congregation, the *Chester Times* noted that the previous week, February 23, he was scheduled to speak to local high school students in the "Frolic Club" of the West Branch YMCA. His talk, titled "It Pays to Be Decent," was part of a seven-week course moderated by his friend Cyril Pyle. ("Frolic Club to Hear 2nd Talk Tonight," *Chester Times*, February 9, 1949.) The West Branch Y was an important community resource for teenagers looking for guidance, and ML would continue to contribute his time there. On April 13, for Holy Week, he'd participate in a YMCA program on "The Personality of Jesus as Revealed in His Words from the Cross," giving a speech on the meaning of the words "My God, my God, why hast thou forsaken me?" ("Holy Week Rites Being Held at West Branch 'Y,'" *Chester Times*, April 12, 1949.)

Twenty-year-old Martin Luther King Jr.'s photo in the *Chester Times,*
February 26, 1949. *Used with permission of the Delaware County Daily Times*

everyone "regardless of race, creed or color." The newspaper even included
a photo of ML above the article.[1] Fellow black seminarians would have
smirked at their young friend's momentary spike of local fame, proud
and jealous at the same time.

But his next scheduled sermon was perhaps more meaningful to
ML himself. On March 9 he was to deliver a sermon at Calvary Baptist,
and impressing his mentor Rev. Barbour would have required careful preparation. The notes of his sermon "Facing Life's Inescapables,"
developed for the most part in Keighton's preaching courses, would be
his starting point.[2]

In the week before his appearance at Calvary, ML pored over his
notes in room 52 of Old Main, his heater turned on, its *tick-tick-tick*ing
sound interrupting the quiet.

You cannot escape yourself, he'd written . . .

But . . . hadn't he tried? Hadn't his decision to live in the North, to attend a seminary almost eight hundred miles away from his family, been in part an escape from the heavy legacy offered by his father? It would have been easy for ML to imagine having taken Daddy King's path instead: a packed Ebenezer Baptist congregation, a confident young minister spouting sophisticated verbal fire, local Atlanta girls smiling at the available bachelor. . . . And when he'd made the decision to study up north, he knew he'd be leaving behind a confused father. His sister, Christine, confirmed it: "I'm sure Daddy didn't think he necessarily needed to go that far from home, but they both knew the future beckoned."[3]

As kind as Crozer had been to him thus far, ML realized he didn't need to remain there. Perhaps he was simply delaying the inevitable. Marcus Wood had heard ML talk about the "guilt" he felt, being up in the North enjoying almost unimaginable cultural freedom—a few of the black students had called Crozer a piece of heaven—while others suffered in the dark recesses of the South. Had ML abandoned his responsibility to his home and his people in selfish pursuit of personal goals?

No, he thought. This was a chance to broaden his perspective. In only six months, he'd begun to see America in a new light. It would have been easy to remain in the South. After graduating from Morehouse, ML could have joined his father at Ebenezer and grown into his role naturally and comfortably—protected by his father's legacy and status, nourished by his kind and loving mother's cooking, the company of his younger brother, AD, and a ready circle of friends. Even now, a life in Atlanta was all set up for him; at any point he could drop out of Crozer and move back home. But if he went back now, or if he'd never left, then his view of the world would have remained firmly rooted in southern soil.

With his appearance at Calvary Baptist only days away, ML went on to his next sermon point: *You cannot escape sacrifice . . .*

That's right. A sacrifice. Had he escaped his old self by leaving Atlanta behind? Perhaps. But he'd also sacrificed familiarity for an experience that could potentially change his life. He wanted to become *better*, in every sense of the word, and that required sacrifice. He thought of others who'd sacrificed in order to become better. Singers such as Marian Anderson, Paul Robeson, and Roland Hayes came to mind, as did one of his favorite boxers growing up.

ML, like millions of others, had listened on the radio to Joe Louis's fights, as the Brown Bomber inspired his fellow African Americans by knocking out Max Schmeling in 1938 and giving his fans hope. He'd been a walking symbol of empowerment. Maya Angelou once wrote, "If Joe lost we were back in slavery and beyond help."[4] After a punishing fight against Jersey Joe Walcott in June 1948 that Louis won with a dramatic eleventh-round knockout, the nation assumed he would soon retire from boxing, but it wasn't until the Brown Bomber submitted a letter of resignation to the National Boxing Association on March 1, 1949, that he made it official. Louis had had enough.

ML inserted the breaking news of Joe Louis's announcement into his sermon notes. He even added a flourish of appreciation, calling him "probably the greatest boxer in history. . . . Joe Louis realized early that he could not stay up all night drinking and [carousing] if he was to be the chapion [sic] of the world."[5]

On the night of Wednesday, March 9, ML stood in front of Rev. Barbour's congregation. Calvary Baptist was a bit smaller than Ebenezer; where his father's church had three sets of pews, Calvary had two sets of pews twenty rows deep, and a narrower floor area. Although its congregation at the time was predominantly black, most of the parishioners had been raised in the free North. As ML took his place behind the pulpit, he knew his voice and words would be reaching a more liberated audience.

As one reads "Facing Life's Inescapables" and compares it to ML's future sermons, what quickly stands out is the rigid, Keighton-inspired format. It reflects the persona ML had presented to his classmates in his early days at Crozer, with his immaculately pressed suit and perfectly shined shoes—the epitome of sophistication and professionalism, refined, tightly wound, and careful:

We say that Jesus has been the most influential character in Western civilization, and as we read his sermon on the mount there
is something about it that penetrates our very souls, but we must
remember that at a very early age he sacrificed his time to God,
and finally he sacrificed even his life. There are people who expect
the best in life without effort. But I tell you . . . whatever your
potentialities may be, they will amount to little or nothing unless
you subject yourself to hard work and discipline.

For a young man officially ordained as a minister only thirteen
months earlier, and with Barbour's judging eyes looking on, some ner-
vousness would have been natural. But that night ML delivered his
eight-minute sermon with as much confidence as he could muster. And
regardless of the tension he felt, he still had his strong yet smooth baritone voice and his air of gravitas, thanks to his musically gifted mother
and the authoritative Daddy King.

Reviews of his early appearances at Calvary were mixed but encouraging. One parishioner described him as "quiet . . . maybe some thought
he was aloof in the beginning." Another recalled, "He stood tall, but
he was not tall, and when he spoke . . . walls vibrated, because of his
speech . . . I'll never forget it."[6]

Calvary Baptist churchgoer Isaiah Bennett distinctly remembers the
first time he saw ML in the pulpit one Sunday. ML had chosen as his
topic Acts 27–28, the story of the Apostle Paul's arduous journey to
Rome, surviving shipwrecks and frequent brushes with death and star-
vation. At one point, when even Paul's companion Luke has lost hope,
Paul stands up and declares to the frightened sailors, "There shall be no
loss of any man's life among you, but of the ship." Isaiah Bennett was
inspired. "It was very touching. It put everybody to thinking there was
a brighter day coming."[7]

ML may have been young and still in search of a preaching style
that suited him, but as he put in more appearances in Rev. Barbour's
church, his skills began to develop. Barbour's daughter, Almanina, witnessed ML's slow transformation firsthand. "A lot of things happened
to Martin Luther King in [Chester]. He learned how to preach here."[8]

ML's Class Schedule
Year I, Term 3, February 22–May 6, 1949

Time	Tuesday	Wednesday	Thursday	Friday
8:00 AM				
9:00 AM	The Gospels	The Gospels	The Gospels	The Gospels
10:00 AM	Chapel service	Optional service		Devotional pd.
10:30 AM	Christian Mysticism	Christian Mysticism	Christian Mysticism	Christian Mysticism
11:00 AM				
11:30 AM	Practice Preaching?	Practice Preaching?	Public Speaking	Practice Preaching?
12:00 PM				
12:30 PM				
1:00 PM				
2:00 PM				
3:00 PM				
4:00 PM			Vespers service (4:15 PM)	
5:00 PM				

No classes on Monday | Eighty-first commencement: May 8–10
ML's GPA for the term: 3.40

The Gospels

Morton Scott Enslin, BD (Andover Newton), ThD (Harvard), DD (Colby)
Course Description: "The Synoptic Problem; Gospels as sources of knowledge of the life of Jesus and of developing Christian thought." (Credit hours: 4; ML's grade: B+)

Christian Mysticism

George Washington Davis, BD, ThM (Colgate-Rochester), PhD (Yale)
Course Description: "The history, nature, value, and psychology of Christian mysticism; the place of mysticism in the total structure of religion. Readings from Dionysius the Areopagite, John Tauler, Thomas a Kempis, St. John of the Cross, St. Theresa, Madame Guyon, Brother Lawrence, George Fox, Toyohiko Kagawa, and others." (Credit hours: 4; ML's grade: B+)

Practice Preaching

Robert Elwood Keighton, BD, ThM (Crozer)
Course Description: "Delivery of sermons in the classroom with criticism by the instructor." *This class was listed at 10:30 in the course catalog, but as that overlaps with ML's Christian Mysticism course, I speculate that it was actually at 11:30.* (Credit hours: 4; ML's grade: A-)

Public Speaking

Robert Elwood Keighton, BD, ThM (Crozer)
Course Description: "Fundamental physical and psychological elements of public speaking." (Credit hours: ⅓; ML's grade: C)

On Tuesday, Wednesday, and Friday, a half-hour period was set aside at 10:00 AM for services in the chapel. On Tuesdays was a mandatory service led by Crozer president E. E. Aubrey. Wednesday services were optional, generally led by a member of the faculty or an invited pastor from an evangelical institution. The Friday devotional period was run by the students themselves and presided over by the chairman of the Devotions Committee. On Thursday, the 10:00 AM slot was a free period, and a vespers service was held at 4:15 PM. This tightly planned service featured a speaker from a prescheduled list, usually a Crozer professor or a guest speaker from another institution.[9]

Classes and Professors: The Gospels of Sacrifice
Practice Preaching; Public Speaking

> *"The congregation sings Amen; the last notes of the organ*
> *quietly die away. There is a settling of the congregation*
> *into the mood and manner of an audience. The minister*
> *stands quietly behind the pulpit, waiting for the excitement*
> *within him to subside so that his voice may have only the*
> *calm compulsion of the pastor. The moment has come; he*
> *is to preach his first sermon to the people of his first church.*
> *For these are his people now, as he is now their pastor."*
>
> —Robert Keighton[10]

Not only did ML preach his "Facing Life's Inescapables" sermon to the Calvary Baptist congregation early in his third term, he also delivered it in front of his fellow students in Robert Keighton's Practice Preaching class. As ML spoke, Keighton would determine whether he was following the formatting and organizational guidelines the professor had been teaching the class over the course of their entire junior year. ML apparently gave Keighton what he was looking for, as he finished the course with a grade of A-.

The same couldn't be said of his performance in Keighton's Public Speaking class, where his grade dropped from a C+ in term 2 to a C in term 3. Once again, I suspect that ML's connection to Rev. Barbour was the reason the course caused him so much trouble. By term 3, word must have circulated around Crozer that ML, Horace Whitaker, and Walter McCall were frequent guests in Barbour's home. The faculty were quite familiar with their school's first black graduate, and some of them had a less than favorable opinion of the man. Dr. Pritchard, for example, called him "almost a buffoon," who made jokes and didn't trust Catholic priests. It's possible that Keighton responded unfavorably to signs of Barbour's influence, and ML's grade suffered as a result.[11]

By the end of ML's first year, it was clear that his preaching style had been influenced by both Barbour and Keighton. From Keighton he'd learned how to shape his sermon in a manner acceptable to a northern white congregation, while at the same time he'd gleaned from Barbour the sort of rumbling sophistication that was perfect for southern black audiences. Both would prove vital to King down the road when faced with the responsibility of crafting a message meant for *everyone*. As Addie Cheeks, a Calvary Baptist parishioner, once said, ML "wasn't just concerned about black people. He was concerned about all people."[12]

The Gospels

Crozer's program of mentally excavating the Bible and stripping away its myths continued in term 3 with The Gospels. In this course, Professor Morton Enslin returned to focus his intensive scrutiny more narrowly on the books of Matthew, Mark, and Luke, attempting to change his students' perspective on three of the most quoted chapters of the New Testament.

The course addressed the Gospels' "synoptic problem," which was, quite simplified, *Which book was written first?* Like other scholars at that time (and today), Enslin believed that Mark should be considered the original gospel. "For centuries this was denied," he wrote in his 1938 opus *Christian Beginnings*, "and Mark was regarded, as it had been by Augustine, a colourless epitome of Matthew and Luke."[13]

Christian Beginnings could serve as a window into Enslin's process as a scholar. Its richness lies in his ability to source, source, and source. He analyzes the analyzers and critiques the critics. After an almost biblical amount of processing, Enslin concludes that Mark was not only written first but also stands tall as the most intense Gospel. Enslin's love for Mark seems naked in its pureness. He calls the gospel "highly dramatic. . . . Constantly [Mark] falls into the historic present, so real to him is the scene."

If *Beginnings* is any indicator, discussing the Gospels is where Enslin came alive. "There is only one way to read this gospel, and that is at a sitting, and it leaves one tense and exhausted." With his pipe at hand, pacing back and forth, he would have emphasized the power of Mark to his class, *needing* them to respect Mark's story: "As the narrative [of Mark] proceeds, the tone of excitement heightens, until in the last pages—the dreadful days in Jerusalem—there is no let-down or breathing-space till the very end, the death. . . . The curtain falls with the audience speechless. Then after a quick moment the curtain rises again for an instant."[14]

As for Matthew and Luke, Enslin felt differently. He would have described Matthew to ML and his classmates using less-than-thrilling words such as "systematic," "comprehensive," and "intended for church use." He imagined Matthew the author creating rounded, perfectly structured text—easy to grasp and, more important, easy to remember. Whereas Mark is a thrilling roller coaster ride, Matthew borrows Mark's framework but creates a milder attraction suitable for the whole family. "[Matthew] implies an organized church life," wrote Enslin, "with a well-defined moral code."

Enslin gave Luke the same underwhelmed, matter-of-fact treatment, describing it as "biographical," a "carefully prepared account of Jesus's actions and teachings." He would have impressed on the class that the Gospel of Luke was not capable of standing alone, that it needed to be considered alongside with the same author's Acts of the Apostles to produce a transcendent vision. "It is distinctly unfortunate that through the years these two halves of a single whole have been divorced from one another."[15]

Overall, Enslin attempted to show the class that although Mark probably drew from existing sources himself, they should consider him principally responsible for igniting the flame of the New Testament. Matthew and Luke then took up Mark's fire and expanded the story of Jesus.

For ML, the in-depth analysis must have seemed far removed from Daddy King's passionate, plainspoken overtures of strength and hope. In just two courses, Enslin had widened ML's biblical views. The New Testament could now live inside his mind far more dynamically than it did in his father's. ML was maturing "offstage"—away from his family. And he wanted more. Later, Enslin would say of ML the student that when it came to absorbing a concept or thought, "all is grist that comes to his mill."[16]

Christian Mysticism

> "We must understand how to fail. Jesus was willing to fail
> so that He might establish a better social order. I repeat
> that: It is necessary to fail to establish a good society. If
> anyone wants to be the chief of society he must first be a
> leader of the common people. . . . If we want to have real
> progress, we need to be subjected to pain and suffering
> to make us want to fight for the cause of righteousness."
>
> —Toyohiko Kagawa[17]

Through Enslin, ML was called on to critique the words of the Bible in a way he had never before attempted. Through Keighton, he honed his skill behind a pulpit. There was, however, a curricular gap left to fill, and that was the fundamental experience of *being* a Christian.

This was where George W. Davis's Christian Mysticism came in. Whereas his Great Theologians course had been dedicated to introducing central figures in Christian history, this class would delve deeper into the hearts of the Christian mystics, men and women who dedicated themselves to experiencing, in as real a way as they could, the presence of God within human life.

Nowadays, the word *mysticism* may bring to mind things such as meditation, New Age beliefs, finding one's inner self, and so on. But these practices, often of Eastern origin, are concerned primarily with a state of mind. Christian mysticism, on the other hand, concerns itself with the state of *living*. The mystics are those who decided to follow Jesus's example of sacrifice in order to fulfill what they believed was God's will.

From what materials are available, it appears that Davis taught his class about the topic using larger-than-life figures in Christian history. The mystics Davis mentioned in class all actively pursued a connection with God, usually through privation, persecution, and devotion. Many spent time in prison, or devoted long periods to monastery or convent life. Davis's course descriptions may have read like a collection of Christianity's greatest hits, but his lectures provided ML and his classmates with essential examples of faith in action.

The only living mystic in the Christian Mysticism course description was Japanese Christian Toyohiko Kagawa. His legacy is difficult to reckon with, which may be why Davis chose him for the class. Kagawa loved America dearly; in 1936 he traveled all over the United States and even declared to a group of supporters that the "Emperor of Japan once said the greatest personality in the world's history is Abraham Lincoln. Even the Great Emperor of Japan considered himself inferior to Abraham Lincoln."[18]

But when World War II broke out, according to Kagawa scholar Robert Schildgen, the mystic chose not to speak out against it, instead broadcasting radio messages that supported the Japanese government's military strategy. To Kagawa, cooperating with his country's government was necessary to preserve the Christian message in Japan. Mahatma Gandhi disagreed, and his advice to Kagawa at a religious conference in 1939 had been direct: "I would declare my heresies and be shot." Kagawa chose not to follow the path of a martyr.[19]

By the time ML entered Professor Davis's class, he and his classmates had most likely heard about Kagawa's wavering stance. By delving deeper into why a man like Kagawa would fall into line during the war to save himself, Professor Davis may have provided the twenty-year-old King with a warning sign. ML was attempting to figure out a way to change society for the better. He needed all the real-life examples he could find, positive and negative, to help him along the way.

Blue Mondays: "In This Experience, I Saw God"

As ML began to log more hours preaching at Calvary Baptist Church, he would have benefited from Crozer's policy of not holding classes on Monday. The practical reasons for such a policy are fairly straightforward: many of the students and faculty would be spending their Sundays preaching at churches across the area or even farther afield (recall Marcus Wood, who commuted to Woodbury, New Jersey, to preach), so it would be hard to ask them to be present and prepared for class the following morning. For divinity students, even just attending a service at a new church meant studying the congregation, the preacher, the choir, and the dozens of other factors that they'd be expected to consider when they had their own church to run. Visiting a new place of worship was an immersive, thrilling experience—a short peek into another world. For the seminarians, Sunday was their Saturday night.

But there was another reason Crozer gave students and faculty the day off . . .

It's called Blue Monday, a condition that is said to affect ministers after they deliver a sermon. Sermonizing requires every ounce of spiritual energy a preacher can muster. For most of the week, ML or any preacher with a Sunday engagement planned an approximately fifteen-minute sermon, crafting and tweaking it for maximum impact. For that one moment in time on Sunday morning, the minister labored to hold the spiritual attention of dozens, sometimes hundreds of people using such devices as current news (*I think we've all heard about the tragedy in Anytown a few days ago . . .*), personal anecdotes (*I was talking with a friend the other day, and he told me . . .*), and shocking first lines (*I'm going to go ahead and say it, and you're not going to like it, but . . . we're in trouble, y'all . . .*), with biblical and literary passages threaded throughout.

It's a workout, a performance, an offering to God of blood, sweat, and tears. Once the preacher steps away from the pulpit, he or she does not usually feel fulfilled. Rather, the preacher has been emptied of light, and Sunday night becomes an exercise in shadow fighting:

> One Sunday evening I left my pulpit with a sense of the most utter frustration I had ever known. The sermon had been terrible in its inadequacy, the delivery pitiful in its awkwardness. Every sentence, every word, seemed to have come only after the most appalling struggle. I literally perspired with the effort to be convincing. Floating through my consciousness were the thoughts: "Why did I ever choose this sermon? What did I ever see in it? Will I get through this side of a complete breakdown?"[20]

This was from, of all people, Robert Keighton. During the week, Keighton taught ML and other students the art and format of the sermon, but on the weekends, Keighton did his best to walk the walk.

But as with all preachers, ML included, self-doubt crept in—*Were they listening? Are they even trying to see a new perspective?*—and this neurotic bender would remain with Keighton through sleep and into the following morning. To Keighton, Blue Monday moods grew "out of the fact that what we wanted did not happen; the change we sought did not come."[21]

Thankfully for ML, he'd always had help and support in dealing with this condition that made Monday classes untenable. His earliest preaching experiences had taken place within the sheltered atmosphere of Daddy King's church in Atlanta. And now as he ventured beyond the protective walls of Ebenezer Baptist, he had the Crozer community and its many amenities to lean on. Just outside his second-floor dorm room was a tennis court where he could work off his anxieties. If he wasn't in the mood to move, the second floor had a student lounge—a perfect location for melancholic preachers to gather and bond over common miseries, *This one man just wouldn't stop snoring!* or *They're all looking at me, but are they **hearing** me?* There was also the rec room down in the catacombs of Old Main, a place to play with friends who knew exactly how you felt as cigarette smoke billowed, the dark and empty chapel directly above.[22]

If what ML needed was solitude, there was the Pearl Hall library only a minute's walk away. He also had his own place of refuge—a temporary Walden Pond, a safe haven from criticism, discrimination, and the spiritual pressure to be not just a great man but *incredible.* As King described it:

> The seminary campus is a beautiful sight, particularly so in the spring. And it was at this time of the year that I made it a practice to go out to the edge of campus every afternoon for at least an hour to commune with nature. On the side of the campus ran a tributary from the Delaware River. Every day I would sit on the edge of campus by the side of the river and watch the beauties of nature. My friend, in this experience, I saw God. I saw him in birds of the air, the leaves of the tree, the movement of the rippling waves . . .[23]

Photographed in January 2016, this is the path ML took into what was then called Ship Creek Woods, behind the Old Main building. Farther down the path is Chester Creek, by which ML used to sit. *Photo by the author*

Moments of conflict swirled through ML's mind as well: sand in his vegetables; Lucius Hall's gun pointed at him; his meetings around campus with Betty and the awareness that even though he was attracted to a white woman, society, church culture, family, and friends would disapprove of any kind of relationship.

Was devoting his life to a church what he really wanted? He had his doubts, and near the end of his first year at Crozer, he wrote them down:

> The church is suppose to be the most radical opposer of the status quo in society, yet, in many instances, it is the greatest preserver of the status quo. So it was very easy for slavery to receive a religious sanction. The church is one of the chief exponents of racial bigotry. Monopoly capitalism has always received the sanction of the church. . . . Since this is the case, we must admit that the church is far from Christ.[24]

He was frustrated. With his own eyes, not just in the South but in the North as well, he'd viewed a deeply flawed society, one that overwhelmed the oldest and purest impulses he still perceived within the church:

> What has happened is this: the church, while flowing through the stream of history has picked up the evils of little tributaries, and these tributaries have been so powerful that they have been able to overwhelm the main stream.[25]

ML himself was flowing through history, picking up influences that instead of corrupting would clarify his place in the world. But here, near the Delaware River, he could stretch his legs and think for himself. He was under no national pressure to become a great man; he was under no obligation to be a leader of the civil rights movement—and he was under no expectation but his own to change the way society had been structured. By that tributary, ML pondered his existence. His first year at Crozer was ending, and he was due back at Ebenezer to serve as the associate pastor. No matter where he turned, a church was waiting for him. The institution, for better or worse, had begun to wrap itself around his mind.

And yet, as he prepared himself for a summer of southern preaching, a haunting thought was ringing through his head: "The church, in its present state, is not the hope of the world."[26]

Year II

Exodus

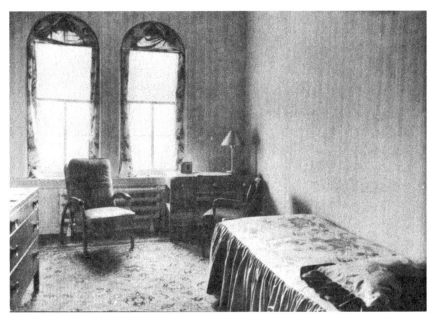

Standard dorm room on the second floor of Old Main, where Martin Luther King Jr. lived. *Courtesy of Colgate Rochester Crozer Divinity School, Rochester, NY*

4

A New Devotion

Term 1, September 13–
November 23, 1949

"The trouble with you fellows from Universities is you think that there is only one type in the World ... the Socratic. But history records Attila the Hun as well as Jesus; Stalin as well as Paul. And by the way I never heard of Attila drinking the Hemlock or Stalin going to the cross. Don't believe that mess about the Pen is mightier than the sword. Give me the sword!"

—J. Pius Barbour to King, 1954[1]

New Leaders, New Friends, New Devotions: "It Takes an Audience Just About Two Minutes"

When ML returned to Atlanta in the summer of 1949, it was clear to his former Morehouse classmates that he'd changed. One of them, Samuel McKinney, spoke of his friend's newfound maturity: "I think he really came into his own when he was in seminary. . . . He grew up quite a bit. He was able to move away from his own family and become his own person. Not that he wasn't already." McKinney, more than other friends, sympathized with ML's desire to leave behind family—especially since they were both PKs: preacher's kids. "We were both 'refugees' hoping to escape an assembly of hot air. Sons of preachers all the time. We didn't want to listen to all that stuff."[2]

But that summer, ML found himself back in the hot air, by his father's side as the associate pastor at Ebenezer Baptist Church. It was his chance to put into practice everything he'd learned at Crozer and develop his oratorical muscles in front of a supportive congregation. "It takes an audience just about two minutes to find out if a man has any sense," his mentor Rev. Barbour once wrote.[3] ML had sense—but could he hold his congregation's attention for three solid months?

With Daddy King on the sidelines with arms crossed, mother Alberta flipping between organ and piano, and brother AD and sister Christine watching from the pews, the twenty-year-old ML barreled his way through fourteen sermons in fourteen weeks. On May 22, in a sermon titled "A Way Out," ML started by mentioning a "very close classmate" who'd confided in ML by telling him about a "crisis" in which his wife and mother had died within three weeks of each other:

> The forms of these crises may be as diverse as the number of human beings. It may result from the death of a loved one, it may result from an unsuccessful love affair . . . or it may result from a child's failure to [live] up to his parent's expectation. . . . When men find themselves in these crisis situations they are forever trying to find a way out.[4]

By early June, ML had begun to settle into the rhythms of the Ebenezer congregation. On June 5, he preached on "Mastering Our Evil Selves," bringing up the issue of race as he discussed the Jekyll and Hyde inside every human being:

> The average white southerner is not bad . . . he goes to church every Sunday. He worships the same God we worship. He will send thousands of dollars to Africa and China for the missionary effort. Yet at the same time he will spend thousands of dollars in an attempt to keep the Negro segregated and discriminated.

On July 24, ML felt comfortable enough to go global. In a sermon he called "Splinters and Planks," he compared the escalating threat of Russia and Communism to America's own civil threat, racism:

> While we see the splinters in Russia's eye we fail to see the great plank of racial segregation and discrimination which is blocking the progress of America.

By the time ML headed back to Crozer, he'd been reforged as a preacher. Yes, he'd had his family, friends, and hometown community behind him, but that's something most of his fellow seminarians lacked, and he'd made the most of it. As he returned to room 52 on the second floor of Old Main, he could reintroduce himself as a young man—still well-dressed—whose oratorical skills had been tested and tempered.

Of course, Daddy King wanted to reintroduce his son to Crozer in a way that any alpha, driven father would: in style. One new seminarian, Francis Stewart, remembered seeing the King family on campus for the first time: "ML Sr. brought King back to the seminary in a big black limousine, and ML Sr. had a big gold chain across his chest . . . typical, classic black preacher. . . . He was planning on having ML take over his church . . . that was his dream . . . but King did everything he could to be as opposite to that type of person as he could be."[5]

———————

A new school year always brought changes, and in the fall of 1949, Crozer had been through plenty of them. Dr. Aubrey had officially left the Crozer presidency, becoming the head of a new department of religious thought just up the road at the University of Pennsylvania. Taking Aubrey's place was an interim president named Dr. Howard Wayne Smith, who'd graduated from Crozer in 1896.

Dr. Smith, in his seventies at the time, didn't plan to hold the post for long. In the local Chester paper, he said that "the interim period will be very brief." Quiet by nature, Dr. Smith had a silent, unassuming way of walking around campus—as if at any moment he might fade away and not be seen again. Students nicknamed him "Creeping Jesus."

They viewed him as a "serious, sober, slow-moving administrator" with a "turtle-like demeanor."[6]

As Creeping Jesus roamed the campus, ML welcomed a few new seminarians to the second floor of Old Main. One was a Japanese man nine years older than ML named Makoto Sakurabayashi, from Yokohama. Despite lingering tensions from the Pacific theater of World War II, Sakurabayashi had made the eight-thousand-mile trip to obtain an "Oriental certificate," Crozer's two-year program for international students. Standing around five feet tall, Sakurabayashi was described by other classmates as "highly cultured."

Quite opposite in manner was fellow international student En-Chin Lin from Foochow, China, who had sloppy eating habits and "belched" during dinner. Despite Lin's table manners, he may have been one of the oldest and most experienced students at the seminary, having completed his bachelor's degree in counseling in 1935 and earned an MS in education from UPenn in 1949. He hoped to start a career as a director of teacher education.[7]

The student lounge, circa late 1940s, located near the end of the hallway on the second floor of Old Main. *Courtesy of Colgate Rochester Crozer Divinity School, Rochester, NY*

There were also the "Yankees," or white northerners who'd come to Crozer more accustomed to the campus culture. Two doors down from ML was new Yankee student Walter Stark, a pacifist and vegetarian who was given a hard time by other students for wearing a leather belt. Now in his late twenties, Stark had grown up on a farm in Michigan and served two years in prison for avoiding the war. His tendency to argue for the absolute goodness of man led to frequent debates with ML. "We had lots of discussions with each other," Stark said. "At that time he wasn't convinced of the nonviolent approach. . . . He didn't strongly oppose it or anything like that, but he had serious questions about whether that approach would work."[8]

When talks about the church, classes, and approaches to social action had run their course, ML, Stark, and other friends would go out at night to cut loose a bit. Stark remembered one evening at a New Jersey nightclub. As the band blared its music, a packed dance floor moved to the beat. For Stark, it wasn't his cup of tea: "I couldn't stand it in there. . . . It was a real low ceiling. Someone was playing and singing and jumping up there. And it was so thick with smoke and the smell of liquor, that that mixture I would have heaved up pretty soon if I had stayed there very long, so I just went out to the car."[9]

Perhaps Stark's opposite among the new students was Francis Stewart, who'd come up from Atlanta, having graduated from Mercer University in 1948. Stewart served in the Air Force during WWII, completing a tour in Italy. He was one of millions of veterans all over the country taking advantage of the GI Bill, but he also had a part-time job at Sears that kept him busy all week, followed by church duties on Sunday at First Baptist Church, a mile and a half away from Old Main. Married with a son, Stewart lived in the housing directly behind Old Main. Eventually Stewart would distinguish himself among the small class of 1952 by being elected student body president, but for now he was an incoming junior in awe of ML's oratorical skills: "Nobody skipped chapel or played when King spoke. He was gifted. He always had something to say when he said it."[10]

At the end of ML's first year, the Crozer student body elected him to lead Friday devotions. His official title was "Devotions Committee chairman." Each Friday morning from 10:00 to 10:30, ML was responsible for leading all his classmates through the student-only church service in the chapel on the first floor of Old Main. There was a presiding speaker—typically someone in his first year, to get his feet wet—and a sermon. Peppered throughout the vespers-like service, according to the program of one such service, were the Nunc Dimittis (the Song of Simeon), a recitation of the Decalogue (the Ten Commandments), a hymn, and various gospel readings.[11]

For ML, it was an honor to be named chair of what may have been the most personal religious experience of the week for his fellow students. He'd earned the respect of grown men—soldiers who'd seen war, pacifists who'd refused the fight, and outsiders looking to rebel against the system. ML himself understood the value of that accomplishment. "It is our job as ministers," ML wrote, "to bring the church back to the center of the human race."[12]

Classes and Professors: An Intellectual Tug of War
Christian Theology for Today 240

> "Christianity is not a balcony experience where we sit and watch the parade of life swing by. On the contrary, it is a descent into the busy road of life where we meet the issue of existence and move on toward fulfillment or disaster."
>
> —George W. Davis[13]

Christian Theology for Today was a required course, divided into two terms of material (numbered 240 and 241). It was ML's third class with Professor George Davis, who'd also taught Great Theologians and Christian Mysticism. Although at first he came off as distant, Davis eventually won over just about all his students, either in the classroom or over dinner and a chat with his wife and sons. To the seminarians, Davis was a "real Christian," said Horace Whitaker. "We all loved Davis."[14]

During summers, Davis served as an interim pastor at the nearby First Baptist Church. In the fall, Davis took Walter McCall to a local apple orchard. They spent days crushing apples together to make cider. Devout yet laid back, Davis would not have objected if he'd heard that Mac usually transformed the results into hard apple cider, which other seminarians sampled when they felt the urge.[15]

ML's Class Schedule

Year II, Term 1, September 13–November 23, 1949

Time	Tuesday	Wednesday	Thursday	Friday
8:00 AM	Christian Theology for Today 240	Christian Theology for Today 240	Christian Theology for Today 240	Christian Theology for Today 240
9:00 AM	Public Worship	Public Worship	Public Worship	Public Worship
10:00 AM	Chapel service	Optional service		Devotional pd.
10:30 AM				
11:00 AM				
11:30 AM	Greek Religion	Greek Religion	Greek Religion	Greek Religion
12:00 PM				
1:00 PM				
2:00 PM				
3:00 PM				
4:00 PM			Vespers service (4:15 PM)	
5:00 PM				

No classes on Monday | Term examinations: Nov. 21–23 |
Thanksgiving break: Nov. 24–28
ML's GPA for the term: 3.22

Christian Theology for Today 240
George Washington Davis, BD, ThM (Colgate-Rochester), PhD (Yale)
Course Description: "The nature and method of theology; the Christian faith in its systematic formulations; the Christian conception of God; man, his nature, need, and destiny; the religious significance of Jesus of Nazareth and his part in salvation; the place and task of the Church as the carrier of the Christian faith and experience." *First of two terms.* (Credit hours: 4; ML's grade: B+)

Public Worship
Robert Elwood Keighton, BD, ThM (Crozer)
Course Description: "The philosophy and psychology of worship; relationship of worship to other human activities; history and development of Christian worship; source materials; creation of actual worship services." (Credit hours: 4; ML's grade: B+)

Greek Religion
Morton Scott Enslin, BD (Andover Newton), ThD (Harvard), DD (Colby)
Course Description: "The origin and development of Minoan-Mycenaean and Greek religion." (Credit hours: 4; ML's grade: B)

On Tuesday, Wednesday, and Friday, a half-hour period was set aside at 10:00 AM for services in the chapel. On Tuesdays was a mandatory service led by interim president Dr. Howard Wayne Smith. Wednesday services were optional, generally led by a member of the faculty or an invited pastor from an evangelical institution. The Friday devotional period was run by the students themselves and presided over by ML as chairman of the Devotions Committee. On Thursday, the 10:00 AM slot was a free period, and a vespers service was held at 4:15 PM. This tightly planned service featured a speaker from a prescheduled list, usually a Crozer professor or a guest speaker from another institution.[16]

In Christian Theology, Davis took his time with the class, emphasizing what he would later say to incoming Crozer students: that it was important for them to develop a deeper understanding of Christian theology, apprehending it on three different levels he referred to as:

1. *The Strata:* Students needed to immerse themselves in the meanings of the Bible and other sacred texts—many of which they studied in their first year at Crozer.
2. *The Sub-strata:* Students should absorb the history of the church, good *and* bad, and better understand how it came to be and where it could possibly go.
3. *The Basis:* Ambiguous for a reason, this level comprises the connective tissue related to the life of Christ and his teachings. As a divinity student rereads the Bible with new eyes, the student should begin to perceive a "thread of unity," an emotional and hopefully satisfying pattern. Only then, Davis believed, can the seminarian be close to the spirit of Christ.[17]

The papers ML wrote for Davis reflect this multitiered process. In one, a B+ effort titled "The Place of Reason and Experience in Finding God," ML once again goes after Karl Barth, this time criticizing not his preaching skills but his thinking, in particular his attempt to "undermine the rational in religion." Attempting to do so, ML wrote, "is one of the perils of our time."[18]

Surprisingly, one of his sources was a book by E. E. Aubrey, of all people, the former Crozer president who had called ML's class the dumbest in Crozer history. Granted, ML failed to use quotation marks when using Aubrey's words, but he did include a bibliographic reference at the end of the paper.

Public Worship

"A church service gathers a congregation—people brought together by a common assent to the suppositions of the church, by precedent conditions of relationships—and they are dismissed with the implications and the obligations of the hour spent together still upon them."

—Robert Keighton[19]

"You will notice that the Negro Church is the only sphere of Negro life that is not a carbon copy of the white man."

—Rev. J. Pius Barbour[20]

In Public Worship, Robert Keighton attempted to simulate for his class the *whole* of a minister's church experience, emphasizing the importance of the congregation and the duty of the preacher not only to attempt to deliver an excellent sermon but to be "with the people . . . beyond the limits of the hour" and "serve in various capacities." With this class, Keighton hoped to take each student into the mind of the congregation and encourage him to better appreciate the act of worship.

But Keighton's focus, as usual, was on the character of the *white* church experience. This may have proven particularly challenging to ML in light of his most recent preaching endeavors. He had just spent the summer learning how to captivate the southern black congregation at Ebenezer Baptist—learning *their* style of worship, his successful turns of phrase answered with exclamations of *Mmhm* or *Amen* or *Yes, keep goin'*. He'd shaken hands near the church front doors, learned the names and personalities of dozens of Ebenezer parishioners, and become familiar with their particular struggles—Jim Crow, an Atlanta population that had tripled in less than thirty years—which were different from those of a white Baptist congregation in the North.

And even now, back in the North, ML was attuning himself to the African American congregation at Rev. J. Pius Barbour's church. Barely a month into his fall term at Crozer, ML was the main speaker at Calvary Baptist's 3:30 PM service for "Homecoming Day."[21] It's unknown what ML said to the congregation, but it's clear that with each passing month, ML felt more comfortable behind the pulpit of a black congregation.

Rev. Barbour, however, believed that ML also needed to get comfortable with the forms of engagement Robert Keighton was teaching him. Barbour did not want ML to only be *for black people*. In Barbour's mind, that would have been tragic:

> The Negro Preachers who have been educated by white people and who have lacked the creative element, native to the Negro, have been dismal failures. But the Negro Preacher who has <u>sharpened his intellect with the White Man's intellectualism</u> and has retained his native gift preaches to thousands all over the country. Ask any fair-minded man what kind of a crowd a Negro with a superb education and the feeling power of his people preaches to.[22]

Whether ML agreed with his Public Worship professor didn't matter to Barbour. Keighton represented the "White Man's intellectualism" that, like it or not, held a grip on the nation through radio programs, mainstream newspapers, and the earliest national television broadcasts. ML needed to learn as much about ministering to white audiences as he could if he hoped to have any kind of influence on the country as a whole.

Greek Religion

ML's Greek Religion professor was Morton Scott Enslin, who along with the dean, Charles Batten, was arguably at the helm of Crozer Theological Seminary during this period of interim leadership. While President H. W. Smith crept quietly through the campus and looked forward to the quick end of his tenure, Enslin was running the *Crozer Quarterly* (at a loss) and serving as the committee chairman for "comprehensive examinations" and "higher degrees."[23]

In his Greek Religion class, Enslin taught students about the symbolic links between Christianity and pre-Christian religions. One of ML's papers described the "cult" of Mithraism, which, if it hadn't been interrupted by Christianity, may have had a chance of spreading throughout the Western world. According to ML's paper, "A Study of Mithraism," the religion was paganistic in spirit, and ML keenly compared the "rites of initiation" in Mithraism with the beginnings of Christianity.[24]

Mithraism was not for the faint hearted. In order to be initiated, one was told to bathe in the blood of a sacrificial bull, immersing oneself completely and tasting the sacred liquid. Believers also ate the flesh of the recently speared bull. ML connected this tradition with the writings of the apostle Paul, who "thought of the [Christian] believer as buried with Christ in baptism and as feeding upon him in the Eucharist."

Enslin was deeply impressed with ML's paper, giving it an A. It probably didn't hurt that ML used Enslin's own book, *Christian Beginnings*, as one of his sources, even quoting (with the appropriate quotation marks!) Enslin's own words.

More than the grade, though, it is Enslin's commentary at the end of the paper that seems especially fascinating today. The first few lines are common professorial feedback: "This is an exceedingly good paper. You have given a very complete picture of the essential details and you have presented this in a balanced and restrained way. And furthermore you know how to write." But then comes Enslin's last line, which seems to transcend time and place: "You should go a long way if you continue to pay the price."[25]

Betty Moitz and Barriers: 94 Percent of White Americans Disapproved

> "No theology is needed to tell us that love is the law of life and to disobey it means to suffer the consequences; we see it every day in human experience."
>
> —Martin Luther King Jr. circa 1949[26]

For Betty Moitz, the summer of 1949 had been a difficult one. Her father, William O. Moitz, an elevator inspector and Philadelphia native, had collapsed at a nearby hospital and passed away on May 9, during Crozer's commencement activities. Mr. Moitz, at fifty-three, left behind his grieving mother, wife, and daughter.[27] The three women remained in their campus home, Miss Hannah still tending to the seminarians' dietary needs. And when ML returned to school the following fall, his and Betty's relationship continued to blossom—though that posed its own difficulties for the young couple.

By this point, they had become more comfortable on campus, sitting on benches and sharing their hopes and dreams in full view of ML's classmates and teachers. When asked if she had concerns about how they might be seen, Betty shrugs. "I never noticed. I always had a tan and dark brown hair."[28] But the twenty-year-old ML was more aware of the potential social fallout.

It's important to understand that in 1949, interracial relationships were a long-standing American taboo. Since the founding of Jamestown and Plymouth, Americans had had issues with mixing. Less than forty miles from Crozer was the state of Maryland, where the first law against interracial marriage was enacted in 1664; the state would keep similar laws on its books for over three hundred years. Even a decade later, a

1958 Gallup Poll would report that an astounding 94 percent of white Americans disapproved of interracial marriage.[29]

Pennsylvania was in fact one of the most flexible states when it came to "miscegenation" laws. Still, that didn't mean ML and Betty could head over to a local café and hold hands out in the open. Members of the Crozer community, despite their liberalism, would have had trouble throwing their support behind such an arrangement. They weren't against it, but they weren't exactly *for* it, either. Glares, scoffs, and head shakes were inevitable.

Cyril Pyle, ML's classmate from Panama, worked in the kitchen and dining hall and witnessed ML and Betty getting closer. "I knew about it, thought it was bad, but I didn't want to get involved."[30] One of the only students who actually supported their relationship was the man who had a hand in orchestrating their meeting: Walter McCall.

Not that ML needed anyone's approval. Soon, their "dates" mainly consisted of Betty driving ML around the city of Chester, ignoring the scowls of society. "I listened," Betty says, "and he'd just talk and talk." But she loved it—his enthusiasm, his anxious hopes "to return South and help people. He was wonderful—a joy to be with and listen to."[31]

When ML's sister came to visit him at Crozer, however, his friendship with Betty crept back into the shadows. It wasn't that ML didn't trust Christine—their relationship had always been strong—it was the fact that Christine was a direct conduit to Mama King, and that was something ML could not risk. Telling his sister about Betty would have meant putting her in the unenviable position of withholding important information from her mother in every letter and phone call home. And if Christine were to let slip that ML had been getting closer to a white woman, ML could only imagine the disappointment in his mother's eyes. Betty knew about these concerns: "He was worried what she'd think."[32]

Betty's own mother wouldn't have been against their relationship. During his early days in the kitchen washing dishes and over the rest of his time at Crozer, Miss Hannah had come to trust ML. As one former student's wife said, "Hannah liked Martin. She thought he was a good person."[33]

Betty Moitz, outside her home on campus and next to her car, 1950.
Courtesy of Dr. James Beshai

Cyril Pyle remembered how Miss Hannah had "gestured" to him about Betty and ML, but the seminarian wanted no part. "I thought it was a dangerous situation that could get out of hand, and if it did get out of hand it would smear King. It would make [his future] hard for him."[34]

5

Mordecai's Fire
Term 2, November 29, 1949–
February 15, 1950

"For us, immortality will mean a spiritual existence. All of the details of what this existence will be like are somewhat beyond our intelligence. But with faith in God we may rest assured that death will not be a period that will end this great sentence of life, but it will be a comma punctuating it to loftier significance."

—ML, age twenty-one,
at Crozer Theological Seminary[1]

ML and Communism: "Capitalism . . . Has Failed to Meet the Needs of the Masses"

"During the Christmas holidays of 1949 I decided to spend my spare time reading Karl Marx to try to understand the appeal of communism for many people."

—ML[2]

On Friday, December 23, 1949, about a month into the second term of ML's middle year, the *Chester Times* ran an article with the headline TRU-MAN, POPE APPEAL FOR WORLD PEACE. In it, President Harry Truman

97

delivered a message to Pope Pius XII that the US "was progressing 'toward a better world' by following the glorious lessons for man taught by the life of our Savior." Truman then laid into America's ever-growing enemy at the time, Soviet Russia, and expressed hope that it would fall into line, become "good neighbors, and . . . join with the multitude in striving to build a world wholly and truly at peace."[3]

The president's concern was likely one of a number of factors that inspired King to begin studying the ideals of Communism. Such global anxieties made the ideology a natural topic of conversation throughout ML's time on campus, but his interest may have been heightened during this term as he studied Marx with Dr. Elizabeth Flower at the University of Pennsylvania (see page 99). His curiosity about the Soviet system may also have been piqued by a celebrity endorsement: as one Crozer student recalled, ML knew that black singer and actor Paul Robeson "had been to Russia and thought that Communism would favor racial integration more than capitalism."[4]

More generally, ML became interested in understanding Marx because he had grown disgusted with American capitalism as it stood in 1949. In a paper at Crozer titled "Will Capitalism Survive?," ML wrote, "I am convinced that capitalism has seen its best days in America, and not only in America, but in the entire world." To King, capitalism had "failed to meet the needs of the masses." He also wrote, in regards to the nationalization of health care, that everywhere "we turn we hear the demand for socialize[d] medicine."[5]

At the end of the paper, ML used a sports analogy to describe America's failed system. "Capitalism finds herself like a losing football team in the last quarter trying all types of tactics to survive. We are losing because we failed to check our weaknesses in the beginning of the game."[6] By studying Marx, ML was starting his own "weakness check." He saw such archaic, broken systems around him—segregation, income inequality—that it was time to see if "the enemy" knew something he didn't.

By the time Crozer's Christmas break began (the same day the *Chester Times* reported on Truman's message to the pope), ML was deep into his exploration of Marx's writings. He spent most of his break with his family down in Atlanta, copies of *Das Kapital* and *The Communist Manifesto* at hand. They weren't the kind of books you'd carry around freely in December 1949, just months before Senator Joseph McCarthy began leveling accusations of "card-carrying Communists" within the US government. ML, now Ebenezer's associate pastor, would have needed to keep this kind of reading private.

As King rose to prominence in the coming years, he would need to be even more careful about his public sympathies. In his 1958 book *Stride Toward Freedom*, carefully modulated so as to be easily absorbed by the white reading public, ML repudiated Marxism, citing its "deprecation of individual freedom" and its lack of a "place for God." The latter was a particular deal breaker for the up-and-coming minister: "As a Christian I believe that there is a creative personal power in this universe who is the ground and essence of all reality—a power that cannot be explained in materialistic terms."[7] But these words were written amid King's rise as a leader of the civil rights movement, when he needed to publicly and unequivocally reject Communism to avoid inviting suspicion from the government.

Back in 1949, ML may have been more open to some of Marx's ideas than he would later be willing to admit. Rev. J. Pius Barbour, always happy to go a few verbal rounds with ML, listened firsthand as ML's young mind attempted to process the storm of concepts raining down on him through books, classes, and heated extracurricular discussions. ML "thought the capitalistic system was predicated on exploitation and prejudice, poverty," Barbour said, "and that we wouldn't solve these problems until we got a new social order."[8]

Classes and Professors: Trial and Error
Ethics and Philosophy of History

> "It is perhaps inappropriate for a white person to reflect on how much has been changed for the better in the decades since Martin Luther King was at Penn, rather than to lament how much still needs the doing. But perhaps I can speak as a woman and thus a member of a group that is itself still struggling for equality."
>
> —Dr. Elizabeth Flower[9]

ML's Class Schedule
Year II, Term 2, November 29, 1949–February 15, 1950

Time	Tuesday	Wednesday	Thursday	Friday
8:00 AM	Christian Theology for Today 241	Christian Theology for Today 241	Christian Theology for Today 241	Christian Theology for Today 241
9:00 AM	Conduct of Church Services	Preaching Problems	Conduct of Church Services	Preaching Problems
10:00 AM	Chapel service	Optional service		Devotional pd.
10:30 AM	The Development of Christian Ideas	The Development of Christian Ideas	The Development of Christian Ideas	The Development of Christian Ideas
11:00 AM				
11:30 AM				
12:00 PM				
1:00 PM				
2:00 PM				Pastoral Counseling (audit)
3:00 PM				
4:00 PM			Ethics and Philosophy of History (audit, at UPenn)	
5:00 PM				

No classes on Monday | Christmas vacation: Dec. 23–Jan. 2 |
Term examinations: Feb. 13–15
ML's GPA for the term: 3.72

Christian Theology for Today 241

George Washington Davis, BD, ThM (Colgate-Rochester), PhD (Yale)

Course Description: "The nature and method of theology; the Christian faith in its systematic formulations; the Christian conception of God; man, his nature, need, and destiny; the religious significance of Jesus of Nazareth and his part in salvation; the place and task of the Church as the carrier of the Christian faith and experience." *Second of two terms.* (Credit hours: 4; ML's grade: A)

Conduct of Church Services

Robert Elwood Keighton, BD, ThM (Crozer)

Course Description: "The conduct, function, and values of the services and ceremonies of the Church; their contributions to the Christian community." (Credit hours: 2; ML's grade: B)

Preaching Problems

Robert Elwood Keighton, BD, ThM (Crozer)

Course Description: "A seminar for seniors designed to meet the practical problems of preaching arising from the experience of the student and the present-day demands of the pulpit." *Though the class was geared toward seniors, ML was permitted to enroll in his middle year.* (Credit hours: 2; ML's grade: B+)

The Development of Christian Ideas

George Washington Davis, BD, ThM (Colgate-Rochester), PhD (Yale)

Course Description: "Introduction to the important persons and terms in the history of Christianity; the development of the ideas of God, the person of Jesus, the Holy Spirit, man, salvation (the work of Christ) and the Kingdom of God." (Credit hours: 4; ML's grade: A)

Ethics and Philosophy of History

Elizabeth Flower, BS (Wilson), PhD (UPenn); Assistant Professor of Philosophy (UPenn)

Course Description: "The issue as it arises in the 18th century: Vico and Herder. The Kantian restatement. The scientific-naturalistic conceptions: Taine, Marx, and Spencer. The historical-critical position of Hegel, Spengler, Dilthey, and Spranger. Contemporary controversies:

Croce, Mannheim, Weber, and Toynbee." *King audited this course, which was held at the University of Pennsylvania.* (Credit hours: 2; ML's grade: None given)

Pastoral Counseling
Seward Hiltner, BA (Lafayette); Visiting Lecturer in Pastoral Counseling
Course Description: "Basic principles of counseling and their application to pastoral work; pastoral function; analysis of pastoral task in terms of work with individuals; methods of individual work; religion and mental health; counseling procedures and skills; limitations of psychology and psychiatry; process of referral; uses of group counseling in the church." *King audited this course.* (Credit hours: N/A; ML's grade: None given)

On Tuesday, Wednesday, and Friday, a half-hour period was set aside at 10:00 AM for services in the chapel. On Tuesdays was a mandatory service led by interim president Dr. Howard Wayne Smith. Wednesday services were optional, generally led by a member of the faculty or an invited pastor from an evangelical institution. The Friday devotional period was run by the students themselves and presided over by ML as chairman of the Devotions Committee.[10]

In an effort to expand his educational experience at Crozer, ML asked the dean, Charles Batten, for approval to study at the University of Pennsylvania. It was an option the seminary offered to a few well-qualified students, and after evaluating ML's grades from his first year and discussing the issue with the faculty, Dean Batten agreed. Instead of attending vespers service on Thursday afternoons, ML would audit a class with Dr. Elizabeth Flower, a thirty-five-year-old professor who'd chosen Ethics and Philosophy of History as the topic of her first-ever graduate seminar.[11]

Studying at UPenn may have helped ML recharge his spiritual battery, as it meant a break from biblical analysis and a tighter focus on humanistic principles. It was also a chance for him to broaden his perspective on northern culture. He'd been to Philadelphia plenty of times for many reasons—girls, church services, sightseeing—but this would be a unique challenge: taking a course at an Ivy League school.

To get to UPenn without a car was a bit of an adventure. ML pushed open the front doors of Old Main and headed down the center walkway. He snagged a seat on the local bus that stopped in front of Old Main for the fifteen-minute ride to catch the train. The bus turned right, then traveled down Seminary Avenue, going past the Chester Rural Cemetery, a graveyard so close to the campus that it could be viewed by students from inside Old Main—a sobering reminder of their own mortality, perhaps, and also the resting place of a few of the wounded Civil War soldiers who had stayed in their rooms and written their names in the building's cupola.[12] After a right turn onto Edgemont Avenue, it was a straight shot to Chester's main train station.

ML boarded the train bound for downtown Philadelphia, and twenty or so minutes later he was there, walking out of the Thirtieth Street station toward UPenn's Bennett Hall. From 4:00 to 6:00 PM, ML sat with at most ten other students in Dr. Flower's classroom. The fact that Flower was a woman must have felt a bit out of the ordinary to ML, since the overwhelming majority of professors he'd had at Morehouse and Crozer had been men. Nevertheless, he made a positive impression on Flower, who later remembered him very clearly, writing that he "sat in the last row, second from the end, at my left. Although the seats were fixed, this did not hinder the . . . community of discussion."[13]

To Flower's recollection, the seminar never specifically addressed the issues of discrimination that would become one of the central focuses of King's life. But discussions of "peace and of conflict" and of taking "a moral stance (as in Gandhi) were much in the air." ML's back-and-forth discussions with Rev. Barbour about nonviolence apparently served him well: whenever ML contributed in class, Flower was impressed by how his thoughts were "already vigorous and well-forged."[14]

Here, in Dr. Flower's words, are what they covered in the seminar:

In addition to standard materials from Hume to Hegel to Marx, we also read Gandhi and Tolstoy—remember that the independence of India was strikingly contemporary—but perhaps Kant was central. . . . Kant's view of equality as tied to the intrinsic moral worth of each individual. . . . Every human [according to

Kant] is a center of freedom and dignity, legislating a common morality for all rational beings."[15]

Flower was careful when considering the impact her seminar may have had on the course of ML's life. "While it is highly unlikely that I had an influence on Martin Luther King," she wrote, "I have since cherished the thought that some of the materials we read and discussed provided their own insight and strength."[16] This thought could very well be accurate, since he spent his Christmas vacation poring over the works of Marx, one of the "standard" topics he would have discussed in Flower's class.

Dr. Flower also crossed paths with ML outside of her seminar. She often saw him at Horn & Hardart, a cafeteria near the UPenn campus, with Dr. William Fontaine, UPenn's "first fully affiliated African American faculty member."[17] Dr. Flower believes that ML took a course with Dr. Fontaine, but there are no records to confirm this. Nevertheless, it is clear that ML was starting to find a bit of a comfort zone in the larger academic world beyond the Crozer campus.

Preaching Problems; Conduct of Church Services

> "The preacher has inevitable moments of despair, frustration, and defeat. It cannot be otherwise. He does not live a secluded existence, nor does he merely accept life; he challenges it and seeks to make it nobler, and these very ambitions lead him over difficult paths."
>
> —Robert Keighton[18]

ML was quickly gaining experience behind the pulpit, but in the process he frequently encountered issues his limited experience hadn't yet taught him how to overcome. Offering guidance with such issues was the purpose of Robert Keighton's Preaching Problems course.

Unfortunately, ML couldn't rely on Keighton for help with his deeper issues, such as how to address the social concerns his Ebenezer congregation faced daily. The South was hundreds of miles away, and Keighton's relation to it thousands. His course emphasized general problems that *any* preacher would face; regional issues needed to be addressed on a case-by-case basis, which was not conducive to class-room discussion.

As a result, ML focused his inquiries in class on a few of the more basic problems he'd encountered as an active preacher:

1) . . . Difficulty in preaching on special days that appear in the Christian year.
2) . . . Difficulty in applying the Old Testament to modern life.
3) I often get criticisms from laymen and unlettered ministers for using a modern translation of the Bible as a source of preaching resurrection.[19]

These were *slight* problems—easily addressable in a classroom environment. According to Rev. Michael Frank, a Cleveland, Ohio, minister for forty-one years and a former seminarian, ML's first difficulty could have simply been related to the fact that he was young and thus "didn't like any form of constraint" placed on his preaching, such as the demands of crafting a sermon to commemorate a particular Christian holiday. It's also not unusual for a young, inexperienced preacher to have trouble relating the Old Testament to the modern world. And ML's third problem reflects a common controversy that persists to this day. As Rev. Frank puts it:

Some Christians, for odd and to me utterly indiscernible reasons, think the King James version of the Bible to carry a kind of authority that other translations don't. But the point is that the original scripture was written in Greek (NT) and Hebrew (OT), and since language changes new translations are appropriate. King was right on this one, and I understand his frustration.[20]

Though Professor Keighton's responses to ML's concerns are unknown, as an experienced preacher he would have recognized the disadvantages of youth and advised his student to push past any discomfort with having his ideas constrained. As Keighton wrote in his book *The Man Who Would Preach*, "A man must learn to preach the things that lay hold upon him rather than the things that he has laid hold upon. He can possess the latter, but he can lose them, too."[21]

As for ML's second class with Keighton this term, Conduct of Church Services, not much has been recorded about it, either. But judging from the course description, ML may have found his role as Devotions Committee chairman helpful in connecting with the subject matter. The course's focus on the "conduct" and "function" of church ceremonies would have related directly to the Devotions Committee's work organizing a weekly service for the student body.

Pastoral Counseling

> "It is our obligation [as preachers] to have some special kind of relationship with our people, whether it be a counseling relationship or not, in connection with all the crises of life . . . working backwards: bereavement, marriage, vocational choice, adult entrance into Christian fellowship, and concern for babies and children."
>
> —Seward Hiltner[22]

Imagine for a moment that you are twenty years old and in charge of a church congregation. It's Sunday, and you have prepared an epic sermon that swirls together some of the timeless ideals of religion and philosophy. As you stand behind the pulpit, your parishioners marvel at your use of passages from the New Testament (probably John, since his words tend to soar). You throw in dashes of the poet Longfellow, or Plato—or even Ovid, to show 'em you've done your homework. You finish with a few personal anecdotes, and you can see half of the congregation with their eyes closed, nodding, some with hands up. You hear their words of approval (*Mmhm*). You've hooked them—or, in the sensationalized words of Rev. Barbour, "I murdered them Sunday."[23]

But after you step down from the pulpit, you are still the associate pastor of a church, and your congregation still needs your guidance throughout the rest of the week. To provide it, you must now become a regular human being—relatable, unintimidating, caring. As you sit at your desk, a woman enters. She is much older than you, married. She and her husband have been loyal parishioners for years, and after taking a seat, she tells you that she has decided to divorce him. "I know it may shock you, especially since we've both been so active in the church. And [my husband] always puts up a good front when he's around here. I just don't see anything to do except get a divorce. Don't you think I'd be justified?"[24]

Hmm . . .

The prospect of facing such a situation at Ebenezer Baptist very well could have been why ML decided to audit Pastoral Counseling. At the time Daddy King, being older and more established, took care of most of their church's counseling needs, but ML knew he would one day need to be more than simply an excellent preacher and church spokesman. As the course's professor, Seward Hiltner, put it, a minister like ML would eventually need to be a "shepherd, friend, guide, therapist, counselor, and spanker in his work as a pastor."[25]

He could not have had a better guide to this subject than Professor Hiltner. He had very recently published a book titled *Pastoral Counseling*, and would go on to teach at Princeton Seminary and attain global recognition in his field. Forty years old at the time, Hiltner was not in any way a stuffy, disconnected professor. His personality ranged from charming to blunt to exacting. He actually had experience as a door-to-door salesman for the Fuller Brush Company, and this background meant a classroom persona that differed greatly from Keighton's wall of dignity or George W. Davis's kindly but authoritative presence. Hiltner's "greatest gift," wrote the *Princeton Seminary Bulletin*, "was an intuitive ability to grasp the essentials of a problem or issue confronting some group of which he was a part. He could state the essence in such a way that those present would say to themselves and to one another, 'That's it.'"[26]

From 2:00 to 4:00 each Friday, Hiltner presented his class with counseling scenarios, all eventually ending with the question *What should you do?* One of his examples was the situation described earlier of a wife who planned to leave her husband. Hiltner described two obvious ways of answering a plea for divorce—both of which are wrong:

> One thing the pastor clearly cannot say is: "Why of course. Don't give it a second thought. I believe in divorce. Go right ahead. . . .

On the other hand, neither does he say: "Why that's terrible. How can you think of such a thing? Divorce is ruining our society."[27]

To Hiltner, a minister must find a middle ground, and that can only be reached through patience and a neutral, nonjudgmental tone. Something like this:

> "You've been trying with might and main to make this marriage work; but you just don't see now how it can be saved without making things worse for every one concerned. And yet you're still not quite sure."

This answer would be standard, perhaps borderline stereotypical, for a psychologist, but coming from a man of the church, a *minister*, it expresses something altogether different: it is *not a sin* to be having these thoughts. It allows this woman to discuss her situation without being judged.

For a twenty-year-old, single, and childless young man like ML, Pastoral Counseling was a perfect opportunity to better understand the gray areas of being a preacher. Even though he could not personally relate to every problem with which a conflicted human being might approach him, he could nonetheless calibrate his tone so that he could be of the most help to each of them. That, in Hiltner's mind, was the most valuable lesson he could convey. ML could preach of legends long past and deliver those words with a voice that immediately turned heads, but there was more to being a preacher than just the Sunday sermon. There were everyday people, struggling through the murk of life, and he would need to show them that he was one of them.

Christian Theology for Today 241; The Development of Christian Ideas

ML's first class each morning was the second term of the required Christian Theology for Today course, with George W. Davis. A former student in this class recalls one of Professor Davis's slightly peculiar habits: "His style of thinking was to read off of his cards [during class]. Very prepared." But he also recalls him as "congenial. He wasn't nearly as stiff as his classes." To ML, on the other hand, Davis's congeniality shone through in his lectures; King later remembered that "the atmosphere" of Davis's classroom was "saturated with a warm evangelical liberalism."[28] Contributing to that feeling, perhaps, was the knowledge that a dinner at the professor's home was just around the corner. Davis enjoyed serving as a host for his students, helping them to grow more comfortable discussing their faith.

True to the professor's efforts, by this point ML was particularly at ease with Davis, if his writing in class is any indication. In most of Davis's classes, ML's work fluctuated between lazy and brutally honest. He seemed allergic to quotation marks, often either forgetting or choosing to forget to properly indicate the words of another author. Perhaps ML believed that Davis was not a stickler for citation, and it appears that the professor wasn't. On the other hand, with comfort comes trust, and ML shared with Davis several personal thoughts about racism that he could have never shared with the likes of Keighton, Pritchard, or Enslin.

In Christian Theology for Today, ML wrote a paper debating the merits of a neo-orthodox perspective versus a liberal one. Neo-orthodoxy had grown in popularity after the violence and moral devastation of World War I, when many sought a conservative and practical philosophy to combat the at times excessive optimism associated with liberalism. ML felt tugged between the two philosophies, but when describing his "leaning toward a mild neo-orthodox view of man," instead of using a published author to support his feelings, he brought up his own childhood: "[Neo-orthodoxy] may root back to certain experiences I had in the south. Some of the experiences that I encountered there made it very difficult to believe in the essential goodness of man."

ML didn't go on to list those experiences, but they could have filled a page. At an early age he'd had white friends taken from him simply because of the color of his skin. Once while waiting for his mother to finish shopping, he'd been slapped in the face by a white woman: "You're the little nigger who stepped on my foot!" ML had done no such thing, and stood in bewilderment until his mother returned. *That's the way things are*, he was told. Growing up in Atlanta in the 1930s also meant regular encounters with the Ku Klux Klan as they held public gatherings and parades, and set off "bombs and dynamite" in random spots as a form of intimidation. When black residents moved into new neighborhoods, the KKK would even target them directly. By phone or letter, the message was sent: *Don't get comfortable in this neighborhood. You don't belong.*[29]

ML opened up to Davis again in another paper for the class, an outline based on the book *Beliefs That Matter* by William Adams Brown. It reflected an issue King had been pondering deeply at Crozer: how for centuries the church had ignored and even perpetuated the problem of slavery. This neglect had given birth to a different kind of church, a personalized communion among those suffering under the maddening sins of the American white man. In his outline, ML included a passage written in 1949 by African American philosopher Howard Thurman:

> During the years of slavery in America it is said that after a hard days work the slaves would often hold secret religious meetings. All during the working day they were addressed with unnecessary vituperations and insulting epithets. But as they gathered in these meetings they gained a renewed faith as the old unlettered minister would come to his triumphant climax saying: "you—you are not niggers. You—you are not slaves. You are God's children." This established for them a true ground of personal dignity.[30]

To ML, the church's passivity on slavery was its greatest sin, and he was determined to foster his own version of Christianity that served as a model for change. No longer would it stand neutral on difficult issues. There would be no dividing line between the church and the greater good of society, especially when it came to race.

———————

ML's other course with Professor Davis during term 2, The Development of Christian Ideas, was a review of major concepts that most of the students already knew. Davis, a liberal theologian to the core, was always concerned with adding depth, depth, and more depth to his students' understanding. He knew that his fellow liberalists, if left unchecked, could focus so intently on nitpicking particular phrases, words, or concepts in the Bible that they'd lose sight of the larger truths they were trying to demonstrate. He urged his students not to simply skate across the surface of an issue but to plunge into it as deeply as they could bear:

> Is there an inner continuity in the Bible, a thread of truth which runs through the sixty-six books as a thread runs through sixty-six pearls, holding them together and imparting a unity to them?[31]

Davis knew better than to give his students a ready-made response to this question. Taking the journey in search of the answer was just as important as the answer itself.

Still, in class as well as in his own book, *Existentialism and Theology*, published a few years later, Davis briefly shared his assessment of how history had interpreted "the person of Jesus." From the "messiah," the "divine Logos," a "high priest," then on to the Middle Ages, when he became a "thin, emaciated ascetic since the ideal man was then held to be one who ignored the world and neglected the demands of the flesh." Davis finally described the twentieth-century interpretations of Jesus: a figure who has been globally fractionalized, "appropriated" by whoever needed him and defined variably as a "ruler," a "comrade," a "man of divine fire," and a "liberator."[32] To Davis, this was not necessarily a bad thing; it simply indicated the large range of influential people attempting to grapple with the internal depths of Christianity's soul.

At the end of one of ML's papers for The Development of Christian Ideas (an essay titled "The Influence of Mystery Religions on Christian-ity"), Davis wrote a nearly 150-word personal comment to his student, giving ML an A but nudging him once more toward pursuing more depth:

> Never stop with the external, which may seem like borrowing, but recognize there is the perennial struggle for truth, fuller [than] life itself. . . . Through experience, knowledge, as through other forms, the outer manifestations of religion change. The inner spiritual, continues ever.[33]

ML Comes of Age: "Have a Deep Belief in Your Own Dignity"

On January 15, 1950, inside the predominantly black Grace Methodist Church less than two miles from the Crozer campus, ML turned
twenty-one years old. This was not a birthday celebration. Rather, ML
was working. At 2:45 PM, at the invitation of the church's pastor, B. A.
Arnold, he stood in front of the youth at Grace Methodist and delivered
a sermon.[34]

Unfortunately, what ML said to the young people that day has been
lost, and all one can do is consider the events swirling around him at the
time and imagine the emotions he must have felt staring into the eyes
of children and teenagers as he himself entered full-fledged adulthood.
Now twenty-one, ML enjoyed certain new rights, the most appealing of
which may have been the right to vote. In 1950, the minimum age to
cast a ballot was twenty-one, but especially back in Atlanta, ML would
have encountered several challenges—literacy tests, poll taxes, a general
vibe of intimidation radiating from the white clerk—designed to keep
African American citizens away from the polls.

ML could have told the African American youths in front of him
about his experiences in the South, or about how he'd arrived at Crozer
a year and a half ago "grimly serious," keeping his suit pressed as he
stayed alert, making sure not to laugh too quickly. Or he could have
brought up his younger days working as a newspaper carrier, moving up
the ladder year by year until he was assistant manager. *Only a white man
could be made manager.* But such blatant racial discrimination would
not have been as familiar to young people in Chester as it was to those
in Atlanta. Instead, he could have gone for the "responsibility" angle,
telling his listeners that delivering newspapers had helped him become
a more diligent worker and better money manager. That, however, was
a truism that could have been uttered by any parent, and ML would
not have wanted to sound like a father talking down to his children.

Perhaps the message he shared with them was similar to one he
delivered at other points in his career. ML had spoken several times to
the youth at churches in the South, and it's been documented that as
early as 1948 he'd been working on one of his more famous sermons,

"What Is Your Life's Blueprint?," delivered in high schools and geared specifically to students.* Here is a snippet of that sermon, after years of practice and revision. Near the end of his life, he could fire off these words without once looking at notes:

> I want to ask you a question, and that is, what is in your life's blueprint? This is the most important and crucial period of your lives, for what you do now and what you decide now, at this age, may well determine which way your life shall go. And whenever a building is constructed, you usually have an architect who draws a blueprint, and that blueprint serves as the pattern, as the guide, as the model for those who are to build the building. And a building is not well erected without a good, sound, and solid blueprint.
>
> Now each of you is in the process of building the structure of your lives, and the question is whether you have a proper, a solid, and a sound blueprint.[35]

He would go on to suggest that a life's blueprint should include:

1. "A deep belief in your own dignity, your own worth, and your own somebodiness. Don't allow anybody to make you feel that you are nobody."
2. "The determination to achieve excellence in your various fields of endeavor. You're going to be deciding as the days and the years unfold what . . . your life's work will be. . . . Study hard . . . burn the midnight oil."

---

* The metaphor of a life's blueprint may have occurred to ML during his first year at Cro-zer, when he worked out the beginning of a sermon based around the construction of the Brooklyn Bridge. He would have seen this landmark a few times while visiting his sister, Christine, in New York, and he'd read about the life of its architect, John A. Roebling, who after creating the design and plan of construction, fell ill and could not oversee the work. But eventually, when the bridge was completed, Roebling, according to ML, "was taken out in a little boat, propped up with pillows, to a position in the East River beneath the great span. There he lay for a long time in silence with the plans of the bridge before him, looking now at the blueprints and now at the bridge, until it was all gone over. Then he sank back among the pillows with a satisfied smile: 'It is like the plan.'" (The material is quoted in King, *Papers*, 6:85, under the title "The House We Are Building.")

3. "A commitment to the eternal principles of beauty, love, and justice. Don't allow anybody to pull you so low as to make you hate them. Don't allow anybody to cause you to lose your self-respect to the point that you do not struggle for justice. However young you are, you have a responsibility to seek to make your nation a better nation in which to live."[36]

What would ML's own life's blueprint have been at this point in time, as he advised the youth at Grace Methodist Church on his twenty-first birthday? He was at the exact middle of his time at Crozer, and his plans for what would come after remained largely unwritten. He had mentors all around him eager to offer guidance: Rev. Barbour, George Davis, Morton Enslin, even his classmate Horace Whitaker. But he was also still pursuing a romantic relationship with Betty Moitz—something he knew full well these men would not approve of. Although they inspired ML and gave him dignity, it was the social limitations even they could not transcend that made him determined to "burn the midnight oil."

As conflicting forces continued to shape his plans for the future, another influence arose that opened ML's eyes to new possibilities. He had discussed Gandhi and debated his principles of nonviolence with Rev. Barbour, but it wasn't until ML first heard the electrifying words of a famous southern preacher that he decided to immerse himself in the life of the Mahatma.

————

On November 23, 1949, Howard University president Mordecai Wyatt Johnson flew to Calcutta, India, to learn all he could about the late Mohandas Gandhi and his nonviolent resistance movement, which had won India its independence from Great Britain just two years before. Johnson was there to evaluate, as one newspaper put it, "the possibilities of using the techniques developed by Mahatma Gandhi in an effort to obtain and preserve peace in the world."[37]

A Baptist minister and a celebrated orator who became Howard's first black president, Dr. Johnson was born in Tennessee in 1890, as southern states were at work rolling back the racial advancements of Reconstruction. He was not shy in telling audiences the plain truth of his past, his voice rumbling through the aisles: "I am the child of a slave. My father was a slave for twenty-five years before the emancipation. My mother was born in slavery. I have lived practically all my life on the territory of former slave states, so when you hear me talk, you are dealing with the real underdeveloped thing."[38]

Johnson often thanked the northern white people who entered the South after the Civil War to establish educational institutions for the disenfranchised. Black people in the South, he said, "could have lost heart and hope, but, thank God, there were some who believed in our highest possibilities and talked with us, for the first time, on the highest level of human intelligence."[39]

Now he was one of approximately thirty representatives from around the world who assembled in India for the World Pacifist

Mordecai Wyatt Johnson at an undated speaking event. *Paul Henderson Photograph Collection, Maryland Historical Society, HEN-00-a2-171*

Conference. The conference descended upon the town of Shantini-
ketan, north of Calcutta, to visit the school founded by Rabindranath
Tagore, a poet and friend of Gandhi's. Tagore had grown disgusted
with the Western style of education and made it his mission to start
a school that could engage a child at every level. After a few brief
sessions at the school, the conference moved on to other cities across
India. For several weeks, Johnson received an immersive master class
in Gandhi's techniques, as he interacted with the leaders and everyday citizens who fought alongside the Mahatma to win their country's
independence.[40]

At the time, India seemed keen to shake off the remaining influence
of the British Empire, and many in the Western world were concerned
that it might fall into the hands of the Communists. To Johnson, the
current situation was entirely the fault of the British and their "stupid
blunder of treating the people of India as the United States has treated
colored citizens in Alabama and Mississippi."[41] As he traveled from city
to city on his tour, Johnson witnessed a populace just emerging from
the shadow of a national bully. It reminded him of his parents' experiences in the aftermath of emancipation, as well as the long road ahead
for all African Americans.

The last week of Dr. Johnson's visit to India included time spent at
Gandhi's ashram, or monastic retreat, in the village of Sevagram. Here
Gandhi's close friends and associates would have exposed Johnson to
the complexities of Gandhi's satyagraha, or truth-force—the Mahatma's
own philosophy of nonviolent resistance, which had sparked such mass
acts of civil disobedience as the nearly 240-mile Salt March of 1930.
Launched in response to the British prohibition on Indians producing
or selling their own salt, this protest led to the arrest of Gandhi and
tens of thousands of his followers.

After his five-week sojourn in India, a fiery Mordecai Johnson
returned to America with a passion to share his experience. It was with
this goal in mind that he gave a talk at Philadelphia's Fellowship House
on a Sunday afternoon in early 1950. As he spoke, a twenty-one-year-old
Martin Luther King Jr. sat in the audience, ready to listen.[42]

It was an unrequired educational event off campus, and ML's interest in the talk "was purely academic," he later recalled. "I never thought

I would be involved in a social movement where [Gandhi's techniques] would be used."[43]

As for the speaker, ML would have known about Johnson from his mentor Benjamin "Buck Benny" Mays, who had been dean of Howard's School of Religion before his appointment to the Morehouse presidency. (Mays had also visited India himself, meeting Gandhi face to face in 1936.) What ML may not have been prepared for was the incendiary power with which Mordecai Johnson could motivate his listeners to rethink the status quo. He had no fear of arguing for change in front of people who were deeply invested in the current system; the previous August, before an audience of two thousand people at a Raleigh Baptist Assembly convention, he had skewered southern Christian culture, declaring in his booming voice that "the intolerance and bigotry in the South exists today because the church has become a prostitute and has sold her soul in order to possess a beautiful body."[44]

The similarities between Mordecai Johnson and Martin Luther King Jr. are also worth noting. Both were blessed with rich, southern baritone voices; both had strict, disciplinary fathers and kind, caring mothers; both delivered newspapers as teenagers; both were Morehouse men and then seminarians directly influenced by the social gospel. During that same speech in Raleigh, Johnson showed his passion for economic justice by telling the thousands in attendance how best to solve poverty: "One of the greatest purposes of the gospel is to bring about on this Earth a society, a movement which can assure the economic future of all mankind."[45] Change the word "society" to "brotherhood" or "beloved community" and his words could have come from King.

Whether ML felt some spiritual kinship with Dr. Johnson or was simply compelled by the power of his oratory, the young man responded fervently to his account of Gandhi's techniques. "His message was so profound and electrifying," ML would later write, "that I left the meeting and bought a half-dozen books on Gandhi's life and works."[46] It's unknown how deep these studies went at the time, but years later ML's sister, Christine, would point to Johnson's lecture in Philadelphia as a formative moment in the development of her brother's own nonviolent methodology, adding, "Never doubt that education is the key to social, economic, and political empowerment."[47]

Mordecai Johnson would have been pleased to have sparked ML's interest, and even if the young man had disagreed with him on certain aspects of his speech, Johnson would have been fine with that as well. As the Howard president reportedly said during another talk, "The greatest tragedy in a democratic society is for a man to graduate from college thinking exactly as the generation that pays his tuition."[48]

ML, studying hundreds of miles away from his parents, adapting to the ways of the North, and drawing ever closer to a white woman, would no doubt have agreed. He was still in the process of charting the path ahead of him, but he knew that from the perspective of Mama and Daddy King, his life's blueprint had already taken the form of an impossible maze.

6

Chosen to Lead

Term 3, February 21–May 5, 1950

Falling in Love: "There Were People Who Knew About Them."

Over the course of ML's second year, his relationship with Betty Moitz grew closer—and more public. From chats in Miss Hannah's kitchen and around campus, the couple had progressed to hanging out with Mac, Whit, and others in the recreation room down the hall from the kitchen. Betty would watch as ML and his friends played pool. "The men who worked in the kitchen and dining room used to go down to shoot pool or play table tennis every evening after dinner," she remembers. "I was surprised how well [ML] played."[1]

And their private time together was no longer limited to Betty driving ML around Chester. "We did go out on dates," Betty says. "He was always trying to get me to go with him to restaurants in Chester. I was embarrassed to let him know I had never been to any of those places. In those days who went to restaurants? . . . You [usually] went to the movies."[2] ML would have known that dining at a predominantly white restaurant was a risky proposition, not only for himself but for Betty as well, but their relationship was a way for him to test the limits of northern culture.

Betty Moitz at her home on the Crozer campus, circa 1951. *Courtesy of Dr. James Beshai*

Such boundary-pushing becomes easier when one starts to fall in love—and according to Betty, that's exactly what was happening: "We were madly, madly in love, the way young people can fall in love."[3]

Many of ML's classmates could see how enamored he'd become. "King was extremely fond of her," Marcus Wood recalled. "But he was also rather proud of the fact that he was able to socialize openly with a white girl."[4] Horace Whitaker also had his eye on the couple. "There were people who knew about them," Whitaker said—himself among them—but "they didn't flagrantly show their feelings toward each other."[5]

ML could only trust one friend with his feelings toward Betty, and that was Mac. Around this time, ML and Betty went into Philadelphia with Walter McCall and his girlfriend at the time, policewoman Pearl E. Smith. The four headed back to Pearl's home, and there was a moment when Betty and Pearl were speaking to each other in the kitchen. "They didn't tell her anything about me," Betty says. Pearl measured Betty up. It was true, Betty was tan, and Pearl gave her a nod of approval: "You know, you could pass [as black]." Mac overheard what Pearl said and "rolled on the floor, laughing."[6]

Their relationship was becoming serious, the most serious one ML had ever been in up to this point. But his friends weren't the only ones he kept in the dark. He also still resisted telling his family about Betty. Reckoning with their inevitable disapproval—and that of society in general—was a dilemma for another day. For now they were content to simply enjoy the beauty of each other's company.

Another reckoning lay ahead for the young couple. As ML's middle year drew to a close and Betty prepared to graduate from the Moore College of Art, Crozer announced that the seminary would be adding two new professors to the staff.[7] One of them was a young man who knew Betty very well: Kenneth Smith, her first serious boyfriend. Starting in the fall of 1950, Smith, the new and single Applied Christianity professor, would take up residence on the second floor of Old Main—only a few doors away from ML's room 52.

Classes and Professors: Historical Perspectives
Outline History of Christianity

> "The religious man has generally been motivated by his desire to win the larger wellbeing of his group, which may include mankind. . . . The greatest evils that beset and baffle him are those which come through the medium of human relationships."
>
> —R. E. E. Harkness[8]

ML's Class Schedule
Year II, Term 3, February 21–May 5, 1950

Time	Tuesday	Wednesday	Thursday	Friday
8:00 AM	Outline History of Christianity	Outline History of Christianity	Outline History of Christianity	Outline History of Christianity
9:00 AM				
10:00 AM	Chapel service	Optional service		Devotional pd.
10:30 AM	Hist. of Living Rels. 101	Hist. of Living Rels. 101	Hist. of Living Rels. 101	Hist. of Living Rels. 101
11:00 AM				
11:30 AM				
12:00 PM				
1:00 PM				
2:00 PM				
3:00 PM				
4:00 PM			Vespers service (4:15 PM)	
5:00 PM				

No classes on Monday | Term examinations: May 2–5 |
Eighty-second commencement: May 7–9
ML's GPA for the term: 3.33

Outline History of Christianity
Reuben Elmore Ernest Harkness, MA, BD, PhD (Chicago)
Course Description: "The rise and development of Christianity to the Renaissance: the Mediterranean world of the early Christian era; reasons for, and types of, persecution; Christianity's defense and its final acceptance by the State; growth of the Imperial Church. Rise of Nationalism and the Reformation: the particular course of the new movement in each nation; the escape of reform forces from England to America; the development of an American Christianity." (Credit hours: 8; ML's grade: B+)

The History of Living Religions 101
George Washington Davis, BD, ThM (Colgate-Rochester), PhD (Yale)
Course Description: "A survey of five of mankind's living religions; the religion of primitive peoples; detailed study of the origins, founders, doctrines, and expressional forms of those religions which have had their origins in India—namely, Hinduism, Jainism, Buddhism, and Sikhism." (Credit hours: 4; ML's grade: B+)

On Tuesday, Wednesday, and Friday, a half-hour period was set aside at 10:00 AM for services in the chapel. On Tuesdays was a mandatory service led by interim president Dr. Howard Wayne Smith and/or his soon-to-be-installed replacement, Sankey L. Blanton. Wednesday services were optional, generally led by a member of the faculty or an invited pastor from an evangelical institution. The Friday devotional period was run by the students themselves and presided over by ML as chairman of the Devotions Committee. On Thursday, the 10:00 AM slot was a free period, and a vespers service was held at 4:15 PM. This tightly planned service featured a speaker from a prescheduled list, usually a Crozer professor or a guest speaker from another institution.[9]

With a voice for radio and a skill for illuminating the seemingly mundane details of history, R. E. E. Harkness had stood as one of the pillars of the Crozer faculty for twenty-three years. By the time ML walked into his Outline History of Christianity class, the beloved professor was both the school's J. P. Crozer Griffith Professor of Church History and president of the American Baptist Historical Society. In short, he was a walking library. If you needed to learn how the Quakers and Baptists of the eighteenth century were connected, you went to Harkness. If you queried Harkness about Roger Williams, the Puritan renegade who founded Providence, Rhode Island, there was a good chance your afternoon would be shot.[10]

ML was fortunate not to have missed his opportunity to study with Harkness, as the professor would retire from Crozer in the spring of 1950. Unfortunately, there is little record of the classroom interactions between the two, and neither man spoke of the other in their later years. "I don't understand that," said a Crozer student turned professor who had also taken a church history course from Harkness.[11] Still, it's clear from the course description that Harkness offered ML and the other students a wide-ranging survey of Christianity's history, with a particular focus on its development in Western Europe and early America—Harkness's specialty. If his frequent journal articles are any indication, he was capable of conveying both enthusiasm and clarity even when describing mysticism during the English Reformation.

Harkness's articles also frequently describe an urgent need for broadened religious consciousness. He would have wanted ML and his classmates to expand their knowledge of Christianity in other times and other places as much as they could, seeing it as the key to understanding Christianity in the here and now:

> Perhaps the most essential requirement is that religion should know itself. For any religious leader we might paraphrase the old adage: "He knows not England who only England knows."[12]

ML could take pride in knowing that he had taken steps to achieve this broadened perspective outside of class as well. He'd left the South, for one. He'd preached in churches in the North, and he'd taken it upon himself to explore social movements on the other side of the world. *He knows not the South who only the South knows.* When King returned home, he would see the region in a clearer light.

The History of Living Religions 101

Delving further into the unfamiliar expanse of religious history, ML investigated the major religions of the world with George W. Davis. Clear-eyed and open-minded as ever, Davis was an ideal professor to introduce students to the basic histories of Buddhism, Hinduism, Judaism, and Islam, and how they intermingled with or ran parallel to Christianity.

In a standout essay ML completed for the class, he contrasted two branches of Buddhism: the more liberal, populist Mahayana branch and the strictly monastic Hinayana branch. A close reading of this paper shows ML working extremely hard to grasp the subtleties of each side, quoting heavily (and at times misappropriating) from his sources. Among the clamor of pasted citations, however, are whispers of his own thoughts. After describing how the Mahayana viewed an aspect of Hinayana as "selfish" and "narrow," ML mentions how the Mahayana created a far more "unselfish" ideal—the notion that as long as believers commit themselves to lives of nonjudgmental empathy, devoted to the service of others, they can attain enlightenment. He adds:

> It is interesting . . . to note the similarities of this [Mahayana] conception of vicarious suffering and the transference of merit to many of the theories of atonement that have appeared in the history of Christian thought.[13]

ML, through one of his sources, also begins to connect the core philosophy of Mahayana Buddhism with the ideals described in seventeenth-century Jewish philosopher Baruch Spinoza's *Ethics*—the idea of "One Reality" and the desire to see the world with as few delusions as possible.

By finding connections among the world's religions, ML was once again broadening his perspective, seeking truth outside his comfort zone. Davis's class was his first direct attempt to understand the world as a unified religious community—a worldview that would be reflected seventeen years later in one of ML's most controversial speeches, "Beyond Vietnam." Delivered in April 1967 at Riverside Church in New York City, this rhetorical storm of anger at the US military's actions in Vietnam included a plea for Americans to conceptualize a "worldwide fellowship" and an "unconditional love for all of mankind":

When I speak of love I am not speaking of some sentimental and weak response. . . . I am speaking of that force which all of the great religions have seen as the supreme unifying principle of life. Love is somehow the key that unlocks the door which leads to ultimate reality. This Hindu-Muslim-Christian-Jewish-Buddhist belief about ultimate reality is beautifully summed up in the first epistle of Saint John: "Let us love one another, for love is God. And every one that loveth is born of God and knoweth God. He that loveth not knoweth not God, for God is love. . . . If we love one another, God dwelleth in us and his love is perfected in us." Let us hope that this spirit will become the order of the day.[14]

Twenty-one-year-old ML could not have imagined the global developments and personal experiences that would lead him to deliver such a plea to a skeptical nation more than a decade hence. But as he continued his Crozer education, the young man was shaping his own philosophy in small but nuanced ways. Classes such as Living Religions were necessary steps toward a future he could not yet see, but was beginning to feel.

Student Body President, NAACP Speaker: "Head and Shoulders Above Anybody Else"

As he stretched his philosophical boundaries and went on dates with Betty, ML was emerging from the shadow of the life that still waited for him down in Atlanta. His role back home was simple and unchanging: be the perfect oldest son who carries on his father's legacy at Ebenezer Baptist, and try to be happy with it. Perhaps in the distant future he would be, but for now it was his life at Crozer that made him happy, and as he allowed his experiences there to enrich him, other students took notice.

Chairing the Devotions Committee provided a particularly good opportunity for him to grab a moment in the spotlight. In order to effectively plan each Friday's student-run devotional period, ML would have had to collaborate with any student who hoped to speak at or otherwise participate in the service, and accommodate everyone in the student body who wished to attend. Each week's service was a testament to his leadership, his ability to connect with fellow seminarians from every background—black, white, and international students alike. Even many first-year students already knew and admired ML, including ex-GI Francis Stewart and vegetarian pacifist Walter Stark, thanks not only to his obvious leadership and preaching skills but also to his lighthearted dorm-room banter.

Thus, it is no surprise that ML was a strong contender for student body president in the spring of 1950. Voting concluded in mid-April, and after a faculty committee and the student government association made their own recommendations, the winner was announced: Martin Luther King Jr.[15]

"It was not all that big of a deal," said Horace Whitaker of ML's victory; the main benefit of winning was simply that you got to say you were the *president*. It did, however, make Crozer history: King was the first black student body president in the seminary's eighty-two years of existence. And the time had certainly come for such a milestone, since seven of the fourteen students in ML's middle-year class were African American. Said Marcus Wood, it "was indeed an honor to us . . . black students to have one of us be the president of the student body."[16]

But Francis Stewart, who would be elected student body president the following year, denied that the students picked ML to make some kind of racial statement. According to Stewart, King was chosen simply because he "was head and shoulders above anybody else. . . . He was a good speaker, a good scholar; he was . . . well liked."[17] In any event, his election was another sign of how much respect most everyone had for ML, and how far he'd come since the days when he tangled with an angry Lucius Hall and took pains not to draw attention to himself in class.

ML's new sense of confidence extended to his preaching. He *knew* he could preach, thanks to his upbringing at Ebenezer and the tutelage of Rev. Barbour, and he felt entitled to judge the way other seminarians sermonized. As the nearly thirty-year-old Walter Stark recalled, "Martin especially told me, '*You don't know how to preach.*' [Martin would] talk about preaching up a storm, and all that kind of thing. He said, '*You white fellas, you don't know how to preach!*'"[18]

ML continued to find work in the pulpits of local churches. For instance, on Sunday, March 5, he had traveled two miles off campus to

Fifth Presbyterian Church,* where he spoke at an 8:00 PM service commemorating "Men's Day."[19] Marcus Wood recalled, with a tinge of envy,
how ML's packed preaching schedule reflected the continued influence of
Daddy King. His young friend "would frequently go out on the weekend
and preach at area churches, because his father—known throughout Baptist circles—would say to his friends, many of whom were pastors: 'My
son is at Crozer; I want you to hear him.'" Although such engagements
were more for the continued practice than anything else, the older and
more experienced Wood couldn't help but notice the monetary benefit
of his friend's packed schedule: "In those days . . . people gave nickels
and dimes in church, along with a few quarters. And King would always
come back on Sunday or Monday with a lot of change in his pocket."[20]

But even when it came to speaking engagements, ML wasn't content
simply to walk through the doors his father opened for him. He was
also making his own arrangements, outside the familiar church setting
in which Daddy King held so much sway. On May 5, 1950, the last day
of final exams, he traveled fifteen miles southeast to Newark, Delaware,
to give a speech in front of the local chapter of the NAACP.

King was there at the invitation of a fellow classmate, a married
preacher named George T. Walton. Although Walton was white, he
was the president of the Newark NAACP chapter, and he asked ML to
provide his perspective on race relations in the United States. ML did
belong to the Morehouse chapter of the NAACP during his years as a
student there, but this is the first reported instance of ML speaking at
an NAACP event in the North.

The meeting was held at the New London Avenue Colored School—
as of 1950, Delaware's schools were still segregated.† Mainly a school
for local black children in the first through eighth grades, the building
was tiny. ML would have had to deliver his speech in one of four common first-floor classrooms or a basement cafeteria to an audience that,
Rev. Walton hoped, would be interracial enough to foster a healthy
discussion.

---

* Fifth Presbyterian Church was renamed Thomas M. Thomas Memorial Presbyterian
Church after its founder, who welcomed any and all races and denominations.
† The building is still there today, now known as the George Wilson Community Center.

During the meeting, the organizers also played a sixteen-minute animated film titled *Picture in Your Mind*.[21] Created by Philip Stapp in 1948 after a trip to war-ravaged France, the film paints a haunting portrait of what the world could become if it continued down the path of racial prejudice. As ML sat near the projector, the narrator described the evolution of man and civilization: "From hunger and loneliness, man banded together . . . to live and work in natural isolation." Over time, these bands of men inevitably split into separate tribes, and when times were tough, those who were suffering assigned blame in a familiar way:

> Within these groups there were other groups, other tensions seeking an outlet. Jealousy, anger, guilt . . . and there was the other tribe across the river, across the hilltop, across the sea, who had different colored skin, ate forbidden food, worshipped other Gods . . . distant, strange. Heard only through the distorted ear of rumor . . . *No amount of education will ever help them.* **Our way is the right way.**[22]

Later in the film, the animation depicts a man standing just in front of a tree, then slowly reveals that beneath the tree, trapped within its roots, is a far wilder man—a demon, one could say. Where the wild man touches the roots, red tendrils begin to spread, creeping up and out of the ground, grabbing the first man around the legs . . .

> Our need to live together, our civilization, our education, have buried in our memory ancient primal impulses . . . but they are not dead. Unexposed, uncontrolled . . . they will control us. These are the hidden roots of prejudice. . . . In time of need they can be turned against us . . .

History does not record ML's reaction to this unusual presentation, but he would surely have agreed with its overall message: humanity, despite our so-called differences, must learn to live together, and not by having "one way of life imposed upon us." Perhaps he would also have admired Stapp for finding an innovative way to convey this message of tolerance, since he himself was seeking new ways to speak to the public about social concerns.

If ML wanted to set himself apart from his father, he would need to prove that he could connect with people outside the familiar setting of a church. So here he was at a Newark NAACP event, holding forth on his chosen, secular topic, which according to the local newspaper was to contrast "popular misconceptions regarding goals of Negroes with what he considers the real objectives."[23]

It was another instance of ML breaking out of his comfort zone in a year that had already been filled with them. His life was beginning to speed up, and the summer of 1950 would be one to remember.

Interlude

The Summer of 1950

"The first civil rights struggle that King had ever been in was with me. It was in Maple Shade, New Jersey, in 1950."

—Walter McCall[1]

ON MAY 28, 1950, ML stood behind the Ebenezer pulpit in Atlanta, preaching the "Three Levels of Fellowship" to the congregation—many of whom, according to ML's close childhood friend Larry Williams, didn't really enjoy this twenty-one-year-old know-it-all telling them how to best live life. They'd grown used to the passionate growl of ML's more experienced father. Closing in on his divinity degree, the younger King could very easily come off as a bit of a snob—a grating reminder for parishioners of the education they themselves had not pursued.[2]

Worse for ML than facing an ambivalent congregation was returning to his childhood home to face the judgment of Daddy King. According to another Atlanta friend, June Dobbs, ML's father had given him the third degree about his academic performance at Crozer. He hadn't earned a grade lower than a B since the end of his first year, but that wasn't enough. "I remember his father saying, 'You ought to be making all As. I pay all your bills,' Dobbs recalls. "He wanted him to be perfect, a scholar and this, that, and the other."[3]

Martin Luther King Sr. also recoiled at his son's evolving political opinions. ML "often seemed to be drifting away from the basics of capitalism and Western democracy that I felt very strongly about," he wrote years later. Daddy King listened patiently to his son, absorbing as much as he could until a line was crossed. "There were some sharp exchanges; I may even have raised my voice a few times."[4]

Daddy King was more impressed with ML's performance behind the pulpit. As each Sunday passed, he could see his son improve as a preacher, starting to seamlessly combine the "Bible's truths with wisdom of the modern world." For the plainspoken southern Bible-thumper who'd graduated from Morehouse in 1930 and never traveled north to continue his studies, his son provided a glimpse of what could have been: "There was a deeper, considerably more resonant quality in his preaching, and on the Sundays he relieved me in the pulpit, I grew increasingly more moved by his growth, the probing quality of his mind, the urgency, the fire that makes for brilliance in every theological setting."[5]

But the elder King also feared that his son, having spent so much time in the North, would not return to Atlanta permanently. "Many of the young went north to school and never came back," he wrote. "This was a loss that hurt the South, perhaps for longer than anyone knows."[6] So he did his best to keep ML rooted to Ebenezer and to Atlanta. Perhaps in pursuit of that goal, ML's father urged him to consider pursuing a serious relationship with his sister's friend Juanita Sellers, whom he'd dated on and off in Atlanta and seen while visiting Christine in New York. Daddy King had no way of knowing that things were already getting serious between his son and Betty Moitz.

Perhaps needing a break from his father's constant scrutiny, ML briefly stepped away from the Ebenezer pulpit and traveled back up north to see Mac, who was staying with relatives at 753 Walnut Street, a brick duplex in Camden, New Jersey. ML knew his trip would be a short one; he had to be back in Atlanta for his brother's wedding. AD was marrying his fiancée, Naomi Barber, on June 15.

753 Walnut Street in Camden, New Jersey, where ML and Walter McCall stayed on and off in the summer of 1950. *Courtesy of Patrick Duff, Camden, NJ*

The previous Sunday, June 11, ML and Mac attended an evening church service, along with Mac's girlfriend, Pearl Smith, and her roommate, Doris Wilson. Afterward, the four wanted to go out for a drink to unwind. They decided to try Mary's Café, a tavern in nearby Maple Shade, New Jersey. According to Pearl Smith's later testimony, she, Doris, and ML took a seat at a table in the taproom. Meanwhile, McCall strode up to the counter, where the tavern's owner, a fifty-four-year-old German immigrant named Ernest Nichols, was tending bar.[7]

It was after midnight by this point, and the tavern was mostly empty. ML and company were still in church attire. Mary's Café was not exactly the kind of place one went while decked out in one's Sunday best; Nichols was used to having patrons who were more blue-collar, especially at night.[8]

Mac asked Nichols for a couple "quarts of beer . . . and four glasses." Nichols stared at his customer in disbelief. The bartender said to McCall that he couldn't serve them alcohol "because it was Sunday."

Mac headed back to the table, confused. Probably at a lower volume, he asked ML and the two young ladies if that was indeed the law. Mac, recalled Pearl Smith, wondered whether Nichols "was refusing to serve us because it was Sunday and a bottled beer was considered package goods." Someone suggested that Mac go ask for four *glasses* of beer instead.

So McCall went back up to Nichols, who no doubt had been watching the four discuss the situation. When Mac asked for glasses of beer, his irritation grew. According to a later statement submitted to the authorities on his behalf, serving beer of any kind at this time of night would have been a violation, and from his perspective, these four were testing him—conspiring to screw him over in some way.[9]

Perhaps McCall could see the annoyed intensity in Nichols, because then Mac shrugged off his previous request and asked for four ginger ales. Surely that would be OK.

But Nichols had already become unhinged. A hidden agenda was being played, somehow, and he refused to take part. He left the bar and stormed outside. Moments passed as Nichols went to his apartment a short distance away. ML, McCall, and the two ladies didn't know what was happening. Then Nichols came back in with a revolver and stood by the door. From Pearl Smith's sworn statement, Nichols "opened the front door and shot out the door and he came back in the tavern and was waving the gun around and using very abusive language."[10]

ML and the others ran out of the tavern. As they did, according to a few reports, Nichols shouted, "I'll kill for less!" The group climbed into McCall's car and sped away.[11]

They decided to head to the Maple Shade police department to file a complaint. According to Pearl Smith, herself an officer of the law, "We got the police and came back down [to Mary's Café] and the police confiscated the gun."[12]

The incident in Maple Shade was still on ML's mind later in the week, when he went to visit Rev. Barbour in Chester and found Almanina Barbour at home. At the time, Rev. Barbour's daughter was a law student at the University of Pennsylvania, so when ML told her what happened, it could have been a case ripped from one of her textbooks. Vividly, Almanina remembered that ML "was furious—livid. I said, 'You don't have to take this lying down.' I advised him to sue."[13]

ML and his friends decided to pursue charges against Nichols, not only for threatening them with a gun but also for racial discrimination. The latter was illegal under New Jersey's antidiscrimination law, one of the first in the nation, which had been passed just five years earlier.

But first up was Nichols's hearing on the weapons charge, which conflicted with the date of AD King's nuptials. This meant that if ML was to testify, he needed to persuade his brother to postpone the wedding.

ML called Mama King in Atlanta around 9:30 AM on the scheduled day of the ceremony and explained the situation. According to AD, ML told his mother that "his suit against the restaurant was coming up the next day," and ML "wanted to know if I couldn't put the wedding off for two more days." AD was still in bed, but his mother passed along the message. At first, AD was annoyed, since he'd "been waiting for the big day for seven years," but he wanted his brother there by his side as best man. After a few moments of head-shaking, AD obliged, pushing back the service by two days. "I will never forgive him . . ." AD jokingly said. "I was mad as the devil."[14]

But ML's attendance at the hearing was good news for the Maple Shade solicitor who prosecuted the case. "He was a very good witness," the lawyer recalled. "He was direct and positive with his answers. You had the feeling he was telling the truth." Mac also credited the assistance of Robert Burke Johnson, a friend of his who was president of a local NAACP chapter.[15] And, of course, Mac's magnanimity shouldn't obscure his own crucial role; had he not insisted, with his typical fearlessness, on confronting Nichols in the first place, they wouldn't have had their day in court.*

Thanks to everyone's persistence, and AD's reluctant sacrifice, the judge found Nichols guilty on the firearms violations and fined him fifty dollars. A hearing on the discrimination charges would have to wait until later in the summer. In the meantime, ML had a wedding to get to.

Right after his courtroom appearance, ML set out on the thirteen-hour drive south. With him were his sister, Christine, who had mainly stayed up north

---

* Years later, ML said of Mac, "He possesses a most radiant personality and the gift of dealing with people of all levels of life. . . . I can say all of these things without reservation because . . . he has been one of my most intimate personal friends." (From King, *Papers*, 3:399. ML wrote this in a letter of recommendation for Mac to preach at First African Baptist Church in Savannah, GA.)

for the summer, and their Atlanta friend "Deacon" Jethro English, a loyal
Ebenezer parishioner since 1925 who had been visiting family in the New
Jersey area. "ML and I almost missed Naomi and A.D.'s wedding com-
pletely," said Christine. "We were traveling by car with ML at the wheel."[16]

Perhaps it was the intensity of the last few days in Maple Shade or
the rush of their initial legal victory, or perhaps ML was simply worried about missing the most important day of his brother's life, but he
decided to ignore the speed limit. "Truth be told," Christine said, "ML
was known for driving with a lead foot."

They'd just started heading south when they heard sirens behind
them. ML pulled over. "We were given a ticket and had to follow the
officer to either the jail or the courthouse. I don't remember which. ML
rode in the back of the police car, Deacon English drove the car ML had
been driving, and I was left as [Jethro's] worried front-seat passenger."

And so, for the second time in less than a week, ML found himself
surrounded by law enforcement, only this time he was the guilty party.
As the three stood near a counter, the clerk told them the fine for
speeding was $25—around $250 in today's currency. "When we heard
the amount of the fine," said Christine, "we could have fainted!" More
than a half-century after the incident, Christine could still remember
ML's exact reaction to hearing the amount. "ML had a look on his face
that was *priceless* as he glanced from me to Deacon English, and back
again . . . poor ML didn't have a penny to his name."

Among the three of them, they scrounged through what they had on
them, hoping to dig up the required amount. If they couldn't, then AD's
wedding would be missing two family members. Fortunately, Christine
had just enough, and they were granted the "freedom . . . to hightail it
to the wedding."[17]

ML and Christine did make it back in time for the ceremony, which
took place, as Christine recalled, "at Naomi's parents' home on McDan-
iel Street in Atlanta." The next day was Sunday, and ML managed to
throw together a sermon at Ebenezer, titled "The Lord God Omnipotent
Reigneth."[18]

His week had started with gunshots and hate, followed by two visits
to the authorities and a court hearing, and it ended with a last-minute

entrance to his younger brother's wedding. ML had squeezed a few months' worth of experience into one jam-packed week.

Back in New Jersey, preparations continued for a grand jury hearing in the Maple Shade discrimination case. The Camden NAACP entered the fray to support what they saw as an obvious race-driven violation. But to secure more evidence that Ernest Nichols had refused to serve ML and company because they were black, Almanina Barbour asked three of her white classmates from the University of Pennsylvania Law School to visit Mary's Café and pose as thirsty customers. Sure enough, they had no problems getting a drink, and were prepared to confirm that fact to the grand jury.[19]

Unfortunately, Almanina's classmates soon had second thoughts. As Walter McCall remembered, "The young white boys who . . . were to testify against the owner discovered that their parents had brought pressure against them and they couldn't appear." Explained Almanina, "They felt testifying would hurt their careers." She then divulged the fact that "all three" became "big attorneys in the city . . . but I won't mention their names."[20]

Their corroborating evidence would have been missed, but according to Nichols's attorney, W. Thomas McGann, the case suffered a more damaging blow when ML failed to return to New Jersey to testify. "Rev. King and his friends," wrote McGann, "never appeared before the grand jury, even though they were notified and asked to be available as witnesses." According to the lawyer, Walter McCall was the only one of the four complainants who made it to the hearing, but his presence alone wasn't enough. The judge dismissed the case.[21]

We can only speculate as to why ML bowed out. He may have seen the loss of Almanina's witnesses as an unrecoverable setback. (Mac would later suggest as much, recalling that "as a result" of the witnesses refusing to appear, "we just dropped the thing.")[22] On the other hand, he may have simply thought himself too busy with other responsibilities to head back north. Not only did he have his associate pastor duties at Ebenezer Baptist, but he had apparently rededicated himself to doing

fieldwork for a sociology professor he'd met while studying at Morehouse, Professor Ira Reid. An Atlanta News column that ran in the
Pittsburgh Courier on July 15, 1950, included the following blurb:

> Miss June Dobbs and the Rev. M. L. King Jr., who are working
> on the survey of the Negro Baptists of America, under Ira D.A.
> Reid, are in attendance at the Baptist Institute which is in session
> at Morehouse College.[23]

Ira De Augustine Reid was a professor at Atlanta University from
whom ML had taken a few sociology seminars as a college student. Reid
then moved to Haverford College in Pennsylvania, where he became
the school's first tenured black professor. In the summer of 1948, right
after ML graduated from Morehouse, the professor reached out to him,
his friend June Dobbs, and other students for help with a mammoth
project: collecting comprehensive data on black Baptist churches and
seminaries across the United States. To do this, he would need young
men and women to sacrifice days and weekends to interview Baptist
ministers in different areas of the country. It was a perfect gig for a
student—flexible schedule, cultural experience, and a little extra cash—
and ML continued to work for the project during his time at Crozer,
pounding the pavement in Atlanta, Philadelphia, and even St. Louis. At
this stage in life, perhaps this took precedence over attending a grand
jury hearing in New Jersey.

One also imagines that if ML had prioritized the Maple Shade pro-
ceedings, they would have made a lasting impression on those close to
him—in particular, the brother who'd held off on getting married so he
could pursue it. But AD didn't seem to retain much knowledge of the
case. Asked about it in 1957, he remembered a few of the basic details
but thought it had taken place in Philadelphia. "I never asked him how
the suit came out," AD said, "and I don't know to this day whether he
won or lost."[24]

But it would be wrong to dismiss the importance of the events in
Maple Shade just because they ultimately petered out. For the first time
in his life, ML had been directly involved in a civil rights case. He
helped file a suit, testified in court, and witnessed the impact an outside

advocacy group, the NAACP, could have on the outcome. Eleven years later, in a *Philadelphia Tribune* article, ML himself would make the connection between the incident and his later work, describing it as something akin to the organized protests of the civil rights movement: "They refused to serve us. It was a painful experience because we decided to sit-in."[25]

And in the immediate aftermath of Maple Shade, ML's preaching does seem to have focused more strongly on social action and combating the ills of the establishment. Where at the beginning of the summer he'd discussed the "Three Levels of Fellowship," by July 2 he was speaking of the importance of "Propagandizing Christianity," urging the Ebenezer congregation to spread the word of the Lord and assuring them that not all propaganda should be considered corrupt. Subsequent sermons are lost to history, but some of their titles, such as "Having the Moral Courage to Speak Out" (July 23) and "The Conquest of Fear" (August 20) suggest the lingering influence of ML's eventful week in June.[26]

Year III

Revelation

A vespers service in the Crozer chapel, circa the late 1940s. The chapel, located on the first floor of Old Main, is where ML and other seminarians had various classes and worshipped throughout the week. *Courtesy of Colgate Rochester Crozer Divinity School, Rochester, NY*

7

Forbidden Love

Term 1, September 12– November 22, 1950

"Martin talked slowly, delivering every sentence with Delphian assurance and oracular finality. . . . That afternoon, in the middle of the day and the middle of the week, he wore a collar, tie, and three-button suit. He was a small-framed person, who walked and talked slowly with a kind of Napoleonic assurance. He looked like a major event about to happen."

—Dr. Samuel Proctor, former Crozer and Boston University graduate, upon meeting ML for the first time[1]

In Love but Struggling: "Man of a Broken Heart"

Term 1 had not yet gotten under way, and already the demands of ML's final year at Crozer were hanging over him. To officially complete seminary, every student needed to pass a battery of comprehensive examinations, both written and oral, during the fall of their third year. It was by no means a cakewalk; both Walter McCall and Marcus Wood would fail their first go-around.[2]

The written portion consisted of "two three-hour written examinations" that were scheduled to begin on Thursday, September 7, nearly a week before the start of the term. According to the exam's study guide, topics would span the entire Crozer curriculum, from the liberal theology espoused by George W. Davis to the practical perspective on the Gospels championed by Morton Enslin.[3]

And ML couldn't just spend the rest of the week preparing, because his other responsibilities demanded attention. As student body president, he was scheduled to address incoming students during orientation that same Thursday. And he was playing host to other members of the King family, who were in town for the annual meeting of the National Baptist Convention (NBC). The event was being held in Philadelphia on September 6–10, and not only was Martin Sr. obliged to make his usual appearance, but Mama King was slated to play the organ for the "women's division," and Daddy King's brother Joel, also a Baptist minister, was in attendance as well.[4]

While ML would have expected his family to swing by Crozer while they were in the area, he may have had a few twinges of annoyance, and not just at giving up precious study time. After all, Crozer and Philadelphia had been *his* second home for the last two years. Now, as student body president and a prominent local preacher, he had a certain reputation to maintain that might be threatened by parental encroachment.

At one point during their visit, ML took Daddy King and Uncle Joel down into the basement of Old Main to show off his pool skills. Uncle Joel was stunned when ML, appearing to have no fear, lit a cigarette in front of his father. Daddy King had never had any patience for smoking, drinking, cursing, or even pool. Uncle Joel, considerably younger than Martin Sr., even remembered when he himself was in college and his brother smacked a cigar out of his mouth. But as they watched ML knock in a few pool balls, puffing away like a natural, Daddy King did nothing. Later, Uncle Joel asked his brother why he didn't try to discipline ML there in the basement. Daddy King remained silent. "Never got an answer," said Joel King.[5] Martin Sr. must have realized that his son had outgrown such heavy-handed parenting.

Though defiant in his leisure activities, in other respects ML was still following in his father's footsteps. He joined Daddy King at the NBC meeting, even persuading Horace Whitaker and Walter McCall to attend. Probably borrowing his father's car, he drove his two friends to the site of the event, an auditorium near the Thirtieth Street Station in downtown Philadelphia.[6]

It was Whit's first time attending such a gathering, and he found it reminiscent of a "mass jungle." Whit watched in frustration as the ministers behind the pulpit onstage competed for attention with vendors strolling up and down the aisles "selling hats" and "shouting" at the attendees. Joel King, too, recalled that attendees would get so wound up at certain speakers that they would scream comments such as "If you pick up that mike, I'll cut your heart out!" The rowdy energy was still good spirited, if surprising to first-time attendees.[7]

At the time, the National Baptist Convention reported a membership of around four million people, predominantly African American. An estimated seven thousand delegates turned out for the annual meeting, which featured singing and pleas from Pennsylvania governor James Duff for tolerance and racial integration. The report issued after the event stated that attendees were pleased "to see the walls of injustice and inequality crumbling daily before our eyes."[8]

As soon as the NBC thunderstorm dispersed and ML's family left the area, it was time for the start of classes—and for the comprehensive oral exam. The test would last for forty-five minutes to an hour and focus on two particular theological areas of the student's choosing, but be broad enough to "discover the student's ability to think in an integrative manner over all the areas of theological education."[9]

Despite ML's demanding schedule, when both the written and oral examinations were completed, he stood out from the rest. In a note by Charles Batten to Morehouse College, the dean informed ML's alma mater of the results. "We have just had a period of comprehensive examinations and only one man was granted honors in them; it was King."[10]

As ML turned his attention from what he'd learned in his first two years at Crozer to the final year that lay ahead of him, it would have been impossible to ignore the changes that were now roiling the school. The interim days of H. W. "Creeping Jesus" Smith were over. After a transition period that stretched over the latter two quarters of ML's middle year, Dr. Sankey L. Blanton was now the seminary's president, and he was eager to change its entire culture.

Dr. Blanton was a man of the South, a fifty-two-year-old North Carolinian who had previously been the dean of religion at Wake Forest University. Blanton brought with him an influx of southern energy, including six of his former Wake Forest students whom he persuaded to enroll at Crozer. One of them, Jack Bullard, remembers witnessing first-hand the transformation Blanton sought. "He represented a change of direction. He wanted to counteract the direction Enslin had been taking the faculty." Whereas Enslin was a brilliant New Testament scholar but an indifferent preacher, Blanton "wanted more of a practical focus. . . . They were interested in *pastors*, not theological scholars."[11]

The plan was not Blanton's alone. Crozer's board of trustees wanted to take advantage of a growing trend in America's postwar religious culture—away from biblical scholarship and toward the populist appeal of charismatic evangelistic preachers—to not just increase enrollment but spike it. Thanks to Blanton's efforts during the transition period, the school was already seeing results: while ML's class had dwindled in his last year to only eleven students, the incoming junior class was a group of twenty-eight students who'd come from as far away as Oregon.[12]

The proposed realignment may have been good for the school's enrollment numbers, but it represented a seismic jolt to Professors Enslin and Pritchard and the other members of the Crozer community who had embraced their academic approach. "Some of the people didn't care for Blanton trying to make it a preacher's school," recalls one Crozer student. "It was supposed to be a scholar's school. There were arguments."[13] Says Bullard, "There was great tension between the faculty and him."[14]

Nevertheless, some faculty members would thrive in the new environment. Robert Keighton fit right in with the emphasis on practicality, while other professors, such as George Davis, were prized for their ability to bridge the growing divide between *scholar* and *pastor.*

As the student body president, ML would have paid close attention to the power struggle among the faculty. But he would also have been keenly aware of another rift that was developing within the student body. As Blanton sought to bring a southern perspective—and more southern students—to Crozer, tension grew between seminarians from the North and those from the South. On one side were young southern Baptist seminarians looking to refine their oratorical skills. On the other were the northern seminarians who had been sold on Crozer's reputation as a liberal, scholarly institution. And yet it wasn't the northern seminarians who tended to be the more academically accomplished. "Usually the southern students were from the good schools in the South," says Jack Bullard, "and the northern students were from run-of-the-mill schools." This only exacerbated the division. "You had a bunch of Southerners who felt they were the cream of the crop."[15]

Standing apart from these domestic conflicts were Crozer's three international students. Joining returning students Makoto Sakurabayashi and En-Chin Lin was new arrival Jimmy Beshai, who'd traveled from Cairo, Egypt, to Chester on an $800 scholarship. According to Jimmy, international students were treated as "adjuncts rather than members of the divinity school," but they participated in all aspects of seminary life as they completed the two-year Oriental certificate program. Besides taking many of the same classes as ML, Jimmy also met with other seminarians in the basement to play pool. "It was the first time for me to play eight ball," Jimmy recalls.

He also remembers what it was like to reside in Old Main: "I lived in a corner room overlooking the campus from one side, and the Delaware River from the other side." Every room came with its own radio, and maids "took care of cleaning the linens. It was a very adequate dormitory. There was a very small but beautiful library . . . and the kind of food Hannah Moitz cooked for us was a mix of German and Pennsylvania meals with frequent Dutch beef porridge. It was good and I missed it on the weekends. No meals were served on weekends, but Mrs. Moitz had milk and cheese in the refrigerator."[16]

Jimmy's room was at the end of Old Main's second floor, only a few doors down from ML's. Walter McCall's room was "adjacent to mine.... He used to wake up the whole floor at six to get ready for breakfast before classes at eight ... waking me up every morning with a loud knock on my door. Walter was taller and more vocal in conversation. We used to call him 'Governor' for that reason."[17]

As for ML, "we often sat together for supper." Jimmy remembers one meal in particular from early in the year. ML took a seat across from Jimmy, naturally curious about how he might be viewed by someone from outside American culture. To start with, ML asked Jimmy about the conditions of racial prejudice in Egypt. Jimmy replied that there wasn't *racial* prejudice but rather *religious* prejudice. After a moment or two, ML asked Jimmy a very direct question: "How do you *see* me?" At first, Jimmy wasn't sure how to respond, but then he settled on a neutral statement: "I see you as an American, like the rest of Americans."[18]

From left to right: James "Jimmy" Beshai (Egypt), Makoto Sakurabayashi (Japan), and En-Chin Lin (China) outside Old Main, circa 1950. *Courtesy of Dr. James Beshai*

ML couldn't help but smile. "Shoot, man," ML said. "I am a *Negro*." To Jimmy, ML wasn't being confrontational—he was simply attempting to develop his global outlook. "I spent more time with Martin than I did with other Crozer students, because Martin was president . . . and he took an interest in international affairs. He was interested in Egypt, and we seemed to pick the same courses by Davis, Enslin, and Kenneth Smith."[19]

Kenneth "Snuffy" Smith was Crozer's new young professor of Applied Christianity, fresh off completing the coursework for his PhD at Duke. Like George Davis, he would play a unifying role at a changing Crozer, fusing President Blanton's emphasis on evangelization with the school's long tradition of theological scholarship.

Smith had graduated from Crozer himself in May 1948, sharpening his Christian perspective under the tutelage of Davis, Pritchard, Enslin, and Keighton. It was Professor Davis with whom he connected the most, and Davis's admiration of Walter Rauschenbusch's *A Theology for the Social Gospel* influenced Smith toward a liberal theology. He was back at his alma mater now "on fire," filled with a desire to create change via the social gospel.*

All of this would make Smith an ideal mentor figure for ML: someone with whom he could spend hours discussing philosophy, someone who would fan the flames of his dedication to social action. But before he could become ML's mentor, he would be his rival: the young professor had also returned to Crozer with the desire to rekindle his previous relationship with Betty Moitz.

Kenneth Lee Smith was born near Exmore, Virginia, in 1925. After a bit of a difficult childhood, Smith learned to distinguish himself through academic achievement. In high school, though, he stood out for more superficial reasons: barely five feet tall with a slow, aw-shucks southern drawl, he seemed to remind many fellow students of a cartoon character. "In the

---

* According to Horace Whitaker, Smith was particularly inspired by the sacrifice of Dietrich Bonhoeffer, the German theologian who vocally opposed Adolf Hitler and helped his Jewish countrymen escape the Nazi regime, for which he was imprisoned and eventually, on April 9, 1945, executed. (Whitaker, notes from interview by Branch.)

comic section of the newspaper, there was a Snuffy Smith," his wife, Esther, explains. "Somebody in high school started calling him that, and it followed him all through his life." In the comic strip, the character of Snuffy was a hillbilly who loved playing cards and drinking moonshine. Smith was of course no hillbilly, but his relaxed, easygoing manner and drawl may have misled a few people meeting him for the first time.[20]

Smith graduated from the University of Richmond in 1945 and went on to Crozer the following fall. He was the first seminarian to grab Betty Moitz's attention in the dining hall, and they began dating. They were involved until May 1948, four months before ML's arrival. When Smith graduated and chose to pursue his PhD at Duke, they agreed to call it off. Their paths were going in different directions.[21]

Now he was back at Crozer. At twenty-five, he was the youngest faculty member by far, and he chose to live on the second floor of Old Main with the single seminarians. Most new professors would have had trepidations about living so close to their students, but Smith was very familiar with the school's liberal, doors-unlocked, interracial culture. Living in Old Main was akin to coming home again.

He fit in quickly with students, some of whom were older than him. During the day, he was a professor in command of his theology, but at night he was happy to go out for an occasional drink in Chester or play eight ball in the catacombs of Old Main. According to Jimmy Beshai, Smith "was very unassuming in his manners. He did not hide that he liked to have beer when he went out."[22] Smith would engage the students in late-night debates, most often around the pool table but also in his own dorm room, which had a bit of extra space that created an office-like atmosphere.

He felt a particular connection with fellow southern Baptists like ML, Whit, and Mac. "We dropped the g's on the ends of our words," Smith explained. "We talked the same way." But he related more easily to the outgoing Mac than to ML, whom he at first found "reserved" and "humorless."[23]

And, of course, one issue in particular came between them. Soon after returning to campus, Snuffy began mentioning to others that he and Betty were going steady. But ML, perhaps with Mac's encouragement, informed Smith that he and Betty were now going out.

The two men—student body president and first-year professor—remained civil, attempting to laugh off the situation. But ML had reason to wonder whether the newcomer could indeed come between him and Betty. After all, Snuffy not only had a history with her but was also close with the Moitz family. "My parents loved Snuffy," Betty says. Miss Hannah knew him so well that she could fry his bologna just the way he liked it.[24] And now he was a full-fledged faculty member.

Eventually, Betty made her choice clear. "Snuffy," she recalls, "asked me to go to dinner several times a week after he came back as a professor. He began to tell people I was 'his girl.' I stopped going out with him."[25] With Smith out of picture, ML began to seriously consider the possibility of a future with Betty.

ML's friends sensed how serious he was getting about Betty Moitz, and all of them, except for Walter McCall, worried about how this would affect his future plans. According to Marcus Wood, "The more we warned [ML] that marriage was out of the question—especially if he hoped to become a pastor in the south—the more he refused to 'break off' the potentially controversial relationship."[26]

ML's counterargument had two components. The first, of course, was the obvious one: He loved Betty. She listened to him, supported him, and greatly admired his ambitions. He could see himself marrying her. The second was a symbolic component: Wouldn't their union also be a powerful statement that barriers can be brought down? It could serve as living proof of his belief in the idea of social integration.

Late one night, after making out with Betty on a bench near Old Main, a smitten ML headed over to Horace Whitaker's apartment. He needed guidance, and though he trusted Mac, it was time to turn to an older and more settled friend.

"They were very serious," Whit remembered, "although he was young." Whit felt a certain sense of dread in telling ML to deny his feelings toward Betty:

Rev. Horace Edward Whitaker, or "Whit," in his Crozer apartment in 1951.
Courtesy of Horace Edward Whitaker Jr.

I'm not saying he wasn't mature enough for that kind of experience, but I remember talking to him about that kind of marital
situation . . . and we had talked about it from the standpoint that
if he intended going back to the South and pastoring at a local
church, that that might not be an acceptable kind of relationship
in a black Baptist church, and I think he would be valuing that in
light of whether or not it was a workable situation, knowing his
own particular sense of call.[27]

Eight years later, King himself would say in a sermon that "there is
more integration in the entertaining world, in sports arenas, than there is
in the Christian church."[28] That was the reality Whit was urging his friend
to consider. Would ML's predominantly black congregation fully accept it
if their preacher had a white wife? Was Betty prepared to handle life as the
spouse of a black southern minister? Or was ML willing to give up on returning to the South? Could he be content to remain in the North and obtain a
position in academia, contributing to the southern cause in some other way?

Whit's mature and tempered words meant a great deal to ML, but they were not enough to convince him to end the relationship. Soon after, ML brought Betty over to the home of Rev. J. Pius Barbour. To his old sparring partner, he proposed a new topic of debate: *Why can't you simply marry us right now?*

ML laid out his two-pronged argument for their relationship, the emotional and the symbolic, and mentor and student went back and forth. Almanina Barbour recalled her father telling the young man that an "interracial marriage would never be accepted in this society."[29] ML countered that they were in the free North, in love, living in a state that had, at least legally, accepted interracial marriage. So why should society continue to get in the way?

As Betty listened, she understood quickly that it wasn't so simple. She loved ML, and her mother liked him as well, but support from ML's side of friends and family appeared to be nonexistent. It wasn't that they agreed with society's disapproval, but they feared that this was one battle with the system he could never win, and never come back from. Rev. Barbour "discouraged the whole thing," Betty says. "He told ML how bad it'd be for his career."[30]

In the end, it was ML's decision to make, and we have no first-hand account as to how he reached it. Some believed that pressure from respected elders like Rev. Barbour tipped the scales; according to Marcus Wood, "A group of local pastors finally got the point across and the relationship ended."[31] But as much as ML respected Barbour, he was never afraid to argue the contrary opinion, and he was likely to see the coordinated word of a group of local pastors as an unwelcome blast of paternal judgment.

Though ML had initially dismissed it, Whit's advice was probably more persuasive in the end. It was Whit who could engage with him not as a concerned mentor but as a friend, a husband, and a father. His role as a family man would have been particularly valuable, since ML had shared one last concern that night in Whit's apartment: how to bring Betty home to meet his parents.

ML had zero qualms about Daddy King finding out about Betty. Thanks to his emotional and intellectual development at Crozer and with Rev. Barbour, he could now debate any objections his father might raise. He might have even enjoyed shaking up the old man's traditional foundations. But, as he told Whit that night, Mama King was a different story. Perhaps Alberta would have gradually accepted Betty, but the thought of even temporarily devastating his mother was something ML could not bear. Eventually, the conclusion proved inescapable. "They cooled it," Whitaker said, adding that if Betty and ML had met in another day and age, they surely would have married.[32]

Rev. Barbour, too, recognized how much the relationship had meant to ML, and could tell that the young man was devastated by its ending. He "was a man of a broken heart," Barbour remembered. "He never recovered."[33]

As for Betty, it was ML's magnetic personality, enthusiasm, and passion that had led her to briefly consider taking such a challenging path. From the moment she met ML in his first year right up to the end, she saw him as "always the same—maybe more determined to return south to help."[34]

Classes and Professors: A Portrait of ML as a Young Man
Religious Development of Personality

ML's daily Religious Development of Personality course was taught by a faculty member he'd never faced in class before, but one he knew well from his many other roles at Crozer: Dean Charles Batten. The moment a new student entered the seminary, there was an excellent chance Dean Batten would be the first person to greet him. When Lucius Hall pointed a gun at ML that first year, it was Batten who arranged a meeting with the students living in Old Main, calling for civility. Batten cut scholarship checks for current seminarians, wrote recommendations for students moving on to another school, and even presided over local weddings and funerals (including the funeral of Betty's father). If there was a void, Batten filled it. "Whatever we look for," he once said, "we will find—what we look for signifies what we are, and what we look for today, will determine what we will be tomorrow."[35]

If Dean Batten had a specialty, it was forging connections between Crozer Theological Seminary and the outside world. He represented the school at conferences, reported updates to the press, and served as the business manager for Morton Enslin's struggling *Crozer Quarterly*.[36] His close affiliation with Enslin placed him in a precarious position as President Blanton's realignment loomed.

ML's Class Schedule

Year III, Term 1, September 12–November 22, 1950

Time	Tuesday	Wednesday	Thursday	Friday
8:00 AM				
9:00 AM	Rel. Development of Personality	Rel. Development of Personality	Rel. Development of Personality	Rel. Development of Personality
10:00 AM	Chapel service	Optional service		Devotional pd.
10:30 AM	Am. Christianity— Colonial Period	Am. Christianity— Colonial Period	Am. Christianity— Colonial Period	Am. Christianity— Colonial Period
11:00 AM				
11:30 AM		The Minister's Use of the Radio?		The Minister's Use of the Radio?
12:00 PM				
12:30 PM				
1:00 PM				
2:00 PM				
3:00 PM				
4:00 PM			Vespers service (4:15 PM)	Problems of Esthetics (at UPenn)
5:00 PM				

No classes on Monday | Term examinations: Nov. 20–22 |
Thanksgiving break: Nov. 23–27
ML's GPA for the term: 4.00

Religious Development of Personality
Charles Edward Batten, BS (Temple), BD (Crozer); Dean of Crozer
Course Description: "The development of religious experience in persons of various age groups; the origin and growth of the individual's religious ideas and ideals." (Credit hours: 4; ML's grade: A)

American Christianity—Colonial Period
Raymond Joseph Bean, BA (University of New Hampshire), BD (Andover Newton Theological School), ThD (Boston University)
Course Description: "The formation and increase of the various colonies with a study of the part religion played in each." (Credit hours: 4; ML's grade: A)

The Minister's Use of the Radio
Robert Elwood Keighton, BD, ThM (Crozer)
Course Description: "The materials, techniques, and possibilities of an effective radio ministry; practice in the writing and production of varied radio programs with emphasis on the sermon. Field trips to broadcasting studios are part of the course." *The course catalog indicates that this was a third-term course, but ML's transcript makes it clear that he took it during this term. Scheduling is speculative, based on the original third-term listing.* (Credit hours: 2; ML's grade: A)

Problems of Esthetics
John Stokes Adams Jr., BA, PhD (UPenn)
Course Description: An attempt to answer the centuries-old dilemma in esthetics: *What is beauty, and how can it be measured?* Selected topics connected to esthetics: historical, methodological, metaphysical. *Description based on ML's class notes. Held at University of Pennsylvania.* (Credit hours: 4; ML's grade: N/A)

On Tuesday, Wednesday, and Friday, a half-hour period was set aside at 10:00 AM for services in the chapel. On Tuesdays was a mandatory service led by President Sankey L. Blanton. Wednesday services were optional, generally led by a member of the faculty or an invited pastor from an evangelical institution. The Friday devotional period was run by the students themselves and presided over by the chairman of the Devotions Committee. On Thursday, the 10:00 AM slot was a free period, and a vespers service was held at 4:15 PM. This tightly planned service featured a speaker from a prescheduled list, usually a Crozer professor or a guest speaker from another institution.[37]

Among the seminarians, however, he was as well liked as he was familiar. In numerous interviews with former Crozer students, Batten was mentioned as being warm, kind-hearted, and able to get along with just about anyone. "He knew every student on campus by name," says international student Jimmy Beshai. "Only [Kenneth] Smith and Batten were spared from criticism during and after dinner at the pool tables."[38] And Blanton import Jack Bullard remembers that Batten "was always very agreeable"; he chuckles at one particular memory of an interaction between Batten and ML.[39]

It was a cloudy day, Bullard says, and he and ML were playing pool in the basement rec room. "Dean Batten would go through the recreation room to his house," and when he came upon ML, he decided to ask the student body president for help with some sort of dilemma. "They went back and forth about it," Bullard recalls, and just about anytime ML made a suggestion, Batten would agree with whatever he said—much to the students' amusement. "And then ML said, 'Dean Batten, if I direct your attention outside . . . if I pointed out that it was a sunny day you would agree with me."

Bullard was impressed at how direct ML was with Batten, even though he was still a twenty-one-year-old student. ML "got away with it," his fellow seminarian says, because he had "such an easy and light spirit."[40]

That spirit would serve ML well in Batten's Religious Development of Personality course. The class was a rare opportunity for students to explore their own religious development, not as scholars or preachers but simply as people. For once, ML did not need to write with the goal of reaching a congregation or engaging with the academic research he'd been studying. He could truly be himself.

The result of this break in the clouds was the most revealing essay ML had ever written to that point. In "An Autobiography of Religious Development," he offered a frank and wide-ranging assessment of his life and his religious beliefs. Batten clearly encouraged such introspection, writing enthusiastic comments in the margins such as "Correct!" and "Right!"* When ML recounted how at the age of six his white friend

---

* The distinctive tone of the comments is particularly noteworthy because it confirms that the class was taught by Charles Batten, and not by George W. Davis as indicated

had been told not to play with him anymore because of the color of his skin, Batten remarked, "How tragic!"[41]

ML even trusted Batten enough to reflect on his strong yet conflicted relationship with Daddy King: "Today I differ a great deal with my father theologically, but that admiration for a real father still remains." And he was unabashed in his description of his own mental and physical advantages:

> From the very beginning I was an extraordinarily healthy child. It is said that at my birth the doctors pronounced me a one hundred percent perfect child, from a physical point of view. Even today this physical harmony still abides, in that I hardly know how an ill moment feels. I guess the same thing would apply to my mental life. I have always been somewhat precocious, both physically and mentally. My I.Q. stands somewhat above the average. So it seems that from a hereditary point of view nature was very kind to me.

To this Batten replied, "Good! I like a man who has an intelligent evaluation of his abilities."

As for the evolution of his religious beliefs, ML's essay credited Morehouse for awakening within him "many doubts" that came with the "shackles of fundamentalism." "This is why," ML wrote, "when I came to Crozer, I could accept the liberal interpretation with relative ease."[42]

ML admitted that he'd never had any kind of sky-opening experience of conversion: "Religion has just been something I grew up in. Conversion for me has been the gradual intaking of the noble [ideals] set forth in my family and my environment, and I must admit that this intaking has been largely unconscious." In response to this comment, Batten may have suggested ML talk to "Mr. Pritchard," but the handwriting on the original document has faded over time.

---

in King, *Papers*, 1:359. The comments demonstrate the positivity for which Batten was known, while Davis's feedback tended to be more muted and to focus more on typos. This matches the information in Crozer's *Annual Catalogue* for 1950 and 1951 (vol. 42, no. 1, and vol. 43, no. 1), in which Batten is listed as the professor for Religious Development of Personality.

ML's unusually candid writing for Batten was not limited to this one autobiographical essay. In a review of a book about personality development, ML wrote about another work he'd attempted to read, a book by Gardner Murphy, which had been "written for the expert, not the laymen." ML freely confessed his confusion: "I was often lost behind the dim fog of psychological obscurities. (Am I just dumb)." Batten replied, "I think not."[43]

And when ML slipped into the affected language of academic papers and Sunday-morning sermons, Batten was there to nudge him back toward honest sentiment. In another review for the class, of a book dealing with religion in education, ML ended by summing up his feelings about the work: "Even though I parted company with him on many points, I was kept spellbound throughout the book." Batten circled "spellbound," then wrote a comment jabbing his sensational word choice: "Isn't this a bit strong?"[44]

For no other professor, in no other class, would ML write with such unembellished candor. Thus, any further analysis of ML's state of mind while at Crozer should begin with his work for Religious Development of Personality, and the refreshing glimpse it offers into his natural written voice.

American Christianity—Colonial Period

Following the retirement of Crozer's legendary church history professor R. E. E. Harkness, the school hired thirty-three-year-old historian Dr. Raymond J. Bean, who fit in easily with the Crozer crowd. "He was a live wire," recalls one former student, "and extremely friendly." Jimmy Beshai agrees; he saw that Dr. Bean had no trouble teaching a class of students from a wide variety of backgrounds. "He was always very open-minded about racial issues."[45]

Bean's mother and father had died when he was five, leaving him to be raised by his paternal grandparents, who "made every sacrifice to care for him and his younger sister."[46] When he started at Crozer, he was only five months removed from earning his doctorate at Boston University. He wrote his dissertation on William Miller, the New England farmer, Baptist preacher, and apocalyptic prognosticator who used the Book of Daniel to try to mathematically predict the Second Coming of Christ.

But Miller would have been a minor subtopic in ML's course with Bean, American Christianity—Colonial Period. Examining Christianity's influence over the American colonies before the Revolutionary War, the class had to cover an absolutely massive amount of ground, starting when Spanish Catholics established St. Augustine and Jacksonville, Florida, in the 1560s and ending around the time new notions of liberalism from Germany began to seep into American culture in the mid-1800s. Bean had about forty one-hour classes to teach the class three hundred years of history.

He was likely to have focused on popular topics such as the misuse of religious principles to justify the Salem witchcraft trials of 1692–1693, and Christianity's widespread acceptance of slavery—the eternal bruise on the Christian church's purity that ML often lamented. The professor may have mentioned that thanks to its Quaker founder, William Penn, Pennsylvania had been the first colony to denounce slavery.

On November 17, 1950, ML handed in to Dr. Bean an essay titled "An Appraisal of the Great Awakening." ML's writing in this essay is dry, but it perks up when he begins describing Anglican revivalist preacher George Whitefield. "The preaching ability of this moving spirit," ML wrote, "cannot be exaggerated."[47]

ML may very well have walked past the statue of George Whitefield on the UPenn campus while attending classes there, and he clearly admired the man for his ability to unify the faithful across all Christian denominations. Whitefield's call for unity was based on rekindling Christians' sense of moral purpose. As he shouted—and ML quoted— "God help us all to forget party names, and to become Christians in deed, and in truth."[48]

Most of ML's term paper is loaded with accidental plagiarism. I say "accidental" not to absolve ML of responsibility but simply because of the following example. In the two columns below, you'll see that ML lifted an entire block of prose from Charles H. Maxson's book. All but the first few words are identical:

The Virginia Gazette tells of the great concourse of people that filled the church of St. Mary Magdalene, London, long before the time of service, and of several hundred persons in the street who in vain endeavored to force themselves into the church and past the constables stationed at the door to preserve the peace. Such was the mad desire to see and hear the eloquent youth who had volunteered to go to Georgia as a missionary.	One of the colonial newspapers tells of the great concourse of people that filled the church of St. Mary Magdalene, London, long before the time of service and of several hundred persons in the street who in vain endeavored to force themselves into the church and past the constables stationed at the door to preserve the peace. Such was the mad desire to see and hear the eloquent youth who had volunteered to go to Georgia as a missionary.
—**Charles H. Maxson**, *The Great Awakening in the Middle Colonies* (Chicago, 1920)	—**Martin L. King Jr.**, "An Appraisal of the Great Awakening" (November 17, 1950)[49]

The cribbing is so extensive and so blatant that if ML had truly wanted to pass Maxson's words off as his own, he would have known better than to provide a source for Dr. Bean to check against. But in fact, in a footnote that accompanies the passage above, ML cites Maxson's book directly, right down to the page number on which the copied text appears (p. 42).

Over his years at Crozer, ML had marginally improved his ability to credit his sources, but in examples such as this, which were many and varied, he continued to demonstrate a poor understanding of proper citation procedures. It seems likely that in his entire academic career, ML never had a professor take him aside and deliver a detailed explanation of the complexities of plagiarism, nor explain to him that the "art of voice merging," while a useful technique for a preacher behind the pulpit, *should not* be utilized in an academic paper.[50]

Certainly, no such explanations were forthcoming from Dr. Bean. For his "Great Awakening" paper, he gave ML an A.

The Minister's Use of Radio

Growing up in Atlanta, ML had often listened to the weekly sermons of radio preachers, not just Daddy King's local rival W. H. Borders but also famed social gospel pastor Harry Emerson Fosdick, whose nationally broadcast radio program reached millions of listeners. Fosdick's voice and passion had a way of capturing the attention of the listener, and ML would draw from Fosdick's language and structure in his own sermons.

So King must have been excited to be one of the first students to take Robert Keighton's class The Minister's Use of Radio. Though he'd had enough of Keighton in his first two years, it was an exciting opportunity to refine his preaching in a medium he'd always been drawn to.

The class would be held in a new radio room on the second floor of Old Main, part of a project begun in early 1949 to found an FM radio station at Crozer. The push had been initiated by a Chester dentist named Nathan Plafker in honor of his recently deceased wife, Pearl Ruth Plafker, and it had the support of Keighton and other Crozer trustees. But a working radio station was still far off and would require tens of thousands of dollars of additional funding. For now, Keighton had transformed two empty dormitory rooms on the second floor into a "one-room studio and a control room." Keighton's equipment consisted of a "brush recording machine and a turntable I have been using in my public speaking classes."[51] It was enough to at least conduct a course.

ML would've had some idea what to expect when he stepped into the classroom for the first time, since several of his friends—Mac, Whit, and Cyril Pyle—had delivered sermons over the radio for the local West Branch YMCA, on a program called *Sunday Meditations*. As Keighton began his instruction, ML took notes, listing the main components a radio sermon needed:

> Did it have a hook? . . .
> Did the central idea make a difference?
> Did it have a pay off or climax?
> Did the sermon deal with a problem that it leads
> to a choice in contemporary living?

Was the development of it clear?
Did pictures come to your mind?[52]

The sermons ML and the other students recorded for the course may actually have been broadcast. Back in 1949, Keighton had indicated that he wouldn't wait for a full-fledged radio station before putting Crozer on the air, saying that the programs produced in their radio room could "be recorded or cabled to nearby radio stations for transcription so that although we may be far from our own station, our radio output is immediate."[53]

Unfortunately, no such recordings of ML from his Crozer years have survived. But as the years passed, ML would become very comfortable in a radio booth—and it all started down the hall from his dorm room, two hours a week, learning how to tailor his slow-cooked southern baritone for the microphone.

Problems of Esthetics

> "In the history of philosophy, the muddle that is esthetics, or philosophy of art, has had a career that quite belies the importance now assigned to it. Kicked around among the philosophic disciplines, relegated to the backstairs for centuries, the highlights of its history are so feebly discernible that many a respectable historian of philosophy can safely neglect it altogether."
>
> —John Stokes Adams Jr., 1951[54]

As ML's professor John S. Adams explained, esthetics is the "philosophy of art," and if you're puzzled by the idea of pushing those two concepts together, you're not alone. Reducing the idea of esthetics to an easily digestible explanation would mean undercutting its profundity. When studying philosophy, as ML enjoyed doing, a student must be comfortable swimming in ambiguous waters. "It is clearer today than ever before," Professor Adams once wrote, "that the history of philosophy is not the history of a particular set of texts, not the patient exposition of what a succession of past thinkers said, but an effort to discern what they were *trying* to say, in the light of their times—a light now quite possibly clearer to us than to them."[55]

It was a heady, humanistic effort, for which ML once again ventured from the cloistered environment of Crozer to the larger world of the University of Pennsylvania.* ML hopped on the bus outside Old Main, then took the train to the Thirtieth Street Station in downtown Philadelphia. From there it was a bit of a walk to the UPenn classroom where Dr. John Stokes Adams Jr. waited to expound upon "the muddle that is esthetics."

Who John S. Adams was is clearer. At the time ML took his class, Adams was a married father with three children. Forty-five years old, Adams had spent most of his professional career juggling the pessimistic philosophy of Arthur Schopenhauer with the melancholic joys of the piano. One close friend called Adams "the finest amateur pianist I have ever heard." Several others also mentioned his "sensitive" spirit.[56] In the coming years Adams's marriage would dissolve, leading him toward struggles with the bottle. But as ML took a seat in his class, Adams stood before him an excellent professor, more than capable of entangling his students in a web of quizzical prompts.

"For centuries," read ML's class notes, "the major problem of esthetics is, 'What is beauty?'" Other questions he jotted down include:

- "Should esthetics confind [*sic*] itself to art material or should its universe be co-existent with the world of nature"
- "Does esthetics today suffer from a lack of more original thinking or rigor in thinking?"
- "Is the problem of the creative process exclusively to be dealt with by experimental psychology"

---

* The fact that ML returned to UPenn for another philosophy course makes it clear that he appreciated the fresh academic perspective the school offered, but one shouldn't assume that he preferred it to Crozer, which had its own allure. Many former seminarians recall fondly how close-knit the faculty, staff, and students were—"one big family." Jimmy Beshai attended classes at the UPenn at the same time as ML, and he felt extremely fortunate not to have studied there exclusively. "Had I just gone to Penn and lived on campus I would have had a different impression of America, less amiable and less challenging." (Beshai, correspondence with the author, May 16, 2015.)

- "Ask yourself, What do you want to hear[:] music, or do you want to hear an obsessed personality entertaining [an] audience?"[57]

Although these kinds of inquiries will always have an answer that is just enough out of reach to create a new question, Adams did toss the class a few solutions. He offered them various thinkers' attempts at defining terms ("Hegel—'Beauty is truth shining through a sensuous mirror,'" ML recorded in his notes), as well as the different moral equivalencies used to assess works of art throughout history (e.g., what's good must be beautiful, or what's ugly must be evil).[58]

Notably, Adams did not rely on religion to answer these complicated questions, so his class would have required ML to think outside the Christian frame of his Crozer studies. Thanks to the seminary's connection to UPenn, ML was discovering what life as a PhD student would soon entail . . .

Call of the Dr.: "A Golden Boy, in a Way"

*"For some time now I have had a great deal of interest in **Edinburgh**, and would like very much to study there."*

—ML

*"It so happens that **Yale** is my preference . . ."*

—ML

*"I have gotten some valuable information about **Boston University**, and I have been convinced that there are definite advantages there for me."*

—ML[59]

As he grew more comfortable looking for answers and new questions outside the religious realm, ML was also growing into his leadership role. The student body president found that seminarians new and old were listening to his sermons and soliciting his opinions. Junior Jack Bullard hadn't known the timid ML who first arrived at Crozer, but he saw how confident he was now. "Anyone who dropped in on campus," says Bullard, "would find that he'd become accustomed to being the leader . . . a golden boy, in a way."[60]

On November 3 the golden boy was a featured speaker at an inter-seminary conference on the Crozer campus. That Friday night, ML's audience included fellow students and respected clergymen from local theological institutions such as Temple School of Theology, Lafayette College, Eastern Baptist Theological Seminary, and the Religious Fellowship House in Philadelphia. For President Sankey Blanton, the event was another chance to nudge the school's reputation in an evangelical direction, so it should come as no surprise that the theme of the conference was "Personal Evangelism."[61]

It's a topic ML would have been extremely comfortable with, since his recent evolution had not erased the influence of his Auburn Avenue upbringing, watching week after week as his father attempted to rip the ceiling off Ebenezer Baptist with his cathartic whooping. There was a duality within ML that he could no longer deny—the young man who lit up a cigarette in front of Daddy King to prove that he now made his own decisions was the same one who thought he had no choice but to break up with the woman he loved rather than risk his mother's disapproval.

By this point, his goal as a preacher was to have the best of both worlds, to merge the bullying power of his father with the refined intellectual framework of a highly educated man. (Charismatic but nuanced forebears such as Harry Emerson Fosdick and Benjamin Mays would have opened his eyes to the possibility.) Though returning to the South to preach "was his whole expectation," as Horace Whitaker put it,[62] he couldn't go back yet. Not until he was able show his father (and himself) how a preacher could sound with power *and* intellect. And to do that, he would be the first person in the history of his family to pursue a doctoral degree.

His father might have hoped that he would at least continue his studies closer to home, but in 1950 there were not enough appropriate PhD programs in the South to make that a feasible option. But with a daunting array of possibilities in the North and even overseas, ML turned to his Crozer professors to point him in the right direction. It would have boosted his prospects considerably that a seminary as renowned as Crozer was supporting his future academic endeavors.

ML's most important consultations were with George Davis, whose office was on the first floor and whose home was just steps from Old Main. Although ML didn't have a class with him in term 1, it was part of Davis's job as chairman of the scholarship committee and as a member of the committee on higher degrees to help advise students on life after Crozer.[63] By the end of the fall, ML had submitted application materials to three schools: Yale, Boston University, and Edinburgh University in Scotland.

Jimmy Beshai listened to ML discuss his graduate school options at dinner, during eight ball down in the catacombs, and while hanging out in the hallway in the middle of the week. ML dreamed of Yale, which had the best reputation, but the university required applicants to score well on a new standardized test, the GRE—a daunting prospect for someone who'd grown up outside the northeast liberal environment in which the exam was designed. Admission to Boston University seemed more attainable; the school had already accepted several African American students, such as past Crozer graduate Samuel Proctor.

Leaving America altogether to attend Edinburgh University seemed like an odd option, but Jimmy could see why ML was interested. "Edinburgh was . . . seen in those days as a European university that promoted liberal theology, and Enslin may have suggested it to Martin and got him to apply for admission." Jimmy was more definitive about which professors were lobbying for BU: "Davis and Smith were strong advocates of Boston."[64]

Snuffy Smith had by now become another important influence on King's academic development. With the Betty Moitz rivalry behind them, ML's reserved attitude around the young professor began to relax, and they were soon trading opinions on theologians over dinner. Smith was fond not only of social gospel prophet Walter Rauschenbusch but also of Reinhold Niebuhr, a "Christian realist." ML mentioned that he'd already been exposed to both theologians while at Morehouse—Rauschenbusch through sermons by Benjamin Mays and Niebuhr through Professor George Kelsey. Rauschenbusch would also have been a topic of discussion in just about every class ML took with George W. Davis.[65]

As the days passed that fall term, Jimmy Beshai and other students had also started to overhear lively conversations among Snuffy, ML, and Mac.[66] Snuffy would fan the two seminarians' zeal for social justice, while serving as a mediating force between them. Left on their own, ML and Mac tended to argue "like cats and dogs," said Horace Whitaker, but adding Smith into the mix provoked discussions that lasted through the night—"bull sessions," the professor called them.[67]

During the last weekend of November, a vicious thunderstorm wreaked havoc on Chester and the surrounding area. The property damage alone amounted to over half a million dollars. Two people were killed; local bridges were destroyed by tidal waves. On the Crozer campus, the nearly century-old silver maple trees that held a special place in the hearts of many students and faculty were uprooted and ripped apart by the wind and pounding rain. It would have been a sad sight to see out of ML's room 52: behind Old Main and into Ship Creek Woods, where ML loved to walk and sit by the water, trees and branches had collapsed.[68]

On these rainy nights, there was always Mac, the radio, and some cards to play. As the smooth and bluesy "A Dreamer with a Penny" played in the background, ML and Mac would share their thoughts on the importance of wealth. "'I'd rather be a [dreamer] with a penny, than a rich man with a worried mind,'" Mac recalled decades later. "We used to discuss this as a part of philosophy of life."[69]

Another bluesy song they enjoyed was Amos Milburn's "Bad Bad Whiskey," often ruminating on the lyric "Bad, bad whiskey made me lose my happy home."[70] ML wasn't much of a drinker back then, and one time he criticized the drinking habits of another black student, Joe Kirkland, who like ML was the son of a preacher and had grown up in the shadow of his successful father. The major difference, more like a vast gulf, was geographical. Kirkland grew up around Philadelphia and saw ML as "sheltered," a southern boy raised without a full understanding of the real world. ML, on the other hand, may have seen Kirkland as jaded—embittered from the illusion of northern freedom.

Once, Kirkland had a can of beer in his dorm room, and when ML saw it, he shook his head: "Don't you know you have the burdens of the Negro race on your shoulders?" Kirkland didn't care in the least,* but for ML, it was always important to show a sense of professionalism.[71]

---

* Rev. Joseph Kirkland pastored at the Church of the Redeemer in Philadelphia, and died in November 1982. According to his wife, Lydia Kirkland, he did not have particularly fond memories of Crozer, considering it "superficial," and he wasn't friendly with anyone on campus except perhaps Mac, whom he remembered for his work as a barber. She also shared one other telling anecdote about his relationship with ML: when King started his "movement" in Atlanta (she may have misspoken and meant Montgomery) her husband called him up and asked, "What's wrong with you? I thought you believed all white people were basically good." On April 6, 1968, two days after King was assassinated, Kirkland spoke at a memorial in his honor at Bethel AME Church in Wilmington, telling those gathered to "be calm and pledge ourselves to the cause for which he lived and died." Kirkland said that whether studying at Crozer or laying down his life for racial equality, ML "was always the same person—humble, quiet and conservative." ("Dr. King Called Mover of Mankind," News Journal [Wilmington, DE], April 6, 1968.)

8

The Recommended Plagiarist
Term 2, November 28, 1950– February 15, 1951

Acceptance and Failure: "Chief Weaknesses"

It was one thing for ML to decide on a middle path between the deep-rooted influence of the charismatic Daddy King and the liberating power of his own intellect, and another one entirely to put it into practice behind the pulpit. It was a delicate balancing act—on the one hand, to stay connected with his southern Baptist heritage despite his years of study in the North; on the other, to not let his intellectual aspirations be swallowed up by showmanship.

Staying connected to his roots had sometimes been difficult during his summers at Ebenezer. Though his sermons were generally well received, when he tried to incorporate what he'd been learning at Crozer, many in the congregation would grow bored with the snooty anecdotes from old books written by white men. It was something he continued to struggle with, if an evaluation he received in early December 1950 is any indication.

During the first three months of his senior year, ML had participated in Crozer's fieldwork program, serving as an assistant pastor at

First Baptist of East Elmhurst, in Queens. The church was only a hop, skip, and jump from where his sister, Christine, lived; its pastor, Rev. William E. Gardner, was a friend of Daddy King's. But when it came time to evaluate ML's performance for the Crozer fieldwork committee, Rev. Gardner did not hesitate to dish out the tough love. He began with praise for ML's "superior mental ability" and "impressive personality," then detailed his weak points:

> I FEEL THAT THE CHIEF WEAKNESSES WHICH THE SEMINARY MIGHT HELP HIM OVERCOME ARE: An attitude of aloofness, disdain & possible snobbishness which prevent his coming to close grips with the rank and file of ordinary people. Also, a smugness that refuses to adapt itself to the demands of ministering effectively to the average Negro congregation.[1]

For a young man who had feared for so long that he would end up preaching exactly like his father, it was hard to find his way back from the opposite extreme. It was easier to lean on his intellect, over which he alone held sway, than to contend with the influences and demands that were beyond his control. That may explain why Rev. Gardner gave ML his lowest marks—three Cs—in categories labeled "WILLINGNESS TO ACCEPT SUGGESTION AND CRITICISM," "UNDERSTANDING OF GROUP WORK TECHNIQUES," and "CONCERN FOR INDIVIDUALS IN GROUP."[2]

On the other side of the balancing act, although ML had confidence in his intellect and his pulpit abilities, his good friend Whit would recall that his preaching at the time was "more style than content." He might, for instance, dramatize the action of putting his sermon notes in his jacket pocket just before speaking. *That's right, ladies and gentlemen. I know this by heart.* Even his slow and deliberate style of preaching—his tendency to draw . . . his words . . . out . . . with his . . . . . . Southern . . . draaaawl—rubbed some the wrong way.[3] Audiences wouldn't complain later in King's life, when he used such rhetorical flourishes to promote the noble cause of civil rights. But all too often at Crozer, they were embellishments without a larger purpose.

Young ML was still building the intellectual foundations that would ground his practiced rhetoric. These efforts would continue in his doctoral studies; the question now was where he would pursue them—Yale, Boston, or Edinburgh.

Admission to ML's first-choice PhD program, Yale, depended on a GRE test that was still months away, so in the meantime he attempted to lock down his other options. He asked two professors, Morton Scott Enslin and Raymond J. Bean, to write recommendations for him to Boston University.

Enslin's recommendation has not aged well, displaying the biblical scholar's eccentric personality at its most exasperating. Watch his sentences roll toward a stone wall:

> He has proved himself to be a very competent student, conscientious, industrious, and with more than usual insight. . . .
>
> He is president of the Student Government and has conducted himself well in this position.
>
> The fact that with our student body largely Southern in constitution a colored man should be elected to and be popular [in] such a position is in itself no mean recommendation.
>
> The comparatively small number of forward-looking and thoroughly trained negro leaders is, as I am sure you'll agree, still so small that it is more than an even chance that one as adequately trained as King will find ample opportunity for useful service.
>
> He is entirely free from those somewhat annoying qualities which some men of his race acquire when they find themselves in the distinctly higher percent of their group.

In Enslin's defense, he may have known the recipient of this letter, BU dean Chester Alter, and believed that what others would see as racial insensitivity, Alter would take as blunt honesty. The line "as I am sure you will agree" suggests that Enslin and Alter may have had prior discussions and been chummy with each other. Both men went to

Harvard, although at different times, and Enslin grew up in Somerville, Massachusetts, only a few miles away from Boston University. Perhaps the tone underneath the recommendation was, between two northeast buddies, *Look . . . King's a good guy. I'm telling it like it is. Give him a chance.*

And as inappropriate as his words now seem, Enslin's name carried considerable weight in 1950. By editing the *Crozer Quarterly* for the last decade, he'd garnered the respect of hundreds of scholars and theologians around the country. "Most of the anecdotes at the dinner table were about Enslin and Keighton," says Jimmy Beshai, "not on account of their racial high mindedness, but more on their high scholarship standards in general."[4] A positive Enslin recommendation was worth the risk, no matter his smug, pipe-puffing tone.

Dr. Bean's recommendation, on the other hand, was valuable because of the new church history professor's links to Boston University. Bean still knew many of the current faculty and staff, having completed his ThD dissertation at BU in 1949. His words of praise were standard, confirming that ML's "work is always of the highest grade" and noting, "The few questions he has asked in class have revealed a real interest in the subject under discussion."[5]

With Enslin and Bean behind him, BU was likely to accept him, even if Yale was more of a toss-up. But like many students applying to prestigious institutions, ML had needed a "safety school." The University of Edinburgh was ML's safety. "Edinburgh was pretty easy to get into at that time," says former Yale seminarian Andrew Burgess, since the UK "was still recovering from WWII and was especially encouraging US students to come there and support the economy."[6]

Sure enough, on December 15, one day after Enslin sent off his recommendation letter to BU, ML headed down a few flights of stairs in Old Main to check his mailbox, #27. There it was: a letter of official acceptance to Edinburgh.

Edinburgh had plenty to recommend it even if ML got in to Boston or Yale. This was an institution that predated America itself, that Charles Darwin, David Hume, and Robert Louis Stevenson had attended. And it offered ML the opportunity to leave behind the racial roadblocks of America for a few years. "Martin," Jimmy remembered, "and most of us in those days, saw Europe as the place to seek for higher education."[7] Of course, ML's parents would have been stunned by the notion of their son living abroad in Scotland; they had a hard enough time accepting that he was living in the American North.

On January 11, 1951, four days before turning twenty-two, ML received his letter of acceptance from Boston University. He heard the good news less than a month after Enslin sent his recommendation.[8]

That left only Yale, and on February 3, ML walked in to a testing room to take the GRE. Although documents are scarce, it's believed that by this point ML had been at least conditionally admitted to Yale. His final acceptance, however, would rely on a high GRE score.

In 1951, the test was only a few years old. To create a standard metric, Educational Testing Service had administered it to hundreds of first-year graduate students. The pool would have been weighted heavily toward students in northeastern academic circles, and against anyone from the segregated South. In other words, it was going to be a very difficult test for ML to do well on.

Just how difficult was it for students like ML? Take the account of black Crozer graduate Samuel Proctor. Hailing from Norfolk, Virginia, he attended Yale Divinity School in the late 1940s. While studying at Yale (on a $2,500 fellowship from Crozer), Proctor was told to go see the dean of the divinity school, Luther Weigle. Dean Weigle had become perplexed by the GRE scores black students were earning. As Proctor recalled:

> One day Dr. Luther Weigle . . . sent for me. It scared me to death. What on earth had I done? "Mr. Proctor," he began, dragging his chair close to mine, "why is it that so many of you colored fellows do so well here, when your Graduate Record Examination scores are so skewed? You are all far above average on the verbal tests and the social science tests, but your mathematics, sciences, and fine arts scores are far below other college graduates in the same majors, both regionally and nationally." . . .

I looked in his eyes and spoke slowly. "Dean Weigle, we do better on verbal tests because we do a lot of debating and discussing. We are a talking people. We survive by images and analysis, analogues and metaphors, so we get to know words. We take flight in language as a buffer for our wounded psyches . . . on the other hand, we are hardly ever considered for jobs in the natural sciences and technology. Our schools have no well-equipped laboratories and our teachers were educated without any hope of being employed in the sciences, either. Therefore, our knowledge in those areas is comparatively sparse.[9]

ML certainly knew words, and in keeping with Proctor's observations, his highest scores were in the Literature section, where he scored in the top 25th percentile (470). However, his Verbal results were less impressive, landing him among the lower half of test takers (350), and his Quantitative results were particularly poor, putting him in the bottom 10 percent (270).[10]

The results wouldn't land in ML's mailbox until March, but he must have known that the scores would not be pretty. Unfortunately, Dean Weigle had retired from Yale in 1949, so ML's application would have faced a new dean who hadn't heard Samuel Proctor's explanation of black students' standardized testing woes. In addition, Weigle's replacement was perhaps less well acquainted with ML's adviser George Davis, who'd earned his PhD from Yale. With these Crozer connections frayed, ML's poor performance on the GRE most likely ensured a denial from his top-choice school.

Besides, according to Jimmy Beshai, Professor Davis and Snuffy Smith continued to advocate for Boston University. "As far as I can remember," he says, they "were the two mentors who persuaded Martin to go to Boston rather than Edinburgh."[11] By the end of February, ML would have mostly made up his mind and chosen Boston University.

ML's family could breathe easy. He was at least staying in America.

ML's Class Schedule

Year III, Term 2, November 28, 1950–February 15, 1951

Time	Tuesday	Wednesday	Thursday	Friday
8:00 AM				
9:00 AM	Philosophy of Religion	Philosophy of Religion	Philosophy of Religion	Philosophy of Religion
10:00 AM	Chapel service	Optional service		Devotional pd.
10:30 AM	Theological Integration	Theological Integration	Theological Integration	Theological Integration
11:00 AM				
11:30 AM				
12:00 PM				
1:00 PM				
2:00 PM				
3:00 PM				
4:00 PM	Kant? (at UPenn)		Vespers service (4:15 PM)	
5:00 PM				

No classes on Monday | Christmas break: Dec. 21–Jan. 1 |
Term examinations: Feb. 12–15
ML's GPA for the term: 4.00

Philosophy of Religion

George Washington Davis, BD, ThM (Colgate-Rochester), PhD (Yale)
Course Description: "The origin, nature, development, function and value of religion both in general and as a Christian phenomenon; the validity of religious experience." (Credit hours: 4; ML's grade: A)

Theological Integration

Sankey Lee Blanton, ThM (Southern Baptist), STM (Andover Newton), DD (Wake Forest); President of Crozer, 1950–1962
Course Description: "An integrative course for Seniors only, in which the student's seminary studies are drawn together into a statement of his own Christian faith and ministerial objectives. Required." (Credit hours: 4; ML's grade: A)

Kant

Paul Schrecker, LLD (University of Vienna), PhD (University of Berlin)
Course Description: An analysis of the concepts within Kant's *A Critique of Pure Reason*. Among other topics: the distinction between phenomena (beings of sense) and noumena (beings of reason); Kant's definition of reality. *Description based on ML's class notes. Scheduling for this course, which was held at the University of Pennsylvania, is speculative; official time unknown.* (Credit hours: 4; ML's grade: N/A)

On Tuesday, Wednesday, and Friday, a half-hour period was set aside at 10:00 AM for services in the chapel. On Tuesdays was a mandatory service led by President Sankey L. Blanton. Wednesday services were optional, generally led by a member of the faculty or an invited pastor from an evangelical institution. The Friday devotional period was run by the students themselves and presided over by the chairman of the Devotions Committee. On Thursday, the 10:00 AM slot was a free period, and a vespers service was held at 4:15 PM. This tightly planned service featured a speaker from a prescheduled list, usually a Crozer professor or a guest speaker from another institution.[12]

Classes and Professors: Means and Ends
Philosophy of Religion

Let's imagine a day in the life of Professor George Washington Davis. You're forty-eight years old, married to a teacher, and have two teen-age sons. When you're not teaching three courses a week at Crozer, you often fill in as an interim pastor at local churches. You frequently invite your students over to your home behind Old Main for dinner and a chat. Currently, you're teaching a Philosophy of Religion class to about twenty students, whom you recently assigned a long essay describing the origin of religion.

On February 9, 1951, one of your students, Martin L. King Jr., hands you his fifteen-page paper, folded long ways, his signature in the bottom right corner. Along with it, you collect nineteen other papers, all roughly the same length—around three hundred pages of material in all. These papers are handwritten and have not been professionally edited or organized; most of them have been patched together using sources you yourself may have suggested. It won't be easy reading, and even if you can make it through each one in about thirty minutes, you're looking at ten hours or more of grading time.

So you take your stack of papers and walk home. Your boys had a busy day at school in Chester, and your wife prepared a nice meal. You enjoy your time with family, maybe listen to a little talk radio, then dig in to that mountain of papers. The second term ends on February 15, and they'll need their papers back before then.

You come to ML's paper, and you begin to read the text. Ah, ML—student body president, former chairman of the Devotions Committee, and that voice! What an incredible talent. Other faculty echo how you feel: that he is one of the brightest students to come through Crozer.

As you peruse his paper, titled "The Origin of Religion in the Race" (meaning the human race), you see that he has listed nine sources on his bibliography page. There are times, however, when what ML writes sounds more like one of the nine authors he listed, so you slow your reading and wonder, your mind a bit cloudy from a long day's work. Still, your concerns build after reading a paragraph like this:

It has been implied above that religion and magic have a common root. At this point we may state this position more fully. The question of the relation between these two attitudes or types of behaviour has often been discussed by anthropologists, and has an important bearing on the problem of the origin and nature of religion. In dealing with this relationship many questions inevitably arise. Have we sufficient grounds for assigning logical or chronological priority to the one rather than to the other? If so, to which of the two does priority belong? Can we place a genetic relation between them? Did the one spring from the other, by way of development or else by way of relapse? Or did they have independent origins? In an attempt to answer these questions at least three positions have emerged.[13]

Hmm . . . This reads a bit too smoothly for a student paper. His questions are clear, profound, and perfectly on target. And, oddly enough, ML even uses the British spelling *behaviour*.

Now, at this point, you as a professor have a choice. You could walk five minutes over to the Pearl Hall library and compare the books that ML has listed to what he wrote. But maybe you look at the clock and realize the library's closed, or maybe you simply balk at the prospect of hunting through each of the nine books ML has cited to find the material he might have cribbed. Perhaps you consider that once you begin investigating ML's paper for plagiarism, it will feel wrong not to check all the *other* students' papers for signs of copying as well.

After all, ML is going places. In fact, at the moment, he *is* Crozer, and in the back of your mind, you may recognize that he came from a different educational background than the one you grew up in. At worst, you might think to yourself, he went to a lot of trouble to assemble a tapestry of thoughts, and he listed far more sources than other students who barely eke by. Or perhaps you just want to finish grading a few more papers before bedtime. In any case, the thought of double-checking ML's attribution skills floats away.

And that's that. "Thoughtful, critical analysis," you write on ML's paper. Grade: A.

But if you *had* gone to the library, and if you'd happened to find D. Miall Edwards's 1940 book *The Philosophy of Religion*, and if you'd turned to pages 47–48, you would have seen that almost every single word in that quoted paragraph came from the pen of D. Miall Edwards. The only words that didn't? The first five: "It has been implied above."

This speculative account is about as close as we'll get to understanding George Davis's inaction where ML's plagiarism is concerned. To be sure, Professor Davis should be forever lauded for introducing ML to so many theologians and scholars that influenced his later work. Davis also unanimously impressed the student body with his welcoming nature and his devotion to the ministry as well as to the life of the mind. But of all the professors who were exposed to ML's attribution issues, Davis may have been best positioned to confront them. By the end of ML's Crozer tenure, he would have taken at least eight classes from Davis, classes that involved writing essays using a variety of sources.

Even in the face of blatant examples of plagiarism like this one, however, Davis apparently chose not to broach the subject. Perhaps if he had discouraged ML from borrowing the thoughts of others, the young man's course work would have become a far more revealing record of his own ideas. But it's certainly easy to understand why Davis would have been reluctant to do so.

Theological Integration

> "I believe [Crozer] is vitally necessary to the balance of theological education in our denomination at this critical time in the history of evangelical Christianity. The concept of religious freedom is being challenged in many lands, our own included."
>
> —Sankey L. Blanton[14]

In prior years, Theological Integration had been taught by Crozer's president at the time, the stern, high-minded academic E. E. Aubrey. Now that President Sankey Blanton was at the helm, he was planning to revamp the entire curriculum for the 1951–1952 school year to bring it in line with his vision of a school for ministers, not religious scholars. Theological Integration would not survive the overhaul, but in its final year Blanton chose to respect tradition and teach the course himself.

Sankey Lee Blanton grew up in rural North Carolina, one of ten siblings in a family of Irish/English farmers. After joining the military in 1916, he fought across Europe during WWI and saw countless friends and allies die in combat. Witnessing such atrocities up close changed Blanton. He felt a new calling: the ministry. "We live not in peace but in war," he said years later. "All of this but accentuates the urgent necessity of the best and highest sort of endeavors, methods and spirits in every kind of educational institution, particularly so in theological schools such as ours."[15]

Across the northeast, Blanton earned degrees and also experience as a pastor in various churches. He found his better half and became a proud father of a daughter and son. In the decade prior to coming to Crozer, Blanton returned with his family to North Carolina, eventually

Crozer Seminary president Sankey Lee Blanton.
From the collection of the Delaware County Historical Society

ending up back at Wake Forest, his alma mater, where he became dean of religion. Now here he was, sitting in front of ML and the ten other seniors as the president of a renowned theological seminary.[16]

President Aubrey had dismissed ML's class as the dumbest in Crozer's history, and turned up his nose at the veterans who swelled the school's ranks. But President Blanton had a real connection with them: many were fellow southerners, and some, such as WWII vet Horace Whitaker, had also heard the calling after watching so many soldiers die in battle. Still, the new president's preacher-centric philosophy hadn't immediately caught on; Blanton recruit Bullard acknowledged that, at least at the beginning, the president was "in the distinct minority."[17]

With Enslin's *Christian Beginnings* still in print, his and Batten's *Crozer Quarterly* publishing regularly, and Dr. James Pritchard creating scholarly waves and national news with his archaeological discoveries, Crozer's brand remained geared more toward the theological scholar than the practicing preacher. Sure, Blanton had Robert Keighton on his side, and George Davis and Kenneth Smith were hoping to carve out hybrid identities as liberal scholarly pastors. Raymond Bean was the resident historian, which, as many in that field would admit, allows for a standing vote of abstention. But it would take a few years for Blanton to create the culture he desired. For the moment, he was still learning the ropes. Perhaps that's why he chose to follow Aubrey's lead and teach Theological Integration—to learn about the culture of Crozer from the students who'd been there the longest.

Little information is available about the actual content of this class, but judging by the course description and President Blanton's own interests, it was bound to have included discussions of each student's future as a minister. For ML in particular, already looking toward the future, the class would have been an excellent opportunity to demonstrate his abilities in front of the new president.

A good showing would have been particularly helpful when in January 1951, right in the middle of the term, ML formally applied for the $1,200 J. Lewis Crozer Fellowship, a grant that would go a long way in supporting his upcoming doctoral studies. Although Blanton wasn't officially on the scholarship committee (the three members were chairman

George Davis, Morton S. Enslin, and Charles Batten), he could still veto the committee's decision.[18]

ML apparently succeeded in making a positive impression. In the years that followed, Blanton would "emphatically" recommend ML for a future job position and urge him to come back to the Crozer campus "as often as you can."[19]

Kant

> "I observed here [in America] a new and timely civilization in the making, a civilization which, unburned [sic] by obsolete traditions and conventions, pioneered to restore civilization to its original function . . . to secure the pursuit of happiness."
>
> —Dr. Paul Schrecker, 1945[20]

The ideas of German philosopher Immanuel Kant had been crucial to the first class ML took at the University of Pennsylvania, Ethics and Philosophy of History with Dr. Elizabeth Flower, but apparently he decided it was time for another go-around. After his morning class at Crozer, he once again set out for UPenn for a course devoted to this central figure in modern philosophy, taught by Dr. Paul Schrecker.

Born in Vienna but a French citizen of Jewish descent, Schrecker was a polyglot obsessed with the work of Gottfried Wilhelm Leibniz (an important philosopher and the co-inventor of calculus); he owned more of Leibniz's printed materials than anyone in the world. Before World War II, Schrecker taught at the University of Berlin, but when the Nazis began scrutinizing the university ranks, he fled to Paris with the help of a secret network of friends and associates. There he devoted himself to translating the works of Kant and Leibniz. When the Nazis invaded France, he again escaped—this time, thanks to the rescue efforts of the Rockefeller Foundation, to a new life in the United States.[21]

A few of ML's notes from Schrecker's class—and there are a lot of them—are peppered with references to Leibniz, a sign perhaps of the philosophical connections Schrecker drew between the two men. More important, of course, was what ML learned about Kant, who would have posed philosophical challenges for the young seminarian.

THE RECOMMENDED PLAGIARIST

First, Kant was not Christian and did not concern himself much with organized religion. Second, he had little interest in directly confronting the problem of human oppression. "It is the people's duty," he wrote, "to endure even the most intolerable abuse of the supreme authority."[22] Clearly, Kant would not lose too much sleep over the plight of a slave; to him, maintaining order, reason, and balance was far more important.

ML would have agreed with Kant, however, in his insistence that the ends cannot justify the means. Both Dr. Flower's class and Dr. Schrecker's would have examined these comments by the philosopher in 1785:

> Now I say: man and generally any rational being exists as an end in himself, not merely as a means to be arbitrarily used by this or that will, but in all his actions, whether they concern himself or other rational beings, must be always regarded at the same time as an end.[23]

Twelve years later, in his famous "Letter from a Birmingham Jail," King would employ a dash of this Kantian logic himself: "Over the last few years I have consistently preached that nonviolence demands that the means we use must be as pure as the ends we seek. So I have tried to make it clear that it is wrong to use immoral means to attain moral ends."[24]

But his letter would go on to propose another principle of which Kant would certainly disapprove. "Now I must affirm that it is just as wrong, or even more so," King wrote, "to use moral means to preserve immoral ends." The Birmingham police may have broken up the recent civil rights demonstrations without resorting to public displays of violence, "but they have used the moral means of nonviolence to maintain the immoral end of flagrant racial injustice."[25] To King, it was wrong to categorically reject the possibility of civil disobedience, if the alternative was to accept a fundamentally flawed system. Kant's reasoning was a finger trap of logic: *Don't use people as a means, but don't disrupt the system if you believe it's using you. Instead, simply stop thinking it is using you.*[26]

Nonetheless, Kant was a critical figure of Enlightenment thought, who encouraged people in his time to "know" the world and exercise their own reason rather than mindlessly accepting conventional dogma.

True to this directive, ML had considered the philosopher's arguments with the help of Dr. Schrecker and Dr. Flower, and would ultimately decide for himself which to embrace and which to reject.

Basketball and Friends: "We Kept Him as a Sub"

Even in the delirium of choosing his next school and wrestling with complex religious and philosophical concepts, ML found time to relax and support his schoolmates. One way he did both was by taking part in an exhibition game between a hastily assembled Crozer basketball team and their rivals at Eastern Baptist Seminary.

The bad blood between the two schools mainly had to do with Crozer's liberal ways. The running joke at Eastern was that they had each Crozer seminarian on their "prayer list," because with the way they were being trained, all of them were going straight to hell. In fact, according to Kenneth Smith, Eastern had been founded in the 1920s as a protest against Crozer's liberalism.[27]

As student body president, ML felt a responsibility to shepherd Crozer's team through this showdown. He'd always loved basketball, often playing at the old Butler Street YMCA in Atlanta during his teenage years. At Crozer, he'd played pick-up games with his fellow students in Commencement Hall. But he had no plans to be a starter in the exhibition game; at five foot seven and 150 pounds, he'd given up hopes of playing against the likes of then–NBA stars George Mikan and Dolph Schayes.

No, according to ML's Atlanta friends, his skills weren't exactly professional level. ML "was one of the subs on our team," one childhood friend remembered, "and we kept him as a sub because he didn't know what teamwork was then." The problem, the friend explained, was that "he was a 'will-shoot.' If he got his hands on the ball, no matter what teammates were free under the basket, he'd shoot, and it didn't make it any better that he often sank the ball. But when we'd give him hell about it later, he'd just shrug his shoulders and say, 'I just felt like shooting.' And what more could you say if the guy had actually made the basket."[28]

But on this night—Thursday, January 11, 1951—ML wasn't too concerned with shooting. Except for him and middle-year students

Raymond J. Dietrich and Billy Reardon, every player participating in the exhibition game was in his first year at Crozer. As he and his nine teammates boarded the bus to the game, he wanted more than anything for the team to have a good time. However, if their idea of having a good time meant winning . . . well, that hope fell away quickly.

After a thirty-minute bus ride, the Crozer team walked into a gymnasium in West Philadelphia at around 7:00 PM. They were about to face a team of Eastern Baptist players who were taller and far more skilled than they were. A box score that ran in the next day's *Chester Times* would tell the sad tale.[29]

Back in 1950, most collegiate box scores only kept track of a few things: field goals (G), free throws (F), and points (P). According to those numbers, four Crozer players (Jesse H. Brown, Reese A. Mahoney, Lawrence J. Seyler, and Calixto O. Marques) played most of the game, while ML apparently contributed a two-pointer and a free throw to the team's futile efforts.[30] As far as I've found, this tiny mention in the

Eastern Baptist Laces Crozer Seminary Five

The · Eastern Baptist Seminary court team rolled up a 104-41 tally on Crozer Seminary at 68th and City Line, Overbrook, Thursday night.

Bud Kenton led the victors with 21 points.

Eastern Bapt. Sem.	G	F	P	Crozer Sem.	G	F	P
Wagner,f	5	0	10	Brown,f	5	0	10
Binning,f	5	0	10	Dietrick,f	0	0	0
McDaniels,f	6	1	13	Mahoney,f	5	1	11
Belli,f	6	0	12	Friend,f	0	0	0
Moon,c	8	2	18	Seyler,c	4	4	12
Leach,c	4	0	8	Redder,c	0	0	0
Notter,g	4	1	9	King,g	1	1	3
Johnson,g	0	0	0	Marques,g	3	0	3
Kenyon,g	8	5	21	Hoffman,g	0	0	0
Wright,g	1	1	3	Fagons,g	1	0	2
Totals	47	10	104	Totals	16	9	41

ML's only recorded basketball game box score at Crozer, January 11, 1951. *Used with permission of the Delaware County Daily Times*

Chester Times and a matching piece in the *Philadelphia Inquirer* are the only instances in which King's name appears in any box score, and their account of the game's final score isn't pretty: 104–41. But in his brief basketball career in the North, ML put the ball in the hoop and sank a free throw, and the entire Philadelphia/Chester area would get to read all about it in the morning.

———————

Three days later—the day before his twenty-second birthday—ML supported another friend, preaching for 1949 Crozer graduate Lloyd Burrus at Zion Baptist Church in Camden, New Jersey. Two weeks after that, on January 28, ML was invited by a Rev. D. W. White to speak at a 3:30 PM service at Temple Baptist Church in Chester. His busy schedule reaffirmed how far he'd come since the lonely days of his first term at Crozer.[31]

The friend who'd first encouraged him to emerge from his shell, Walter McCall, had also come a long way since his first year. Sure, he still struggled to make ends meet, and that made it tough to find study time as he prepared to retake his failed comprehensive exams. But by the middle of his final year, he'd developed a knack for inspiring younger people to pursue their life's goals. Speaking at a banquet in Linwood, Pennsylvania, in January 1951, McCall shared this gem with a crowd of a hundred: "We of the young generation must live up to our best, and as children of God, must discipline ourselves to seek to find and to give our best as we take our places in the world."[32]

But Mac's contentious nature could still land him in a great deal of controversy. During the winter of 1950–1951, he received unwelcome news from Pearl Smith, who'd been in Maple Shade, New Jersey, with Mac and ML the night they faced off against Ernest Nichols. Pearl told Mac that she was carrying his child, and that he had a choice: either acknowledge that the baby was his and do his part, or she'd take him to court. (In an era before DNA testing, of course, there was no way to definitively prove paternity.) Mac flatly said no, and Pearl Smith initiated a lawsuit.

Of all Mac's friends at Crozer, only a few would have known about his situation. The Crozer faculty kept the case tightly under wraps, fearing both a public backlash and a strike against their liberal reputation.

(Other seminaries: *Way too free over there . . .*) They wanted the conflict out of their hair as soon as possible. According to Horace Whitaker, it may have been George Davis who stuck his neck out for McCall, vouching for Mac's integrity and convincing the court to declare Mac innocent of Pearl's accusation. It will remain a mystery, however, as to whether McCall was telling the truth, or whether he relied on Crozer's influence to get out of a problem of his own making.[33]

What ML thought of his friend's crisis is also unknown. But Mac's ability to get into trouble may have helped keep ML focused on his own goals. If he was ever tempted to take a situation too far—if he ever wondered, for instance, whether he'd been wrong to end things with Betty—there was Mac, demonstrating the dangers of treading too far over the line.

Near the end of each term, seminarians often invited their classmates to visit their home during the short break. As ML, Whit, and Mac headed down to Atlanta (ML was due to give a sermon at Ebenezer the following Sunday), another trio of students left the Crozer campus headed for Waynesboro, Virginia, hometown of first-year student William W. Coleman. Coleman was at the wheel, and with him were Makoto Sakurabayashi, ML's friend from Japan, and Nolton W. Turner, a senior who'd joined ML's class in their second year. While driving along Route 1 between Baltimore and DC, Coleman lost control of his car and slammed into a stone wall.

All three men were seriously injured. Sakurabayashi broke his nose, but he would recover in time for term 3. Turner broke his leg and had to withdraw from Crozer temporarily. William Coleman, however, was never the same. He broke his leg both above and below his knee, and suffered a brain hemorrhage. He would leave the school as well, and pass away the following year.[34]

ML and his friends returned to the seminary in late February to find a campus shrouded in sorrow. The accident "had a sad impact on all Crozer students," Jimmy Beshai recalls.[35] With Turner's departure, ML's graduating class had shrunk to ten seminarians—barely two-thirds the number they'd started with in September 1948.

9

A Divine Cause

Term 3, February 20–May 4, 1951

Wrapping Things Up: "You Will Hear from Me"

On Thursday, February 22, 1951, Galja Barish Votaw, a longtime
columnist for the *Chester Times*, wrote a sweeping report detailing
both the history and the current state of Crozer Theological Seminary.
Votaw highlighted the seventeen hundred Crozer alumni serving all
over America and the world, and the fifty-three active students on
campus. She referred to the latter group admiringly as "completely
interracial. . . . Negro, Oriental and European students live and study
harmoniously on the campus to the enrichment of the lives of all."[1]

Of course, this ignored the friction caused by the school's still-
ongoing turn from the scholarly to the practical. Votaw's rosy assessment seemed to take President Blanton's plans as a fait accompli,
referring to the institution as "a professional school first and fore-
most . . . where the teaching of all subjects is done with an eye on
preparation for ministry."

ML warranted a mention of his own, though a somewhat garbled
one. "This year," Votaw wrote, "there are five Southern Negroes on
the campus and one of them, Martin Luther Smith, from Atlanta,

Ga., is the president of the student council."[2] One wonders if ML and Snuffy Smith, rivals who became friends, had a laugh at now becoming relatives.

But ML wouldn't have spent much time worrying about a mistake in the local paper. Though his time at Crozer was coming to an end, his status as a community leader was still keeping him busy. The weekend after Votaw's article published, Crozer held a three-day ministry conference for college students from over forty schools around the country who were curious about the Christian ministry. Events included discussion panels and speeches from fourteen "church officials." ML is not among the documented participants, but as student body president he was likely on hand to answer the students' questions about seminary life.[3]

Rev. Samuel D. Proctor did take part in the conference, leading a discussion group, and it was here that he met ML for the first time. By this point Proctor had transferred from Yale to Boston University to finish his PhD, so the two men would have had a lot to talk about. ML's "goal at that time," according to Proctor, "was to succeed Dr. Benjamin E. Mays as Morehouse College's president."[4] ML may have been thinking of emulating not only his former Morehouse mentor but also Mordecai Johnson, who served simultaneously as president of Howard University and as a highly sought-after preacher.

"After lunch, I went over and talked with the young man in his dorm," Proctor remembered. ML wanted to pick Proctor's brain, asking him to reflect on books that "influenced" him. They discussed the classic works of Walter Rauschenbusch, Reinhold Niebuhr, and Harry Fosdick. Proctor was struck by ML's confidence. Having grown comfortable in his role as Crozer's student leader, he had a calm and canny way of speaking—or, as Proctor recalled, a "Delphian assurance."

Proctor came away impressed by ML. "It was immediately clear to me that I was talking to a prodigious candidate for leadership."

On Sunday morning, February 25, ML returned to Fifth Presbyterian Church to preach the 11:00 AM service at the invitation of a supply pastor named M. C. Spann. Later in the term, on the night of April 15, he headed over to Edwards Street and spoke to the congregation of St. Daniel's Methodist Church for a "Young People's Day" service, at which two children's choirs from other local churches performed.[5]

The St. Daniel's appearance was ML's last reported sermon as a Crozer student. Since coming north in the fall of 1948, ML had publicly delivered dozens of sermons in and around Chester, Philadelphia, New Jersey, and New York. Throughout his three years, he'd collected sermon material using a preprinted "topic, text and subject index" form. Most of the material was derived from Bible passages, and the left-hand side of the form allowed ML to catalog such quotes: book, chapter, and verse. In the space on the right-hand side, he could write general comments on how to use the material. ML's index includes biblical references such as Matthew 23:25 (greed and self-indulgence) and Isaiah 40:15 (the sins of nationalism).[6]

There were also many verses not in his index that he had learned by heart. Marcus Wood remembered ML's continued fascination with the prophets of the eighth century BC. "King was often heard in his room reciting the famous passage from Amos 5:23—'Let Justice run down like water, and Righteousness like a mighty stream.' . . . King saw himself as an Amos to the society in which he lived. As a reformer, he too would have to turn our nation upside down."[7]

———————

Though he was working hard right up to the end, in some respects ML had it easy compared to many of his fellow seminarians, who'd burnished their skills and reputations as ministers over the past few years but couldn't support themselves solely with random preaching assignments around the area. Francis Stewart, who during this term was voted the next student body president, still worked at Sears on the weekends. Horace Whitaker worked as an assistant director at the West Branch YMCA. Walter McCall continued to cut hair in his dorm room and wash dishes in the kitchen. Even Marcus Wood, who had his own pastorship in Woodbury, New Jersey, took shifts as a waiter in the dining room of Old Main. "I stood over his table many times and watched him using his amazing gift for rhetoric upon fellow-students

and guests alike," Wood recalled. "His father provided whatever financial aid was necessary."[8]

Which meant that ML still had time for dating. Though Betty
Moitz caused him the greatest heartbreak, ML is known to have gone
out with several other women over his years at Crozer. The timing of
these interactions isn't always clear, but at one point, he explored a
connection his family would have found more acceptable: while visiting Rev. Barbour's home, Olee Barbour introduced him to a young
black woman from Chester named Annette McClain. According to
McClain, the two of them went "to the movies a couple of times"—but
only as friends. Even so, she got to see a part of his life that Betty
never did, attending a Crozer lecture where "I met his mother." The
young woman would remember ML for his kindness: "He was always
a gentlemen and had a very high regard and respect for women."[9]

ML also saw a young woman named Isabelle Durham, who lived
about twenty-five miles away in the northwest Philadelphia neighborhood of Roxborough. Once, ML went with Isabelle's family to
a restaurant, but they were denied service because they were black.
Although she wasn't entirely sure of the details, Durham's sister, Mil-
dred Benn, recalled ML being visibly annoyed. "You will hear from
me," Benn believed ML said to a restaurant employee. "I will have
this establishment closed." Though it was most likely a coincidence,
the restaurant soon "had a sign out front that said they were closed."[10]

His sister's friend Juanita Sellers also became a serious prospect
at one point. Perhaps because she had known ML since his Auburn
Avenue days and had earned his father's seal of approval, she was
the closest ML came to marrying someone from the Atlanta community. But June Dobbs, who was friends with Christine and Juanita
as well as ML, saw hesitation on both sides. Juanita had always been
more comfortable in cities, and she knew that ML's calling wouldn't
necessarily allow him to settle in an urban environment. According
to June, "ML always said back then, 'The church that calls me first,
that's where I must go.' . . . Juanita was getting scared, because she
didn't want to get involved in any country town."[11]

ML, on the other hand, assumed that whomever he chose to be
his wife would sacrifice her own hopes and dreams to follow him and

support his career. Eventually, Juanita would make it clear that she had her own ambitions, signing a contract to work as a teacher. She noticed that right after she agreed to work, ML started to fade from her life.[12] Though his family's inevitable disapproval was enough to scuttle his relationship with Betty, their approval wouldn't be enough to save his relationship with Juanita.

———

"The old order changeth, yielding place to the new."
—Tennyson, quoted in the *Chester Times*[13]

It was a time of endings, not just for ML and his fellow seniors but for the whole Crozer community. As students, faculty, and staff contemplated President Blanton's plans to do away with the Crozer they'd known, they also looked on sadly as the natural beauty of their campus was literally cut down.

After the vicious thunderstorm of November 1950, Crozer's long-time superintendent of buildings and grounds, Bert Williams, made what was for him an excruciating decision. Seventeen of the giant silver maple trees that shaded the campus were so damaged that they would need to be removed. By April, the trees had been felled, and students were paid to help cut the large trunks and branches down to size so that they could be disposed of. In economic terms, it was a great gig—85 cents an hour and no commute—but for the many Crozer students who'd been angered by the decision to remove them, it would've been a bittersweet experience to profit from destroying the very thing they loved.[14]

It would have been especially sad for ML, who'd enjoyed his spring walks through Ship Creek Woods toward the tributary that rolled into the Delaware River. Damaged trees all around Ship Creek were also cut down, and the view along the path and from the window of ML's dorm room would never be the same.

ML's Class Schedule

Year III, Term 3, February 20–May 4, 1951

Time	Tuesday	Wednesday	Thursday	Friday
8:00 AM	Christian Social Philosophy II	Christian Social Philosophy II	Christian Social Philosophy II	Christian Social Philosophy II
9:00 AM	Adv. Philosophy of Religion	Adv. Philosophy of Religion	Adv. Philosophy of Religion	Adv. Philosophy of Religion
10:00 AM	Chapel service	Optional service		Devotional pd.
10:30 AM				
11:00 AM				
11:30 AM	Christianity and Society	Christianity and Society	Christianity and Society	Christianity and Society
12:00 PM				
12:30 PM				
1:00 PM				
2:00 PM				
3:00 PM				
4:00 PM			Vespers service (4:15 PM)	
5:00 PM				

No classes on Monday | Term examinations: May 1–4 |
Eighty-third commencement: May 6–8
ML's GPA for the term: 3.89

Christian Social Philosophy II
Kenneth Lee Smith, BA (University of Richmond), BD (Crozer), PhD (in progress, Duke)
Course Description: "Post-Kantian thought in the nineteenth century (Schleiermacher, Ritschl, and Troeltsch); the genesis and development of the 'Social Gospel' (Maurice and Rauschenbusch); the cultural crisis in contemporary society and the Christian response in the thought of: Catholicism, Anglo-Catholocism, Neo-Protestantism, and Liberalism; summary and constructive statement." (Credit hours: 4; ML's grade: A)

Advanced Philosophy of Religion
George Washington Davis, BD, ThM (Colgate-Rochester), PhD (Yale)
Course Description: "The religious view of the world, nature and the supernatural, God, evil, determinism, the relation of morality to religion, revelation, immorality; the reasonableness and finality of the Christian faith." (Credit hours: 4; ML's grade: A)

Christianity and Society
Kenneth Lee Smith, BA (University of Richmond), BD (Crozer), PhD (in progress, Duke)
Course Description: "The social principles of Christianity and their bearing on contemporary life; the church as an institution and its relation to the social, political, and economic orders; analysis and interpretation of certain practical issues; education, war, racial prejudice, and world order." (Credit hours: 4; ML's grade: A-)

On Tuesday, Wednesday, and Friday, a half-hour period was set aside at 10:00 AM for services in the chapel. On Tuesdays was a mandatory service led by President Sankey L. Blanton. Wednesday services were optional, generally led by a member of the faculty or an invited pastor from an evangelical institution. The Friday devotional period was run by the students themselves and presided over by the chairman of the Devotions Committee. On Thursday, the 10:00 AM slot was a free period, and a vespers service was held at 4:15 PM. This tightly planned service featured a speaker from a prescheduled list, usually a Crozer professor or a guest speaker from another institution.[15]

Classes and Professors: Things Get Personal
Christian Social Philosophy II; Christianity and Society

> "When [King] came to Crozer, he was a biblical literal-
> ist. . . . He believed the Bible word-for-word. When he left
> Crozer, he could no longer believe that. It sort of shook
> him up. And a lot of other things at Crozer shook him up."
>
> —Kenneth Smith[16]

By his third term as a Crozer professor, Snuffy Smith had endeared himself to the entire student body. He'd lived in Old Main, making himself available to seminarians for breakfast, lunch, and dinner, and he'd encouraged them to debate important issues—even with him. As ML mentioned to an early biographer, "Smith loved an intellectual quarrel with his students."[17] His classes became a must to attend.

There were at least eleven students in Christian Social Philosophy II, a hearty size for a Crozer class. ML was one of them—and he apparently found it tricky to transition from seeing Smith as a pool room debate partner and informal adviser to interacting with him as a professor in a classroom setting. "King was always waiting for me when I came to class," Smith recalled. "He was always dressed in a suit, white shirt, a tie, and his shoes were shined. It took him a long time to loosen up." Nevertheless, he remembered ML as having "deep concentration on what was being said, and . . . penetrating questions."[18]

ML hopped into Christian Social Philosophy II without taking the first section. Due to his previous two and a half years of study, he wouldn't have had any trouble catching up with the content. According to Smith, the class "covered the ethical and social thought of the Church from New Testament times to the present. Its major purpose was to analyze and to assess the various historical 'strategies' which have characterized the relationship between Christ and culture."[19]

To that end, King was assigned a forty-five-minute oral report on contemporary French Catholic philosopher Jacques Maritain. Though ML was the only third-year student in the class, he knew his audience quite well. As he stood in front of the class to deliver his report, he

would have seen three friends who'd joined him during that basketball blowout at the hands of Eastern Baptist, and international student
Makoto Sakurabayashi, who presented his own oral report critiquing
the strong and weak points of the social gospel—overcoming both his
recent car accident and his second-language anxiety. Also in the class
was second-year George W. Lawrence, a married father of two who lived
in an apartment behind Old Main; his wife had made sandwiches for
Mac and ML for their long drives south to Atlanta.[20]

ML's oral report laid out Jacques Maritain's views on "the disease
of modernity," which to Maritain "occurred when modern philosophy
abandoned its dependence on theology." Maritain blamed the global
surge of Communism on this very fact: as soon as philosophy dismissed
its need for God, Communism came roaring in to replace it. "In other
words," ML said in his report, "Maritain feels that atheism was one of
the causes for the rise of Communism rather [than] a mere consequence.
He attempts to prove historically that Marx was an atheist before he
was a Communist."

One can imagine the young preacher looking up at his classmates,
friends, and Professor Smith with a bit of dramatic flair when he added,
"But he does not stop here." According to ML, Maritain believed that "Communism arose as a revolt against Christianity itself. It originated chiefly
through the fault of a Christian world unfaithful to its own principles."[21]

While Christian Social Philosophy examined a broad swath of history, ML's
second course with Smith, Christianity and Society, focused specifically
on present-day issues. As the class delved into such topics as democracy,
family concerns, the role of the United Nations, the strong influence of
the labor movement, and nuclear warfare, Smith noted how ML started to
open up, displaying a "lively interest" and offering "incisive observations."
The professor recalled that ML enjoyed connecting historical moments
with contemporary struggles, that he "was interested in the strategies of
the past only as they provided insights for the development of a Christian
social ethic adequate to meet the needs of contemporary society."[22]

It reminded Smith of someone. "At the time his favorite author in the field of ethics was Walter Rauschenbusch, and it was evident that he had read and pondered all of his major works." There was a sense of urgency to Rauschenbusch's social gospel that ML could relate to, the same desperation he heard in Daddy's King's voice: *Things need to change!* Rauschenbusch was not from the South, but he faced comparable problems preaching at a Baptist church in New York City's crime-ridden, poverty-stricken Hell's Kitchen. As families lined his pews with barely enough money to afford food, shelter, and clothing, Rauschenbusch dedicated his life to bridging the gap between church and society. *The church must help cure society's ills!* A man like ML, who believed the church had become archaic and disconnected from the needs of its people, welcomed having his doom and gloom lifted by the eternal optimism of Walter Rauschenbusch. ML would echo Rauschenbusch's ideas whenever he needed to pitch his message toward a white audience.[23]

The discussions with Smith continued in the rec room of Old Main. With Rauschenbusch in ML's corner, Smith chose to counter with the ideas of Reinhold Niebuhr, the *realist*. Wherever Rauschenbusch stood for sunny optimism, Niebuhr waited around the corner, leaning against a building: *Sounds great, Walter, but how do we really **do** it?* "We engaged in frequent debates," Smith said, "about the relative merits of the social ethics of Rauschenbusch and Reinhold Niebuhr, whom, I must confess, I followed somewhat uncritically during those early days of my teaching."[24]

Niebuhr's carefully moderated beliefs were a perfect template for a young professor just starting out in the classroom. In 1942, Niebuhr wrote that "we need the idealism of the Christian gospel to save us from cynicism and complacency. But we also need the realism to save us from sentimentality. In America at least the dangers of a perverse sentimentality have been greater than the perils of cynicism."[25] This cautious, middle-of-the-road approach was particularly helpful when leading discussions among full-grown adults with their own established beliefs.

ML's position, however, was a bit different. The South *needed* change, and both black southerners and white society needed to believe that such change was possible. This required the sort of idealistic efforts

Rauschenbusch wrote about in his book *Christianity and the Social Crisis*, which ML read and absorbed:

> A minister mingling with both classes can act as an interpreter to both. He can soften the increasing class hatred of the working class. He can infuse the spirit of moral enthusiasm into the economic struggle of the dispossessed and lift it to something more. . . . On the other hand, among the well-to-do, [the minister] can strengthen . . . consciousness . . . [that] the working people have a real grievance. . . . If the ministry would awaken among the wealthy a sense of social compunction and moral uneasiness, that alone might save our nation from a revolutionary explosion.[26]

ML had a strong connection with Rauschenbusch's urgent message of social change, but his debates with Professor Smith would have helped him to appreciate the importance of having the tempered realism of Niebuhr in his back pocket.* Just as Rev. Barbour urged him to synthesize white and black preaching styles, Smith encouraged him to strike a balance among differing philosophical influences.

"It is a pity that [there isn't] a recording of Martin and Ken in discussion," Jimmy Beshai says. "I felt that they were good friends. More than professor and student." And ML himself remembered Smith fondly, telling a biographer later that he "had a tremendous capacity to grapple with big ideas."[27]

---

* In a 1956 editorial, Reinhold Niebuhr commented on the nonviolent movement going on in Montgomery: "The local leader is the Reverend Martin Luther King. He scrupulously avoids violence and calls his strategy the 'way of love.' It is the most effective way of justice." Niebuhr, however, disagreed with using the word *love* as King had framed it. "Love is a motive and not a method. . . . It is justice, rather than love, which becomes relevant whenever one has to deal with conflicting wills and interests. In this case of a race suffering long from the pride and arrogance of another race, one can have little question about the justice of the boycott against the segregated buses, nor of the adequacy of the method by which justice is being achieved." In typical Niebuhrian fashion, he supported the effort but advocated tempering the romanticism. (Reinhold Niebuhr, "The Way of Nonviolent Resistance," *Christianity and Society* 21 [Spring 1956]: 3.)

Advanced Philosophy of Religion

Advanced Philosophy of Religion was ML's final class with George Davis, who had persuaded him to pursue his doctorate at Boston University. Davis also encouraged him to study with BU professor Edgar S. Brightman, who specialized in the branch of religious thought known as personalism. So in Davis's final class, ML would take the opportunity to learn as much as he could about Brightman, taking a deep dive into one of his most influential books, *A Philosophy of Religion*, published in 1940. Davis was the ideal professor to introduce the topic; according to Snuffy Smith, "Brightman was by far the single most important philosophical influence upon Davis's theology."[28]

Brightman's view of personalism can be outlined very generally as follows:

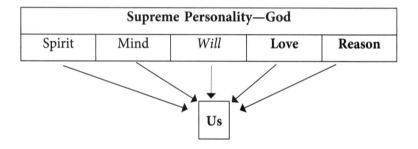

Edgar S. Brightman:
"Personalism is the belief that conscious personality is both the supreme value and the supreme reality in the universe."

"'God is a spirit,' a being whose *esse* is to be conscious, to experience, to think, to will, to love, and to control the ongoing universe by rational purpose."

"Unless religion allows man to retain some degree of self-respect and of intelligence, it is doomed. A God about whom we dare not think is a God a thinking mind cannot worship."[29]

According to this philosophy, there is God, or the Supreme Personality, a parental figure who invisibly invests human beings with five factors, the most vital of which are Love and Reason. Possessing these factors, then, connects us to the Supreme Personality. Simply by being human, we are fundamentally tied to God.

Thus, anything that seeks to deny or diminish an individual's personhood is an affront to God. Perhaps you were once enslaved by a master or considered three-fifths of a human being, or you were not given certain educational advantages or were prohibited from sitting in a particular seat on a bus. "Every act of injustice," ML would write later in life, "mars and defaces the image of God in man."[30]

During late April 1951, ML wrote an essay for Davis's course that used personalism as a lens to examine the nature of evil. The paper, titled "Religion's Answer to the Problem of Evil," is long and plagiarized, but contains a few nuggets of insight into how twenty-two-year-old ML was processing Brightman's ideas.

ML's main beef with Brightman was how the professor viewed the actual power of the Supreme Personality. Although Brightman considered God's existence to be infinite, he saw the existence of evil as evidence that God's ability to affect the world, his *will*, is finite. ML's paper does not propose an alternate conception, but it does suggest ML's displeasure with the notion of a less-than-omnipotent God who cannot prevent evil from happening. Later on, during the civil rights movement, King would argue for the existence of an infinite, all-powerful God who could intervene in human history to aid those denied full personhood. Perhaps, echoing ML's embrace of Walter Rauschenbusch's optimism, the needs of his movement required him to proclaim an absolute God of goodness and hope. But the certainty with which he proclaimed it likely has roots in the studies he began here—and in the deep conviction of a mind that spent years pondering the very nature of man's personality.

For now, ML would answer the problem of evil by leaning on his faith, concluding his paper with a sermonic flourish: "After we have climbed to the top of the speculative ladder we must leap out into the darkness of faith. But this leap is not a leap of despair, for it eventually cries with St. Paul, 'for now we see through a glass darkly . . . but then shall I know even as I am known.'"[31] Though his academic prose would always be mired in self-consciousness, when it came to writing a sermon, ML had no trouble letting loose. And Professor Davis seemed to approve of the overall effort, awarding the essay an A-.

As Davis advocated, King would go on to study with Edgar Brightman at BU, becoming, as Jimmy Beshai recalls, "an advocate of personalism."[32] Unfortunately, ML's new mentor would pass away less than two
years later at the age of sixty-eight.*

The Graduate: "I Do Remember Moments That I Have Been Awe Awakened."

Degrees Awarded at Crozer
May 8, 1951

Bachelor of Divinity		
1. Edwin Alonzo Brooks	Alexandria, VA	BA Bucknell University 1948
2. Eugene Hildreth Drew	Rensselaer, NY	BA Alderson-Broaddus 1948
3. James Joseph Greene	Portsmouth, VA	BA University of Richmond 1949
4. Martin Luther King Jr.	Atlanta, GA	BA Morehouse College 1948
5. Joseph Timothy Kirkland	Philadelphia, PA	BA Virginia Union 1948
6. Walter Raleigh McCall	Marion, SC	BA Morehouse College 1948
7. Wendall Atlas Maloch	Emerson, AR	BA Hillsdale College 1948
8. Cyril George Pyle	Canal Zone, Panama	BA Virginia Union 1948
9. Horace Edward Whitaker	Seaview, VA	BA Virginia Union 1948
10. Marcus Garvey Wood	Charles Town, WV	BA Storer College 1948

Oriental Certificates		
1. En-Chin Lin	Foochow, China	BA Fukien Christian University 1935; MS in Ed. University of Pennsylvania 1949
2. Makoto Sakurabayashi	Yokohama, Japan	BA University of Tokyo 1942

---

* ML would have known prior to arriving at Boston University that Brightman's health
had taken a turn for the worse. In the April 1950 edition of the *Crozer Quarterly*, Brightman, a frequent contributor, explained why he'd been delayed in replying to an earlier
critique: "Circumstances beyond my control, including the excessive heat of the summer
followed by a heart attack that incapacitated me for some time, prevented me from avail-
ing myself." Rest assured, wrote Brightman, he'd finally recovered and would resume his
regular teaching duties at Boston U.

On Sunday, May 6, at 3:30 PM in the chapel of Old Main, Martin Luther King Jr. and the other students sat in pews, awaiting President Sankey Blanton's baccalaureate speech. Its theme was "The Cure for All Souls," but it would not be the most compelling message ML received from the faculty in his last days at Crozer. By this point, with classes finished, he'd most likely been informed that out of the ten students being awarded their bachelor's in divinity, he would be named the most outstanding student. On top of this, George Davis, Charles Batten, and Morton Enslin had agreed to award ML the J. Lewis Crozer Fellowship; the $1,200 grant would be applied in four installments toward his studies at Boston University.[33]

ML was a remarkable student in a remarkable class: for the first time in the history of Crozer Theological Seminary, the majority of its graduating seniors—six of the ten—were black. Leave it to the ever-affable Dean Batten to salute the moment with a line in the *Chester Times* that would have carried significant weight back in 1951: "It is indicative of Crozer's interracial policy."[34] To be sure, that policy wasn't a cure-all. ML and the five other black graduates had contended with an all-white faculty and staff that wasn't always sensitive to their specific backgrounds and issues. When Robert Keighton indicated his animosity toward black preaching styles, they'd gone off campus for more supportive guidance from Rev. J. Pius Barbour. And even here in an enclave of northern liberalism, they'd endured outbreaks of bigotry from the likes of Lucius Z. Hall. But all things considered, they would look back fondly on their time in the inclusive environment of Crozer. Perhaps Marcus Wood summed it up best: "We had spent three years in a miniature kingdom of God. . . . We all were concerned that as we moved up in life that we would make all of society a free society, a society where one would not be known by his race, creed or color."[35]

Monday, May 7, was given over to alumni events, with commencement exercises scheduled for the following Tuesday. In his last act as student body president, ML made sure his class would go through their historic day in style. Although they were officially receiving a *bachelor's* degree in divinity, each man had already earned another BA; in fact, a four-year degree was required simply to be admitted to Crozer. ML wanted to elevate the ceremony beyond the college graduation they'd already experienced. He managed to persuade the administration to open their wallets and augment each graduate's robe with a hood. "This was something that had not been done before," recalled Marcus Wood. "Some of the seminary staff did not want to go along with it, but the class insisted." Since academic hoods have specific colors corresponding to the subject of study, each seminarian would receive a scarlet hood, for theology. Where once ML had overdressed to hide his social anxiety and loneliness, now he was going out on a limb to upgrade his fellow graduates' style.[36]

Commencement began on May 8 at 10:30 AM. As the longest-standing member of the Crozer faculty, Robert Keighton led the short procession from the front entrance of Old Main over to Commencement Hall. Everyone took their seats, and Dr. John R. Humphreys, Crozer class of 1901, provided the invocation. Next came a hymn, then a prayer led by Dr. Frederick Allen, class of 1911. Humphreys and Allen's grandfatherly presence was a salute to the seminary's history, and a reminder to the young graduates eager to change the world that their calling was not a sprint but a marathon.[37]

Next came Dr. Vernon B. Richardson, who'd graduated from Crozer in 1938. Tasked with delivering the commencement address, Richardson chose a broad theme: "The Preacher's Heritage." He knew from experience how Crozer put its students' religious beliefs through the ringer, and he encouraged the graduates to look at the New Testament with fresh eyes. "Let no one ever fail to be awed by the mystery of a body of literature so profound being produced so quickly over so wide an area by so many minds responding to one life so briefly lived." Richardson also warned graduates of preaching too impulsively. "The danger there is in appealing to man's shallow nature, satisfying his daily needs without releasing his deeper nature." Near the end of his speech, Richardson urged the ministers in Commencement Hall to commit fully to their role in society, saying that a preacher "must be acclimatized to a cultural and intellectual environment in many ways strangely different from his own. He must come to grips with ideas in the Gospel framework whether or not those patterns of thought are personally pleasing to him."[38]

After Richardson came good ol' Sankey Blanton, who'd completed his first full year as president of Crozer. Blanton would eventually accomplish his mission to turn Crozer into an evangelical-minded seminary. In exactly three years, a "Blanton exodus" occurred. Morton Enslin relinquished control of the *Crozer Quarterly* and left the school, eventually landing at the St. Lawrence Theological School as a professor of biblical languages and literature, while James Pritchard headed west to join the Church Divinity School of the Pacific in Berkeley. As the right and left hook of Crozer's biblical reality check took their scholarly approach elsewhere, the school also lost Dean Charles Batten, master of community outreach and friend to every student. Batten accepted a position as director of Christian education at the Parish of the Epiphany Episcopal Church in Winchester, Massachusetts. ML would never forget Dean Batten's unconditional support, confessing in a letter he wrote to Batten in 1956, while in the throes of the Montgomery bus boycott, that no matter how old he became, "I would feel strange not calling you 'Dean.'"[39]

His lasting impression of President Blanton would be more apprehensive. In response to the faculty exodus, ML wrote to fellow alum Francis Stewart that he believed Blanton "was desirous of getting rid of these men from the very beginning. What the outcome will be I don't know. . . . I do hope that it won't be disastrous."[40]

But back in 1951, ML was not too concerned with Crozer's longevity. This was *his* day, and after James Greene walked across the stage, Martin Luther King Jr. went up to Sankey Blanton and then George Davis to receive his divinity degree and scarlet hood. In the crowd sat his sister, Christine; his brother, AD; his mother, Alberta; and, of course, Martin Sr., who'd ended up truly impressed (and somewhat perplexed) by his son's development at Crozer. "ML was moving forward into a modern, advanced sort of ministry requiring lengthy and dedicated study," Daddy King remembered. "I admired his mind's receptivity and the genuine passion he had for learning."[41]

It was a day of honors for ML. First his divinity degree, then the J. Lewis Crozer Fellowship, and as the icing on the cake, the Pearl Ruth Plafker Memorial Award, described in the Crozer catalog as follows:

An award of fifty dollars is made annually by Dr. Nathan V. Plafker in memory of his wife, to that student of the senior class who, in the judgment of the faculty, has maintained throughout his course in the Seminary a good academic record, and who has, by his character and cooperation, made a distinct contribution to the community life of the campus.[42]

It was Nathan Plafker who had helped introduce ML to on-air preaching through his radio station project (which he'd also initiated in honor of his wife, Pearl). Now he was recognizing ML's academic accomplishments at Crozer with a fifty-dollar check. The award served as a rough equivalent to the title *valedictorian*, which wasn't mentioned in any of the Crozer literature of the time, but as the award description indicates, it took into account not only a student's grades but also his "distinct contribution to the community." We may never know if ML had the highest GPA in his class,* but we do know that with impressive grades, his service as Devotions Committee chairman and student body president, and his regular work as a preacher in the Chester and Philadelphia community, he stood well above his classmates as the most all-around impressive student at Crozer.

Commencement ended with a few more gift exchanges. As was a tradition, the graduating class gave their own fifty-dollar donation to the seminary, a tangible display of their appreciation. And Crozer sent each graduate off with a collection of books courtesy of the "American Baptist Publication Society of Philadelphia as a nucleus for a personal library."[43] The students headed back to Old Main, where it had all started, and had one last lunch together in the dining hall.

After eating, it was time for photos. ML posed with the entire graduating class and the two international students who had completed the Oriental certificate program, En-Chin Lin and Makoto Sakurabayashi. Though the group's paths were diverging, they would remain bonded by their shared experiences at Crozer. Sakurabayashi, for one, would continue to feel a connection to ML despite time and distance; seven years later, when was back in Japan, he wrote a kind letter to King after learning that he'd been stabbed with a letter opener in Harlem.[44]

---

* See the class schedules in each chapter for term-by-term rundown of ML's own GPA.

ML's graduation photo. Though the only available version of the image is blurry and faces are difficult to make out, it depicts, from left to right: (front row) James J. Greene, En-Chin Lin, Makoto Sakurabayashi, Wendell A. Maloch, Marcus G. Wood; (back row) Joseph T. Kirkland, Eugene H. Drew, Martin Luther King Jr., Horace E. Whitaker, Cyril Pyle, Edwin A. Brooks, Walter R. McCall. *Courtesy of Rev. Marcus G. Wood, Co-pastor, Providence Baptist Church, Baltimore, MD*

ML had entered Crozer Theological Seminary as a man of the South—sheltered and guarded by an influential family, raised in a segregated community where neighbors looked out for one another. He'd come to Crozer in hopes of expanding his horizons, and found that the school was the ideal environment for doing just that. It wasn't always easy; as fellow seminarian Francis Stewart put it, the experience had been "a constant bombardment of shock treatment for all of us. . . . Some . . . just couldn't take it." But ML bore up under every onslaught. He'd had guns pointed at him, sand thrown into his food. He'd accepted demystified, humanized views of Moses and Jesus Christ, absorbing Crozer's white intellectualism without abandoning his black roots. He'd preached at northern churches in New York, New Jersey, and Philadelphia, and experienced the differences between congregations there and back home in Atlanta. He'd written dozens of new sermons reflecting his broadening perspective, and he'd listened to the powerful and stormy voices of J. Pius Barbour and Mordecai Johnson, both sparking his interest in the methods of Mahatma Gandhi.

He'd fallen in love with a white woman and been left brokenhearted by society's disapproval, yet the peaceful soul who had counseled him to end things, Horace Whitaker, became a lifelong friend. His old friend Walter McCall had helped him to open up—even sparking his first foray into civil rights litigation. And when he needed time away from social concerns or liberal philosophy, he'd been able to walk deep into the Ship Creek Woods and commune with nature.

At Crozer, ML's spiritual self had awakened, but he would continue to pursue religion with a sense of hope mingled with melancholy. He still wanted to *feel* the Holy Spirit, and at twenty-two, he'd not yet experienced an unmistakable religious epiphany. In a paper he wrote for George Davis five weeks before graduation, ML shared a bit of his tightly controlled uncertainty:

> I do remember moments that I have been awe awakened; there have been times that I have been carried out of myself by something greater . . . and to that something I gave myself. Has this great something been God? Maybe after all I have been religious for a number of years, and am now only becoming aware of it.[45]

A summer of preaching down at Ebenezer awaited, and in September a new chapter at Boston University would begin. Thanks to his development at Crozer, ML had started to realize his desire to give himself to a greater cause—a cause he hoped God would help him see.

Epilogue
Beyond Crozer

"I am convinced that for men who love the risks of faith and the divine adventure, who can live hard and like it, the ministry presents the noblest and most rewarding of careers. The task is especially difficult in these days, and it is a good thing for the ministry and for the Christian church that the task is so challenging, and that it taxes every power of manhood. Nothing is to be gained by making the entrance into the ministry easy."

—Martin Luther King Jr.[1]

Not much of ML's Crozer is still around today. In 1970, the seminary merged with Colgate Rochester Divinity School in Rochester, New York, giving up the Chester campus. The silver maple trees that survived the storm of 1950 have long since been cleared out for a parking lot, and for a while Old Main was turned into an extension of the Crozer-Keystone Medical Center. But the hospital has moved out, and as of this writing the Old Main building is locked up and in a state of limbo.

In January 2016, Dr. James Beshai—"Jimmy from Egypt"—allowed me to drive him from his home in Lebanon, Pennsylvania, to the former Crozer campus. Even though Jimmy was pushing ninety years old, his memory has remained incredibly sharp. We entered Old Main together, and soon enough Jimmy was pointing out the location of the chapel, the kitchen, his classrooms, and his dorm room. "Right here"—Jimmy indicated a doorway at the north end of the second floor. "This was where I lived." Although it gave me chills to watch Jimmy recall so clearly his time living only a couple doors down from King, I was less impressed by the overall condition of the building. Truth be told, time has not treated the Crozer legacy well.

The exterior of Old Main still has the power to connect visitors with its long and storied past. Its stone facade hasn't changed, and surrounding it are a few more of the original buildings, such as Pearl Hall. There's even a sign in front indicating that a man named Martin Luther King Jr. lived inside Old Main from 1948 to 1951. But once you push open the front doors, there is very little to be discovered. In the chapel, the original wooden ceiling design remains, along with a few stained-glass windows. Up in the cupola are the signatures of the wounded Civil War veterans—the ghosts of Old Main. But ML's room 52 is nothing more than a six-by-eight-foot blue-carpeted office that's now used as disorganized storage space. ML's ticking heater is still there, but that's all.

Old Main and Pearl Hall from a distance, late August 2014. *Photo by the author*

When I shared my disappointment with Jimmy on our ride back to his home, he agreed, believing Old Main should be transformed into a center for social justice. We brainstormed ideas about what such a center might include. Classes and lectures on social activism and the principles of nonviolence could be held on the first floor, where the chapel used to be. On the second floor, visitors could take a trip back in time to 1950, entering a restored version of ML's dorm room, with a collection of books to peruse, and a radio room like the one Robert Keighton set up, with King's sermons available for listening. Such a center would be a far greater tribute to King's legacy than yet another highway bearing his name. The more we can learn about the institution where King began to develop his philosophy, the easier it is to understand that philosophy and put it into practice ourselves.

But understanding the influence of Crozer depends on more than re-creating its physical details. More important are the people he connected with during his years in the seminary, many of whom continued to touch his life in the eventful years that followed.

Horace Edward Whitaker remained King's friend, mentor, and confidant, a living reminder of the value of integrity. After graduation, the two men kept in touch through letters, and a quick peek into the contents shows the depth of their friendship. In a letter Whit wrote to ML in October 1952, he even got in a few playful jests: "Your mother said you had taken all of her pots and pans and cut-outs for Boston. I can imagine that is some apartment you are keeping. You can't wash dishes or can you?"[2]

He followed it up with a more meaningful jab—the kind only he could deliver: "By the way you told me two years ago you would be married by the next summer. Apparently you are still meeting these girls who are one-time wreckers." The reference to "two years ago" is especially noteworthy: it corresponds exactly to the moment in the fall of 1950 when ML turned to Whit in distress over his relationship with Betty Moitz.

The two men continued to correspond through ML's years at Boston, and when the Montgomery bus boycott started and King became a national figure with the weight of an entire movement on his young shoulders, he visited Whit in person at his ever-growing church in Niagara Falls, New York. It was around the summer of 1956, and *Dr.* King had traveled alone to once again confide in Whit about his responsibilities and his doubts. He'd already received death threats by phone, and a bomb had blown up the front porch of his home. Now speaking family man to family man, ML told his friend he wasn't even sure if the Lord *wanted* him to perpetuate the boycott. Whit understood his spiritual concerns—he'd *always* understood. Although his young friend had changed so much since their years at Crozer, Whit still had no trouble lending support and care.[3]

The next day, ML preached at Whit's church, the sermon title echoing the uncertainty of ML's situation: "Going Forward by Going Backward." He reminded Whit's congregation of Luke 2:41–52, in which a twelve-year-old Jesus separated himself from his parents and remained behind at the Temple in Jerusalem for several days. According to Whit, ML's message was for the parents in the congregation—that when it came to their children sometimes they needed to look behind them for the values they'd lost sight of in order to move forward again. Since it was Men's Day at Whitaker's church, ML would have mainly been targeting fathers. At the time, ML had just become a father himself—eight-month-old daughter Yolanda was at home with Coretta, his wife of three years—and he of course was still contending with his own father, who hoped ML would step away from all the danger surrounding him in Montgomery.[4]

In 1962, it was Whitaker who wrote to ML for advice. Whit had been considering a move into academia, as a "college minister at one of the Southern State Colleges." It would mean a complete shift in lifestyle—a shift he was unsure would be wise. "I am wondering," he wrote to ML, "whether or not I have the personality and some of the skills that such a work would require. I think I would enjoy doing the work, but only if I could feel that I could measure up to reasonable expectations."[5]

Less than two weeks later, ML replied to Whit, extending the sort of support his friend had always given him. He wrote that Whit would be "exceptional" at a college. "Your background, training, and general commitment would serve to give you real qualifications for such a responsibility. . . .

The present-day students are in need of guidance more than ever before." Whit would ultimately decide not to make the change, after all, instead accepting the pastorship of Zion Baptist Church in Portsmouth, Virginia.

Horace Edward Whitaker lived to be ninety-four years old, passing away in 2012.

———————

Betty Moitz and ML went their separate ways after May 1951. "He sent me pages to type of his [Boston University] dissertation," Betty recalls, "and McCall checked in to make sure I was still up for it." But that was the extent of their relationship. Betty married, and soon she was like the rest of America, watching ML grow into a global icon.[6]

The last known message ML received from the Moitz family was actually from Miss Hannah, Betty's mother and Crozer's cook. In December 1960, Hannah and Betty attended a morning service at Phila-delphia's Unitarian Church of Germantown, where ML preached one of his time-tested, oft-repeated sermons, "The Three Dimensions of a Complete Life." Before going into his sermon, ML told the congregation how fond he was of the Philadelphia area: "I never feel like a stranger when I return because I lived in this community some three years. . . . I met many, many people in this area, and I feel that I have some real genuine friends in Philadelphia. So it is always a rewarding experience to come back to this area."[7]

ML went on to preach to Miss Hannah, Betty, and the rest of the congregation about the length, breadth, and height of life—of our inward, outward, and upward reach toward ourselves, others, and God, respectively. Miss Hannah was so inspired by his words that she sent him a Christmas card:

So sorry we had to miss talking with you. Since we were with our good neighbor, we had a problem getting home in the storm. You did give us a wonderful message. I must say I never heard a sermon that gave me so much to live by. Just wish I could hear more like them. I wish I could meet your lovely wife and family—God bless you all!

Much love, Hannah R. M. & Betty![8]

By this point, of course, King had found Coretta Scott, and the two shared a far more powerful love that deserves its own book. As a married father in a public battle for racial equality, it makes sense that he would not want to dwell on a long-ago relationship with a young white woman. In fact, the closest he came to acknowledging it publicly was in a secondhand report attributed to a "close friend" in an article written by *New York Post* journalist Ted Poston, which was later quoted in Lerone Bennett's 1964 King biography *What Manner of Man*. Even this account is muted. "She liked me and I found myself liking her," ML supposedly told his friend. "But finally I had to tell her resolutely that my plans for the future did not include marriage to a white woman."[9]

Though he may have attempted to downplay the relationship's significance, there are certainly signs of its influence in Dr. King's later work. In April 1961, he had this to say to a group of graduating seminarians at Southern Baptist Theological Seminary:

> The church can make it clear that all of the talk about intermarriage and all of the fears that come into being on the subject are groundless fears. Properly speaking, individuals marry, not races. And people, in the final analysis, in a democracy must have the freedom to marry anybody they want to marry. And so no state should have laws prohibiting this.[10]

This was still a highly controversial opinion in 1961, when seventeen states had anti-miscegenation laws on the books—including Kentucky, where King delivered the speech. It was not until the Supreme Court's unanimous *Loving v. Virginia* decision in 1967 that all intermarriage laws were declared unconstitutional.* But for King, it had never been enough to simply tolerate another race—one needed to love unconditionally.

---

* Of course, not even a Supreme Court decision would settle the issue in the eyes of every American. As recently as 2000, when the citizens of Alabama voted on whether to officially remove the invalidated ban on interracial marriage from the state constitution, the initiative passed by a vote of 60 percent to 40 percent. This means that around 526,000 people—more than two and half times the population of Montgomery—voted to *keep* the already powerless law on the books. (Somini Sengupta, "November 5-11; Marry at Will," *New York Times*, November 12, 2000.)

That's how Betty remembers ML, as a man who "was a hero not only to black people [but] to all people."[11] For a time, happily married with children of her own, Betty too seemed to play down the intensity of her relationship with King, claiming in a 1998 documentary that it was she who put an end to talk of getting married, and that ML was more angry than brokenhearted that society wouldn't allow their relationship to go forward.[12] But now, when Betty looks back on her time with ML, she can appreciate the genuine love and affection they shared. "Our romance was short and sweet," she says.

———————

In 1958, King wrote a letter to **Rev. J. Pius Barbour** to tell him about his new book *Stride Toward Freedom*. He recommended that Barbour especially read the chapter titled "Pilgrimage to Nonviolence," in which he outlines the development of his nonviolent philosophy. Though the chapter doesn't discuss Rev. Barbour specifically, it does mention ML's studies at Crozer, and focuses on the sorts of complex philosophical issues he and Barbour used to enjoy debating. That's why ML added, "I wrote that chapter for you."[13]

Whenever you see an interview in which Martin Luther King Jr. ably defends his ideas in the face of vehement opposition, you can thank Rev. Barbour for teaching him to hold his own in a heated debate. Even after ML left Crozer, Rev. Barbour never hesitated to restart their war of words. In a December 1954 letter, very shortly after his young pupil decided to become pastor at Dexter Avenue Baptist Church in Montgomery, Alabama, Barbour told ML how he felt about the decision to go back south to preach: "You need not tell me about Dexter; I know Montgomery and its superficial intellectuality. A plant-hand in the North has more WORLD WISDOM than a college Pres. in the SOUTH. . . . Something wrong with SOUTHERN INTELLECTUALITY. I know what it is: it does not have the atmosphere that breeds profundity . . . all abstraction."[14]

ML may have disagreed with Rev. Barbour's unfiltered northern bias, but he always appreciated that his mentor was willing to speak openly and think deeply. In the same 1958 letter in which he told Barbour about his book, ML wrote that he missed the reverend's provocative editorials in

National Baptist Voice magazine. "The present Voice is so shallow that I unconsciously find myself throwing it in the waste basket when it arrives."[15]

Another of Barbour's published provocations stands out as particularly relevant today. Ira De Augustine Reid's survey *The Negro Baptist Ministry*—the same project for which ML did fieldwork during his time at Crozer—includes a passage from Rev. J. Pius Barbour titled "A Defense of the Negro Preacher" that still carries a defiant sting in the twenty-first century:

> The white liberals must stop sipping tea with well-to-do Negroes and drawing the conclusion that the Masses are doing all right. THE MASSES ARE NOT DOING ALL RIGHT. They are scuffling and scuffling like everything . . . cheated at the grocery store; laid off suddenly; harassed by prejudiced bosses; double-crossed by prejudiced labor leaders—the poor Negro worker has to fight tooth and toe nail to exist."[16]

A day after King was assassinated in 1968, Rev. Barbour was interviewed by the local Chester paper. Barbour, deeply affected, recalled ML as a young man in his parlor, debating the issues of life. He missed that man, full of energy and curiosity. At such a tragic moment, Barbour could have chosen to inflate King's reputation as an icon even more. But he didn't. Instead, he remembered ML as someone we all could relate to. "He was a great historian, and he had no delusions about greatness. He was just Martin Luther King, preacher."[17]

Rev. Barbour himself passed away in 1974.

Perhaps we all need to thank **Marcus Garvey Wood** for entering room 52 in the fall of 1948 and quieting the rumbling anger of Lucius Z. Hall—his gun aimed directly at a frozen ML. Without Wood's intervention, the civil rights movement might have turned out quite differently.

Because he commuted to Woodbury, New Jersey, every weekend to preach, Wood was always somewhat disconnected from social life at Crozer. But he had friends like ML, Mac, and Whit, who visited him in Woodbury, and after graduation, he and King stayed in touch. Wood,

too, became active in the civil rights movement as pastor of Providence
Baptist Church in Baltimore, and his letters to ML offered full-throated
support for King's work—along with some weighty biblical imagery.
Take, for instance, this letter Wood wrote in February 1956, during the
Montgomery bus boycott:

> It was one of the happiest moments of my life when I read a few
> weeks ago of the wonderful work you are doing for your people
> in the South. I wish I were there to help you. You are becoming as
> a prophet of this day and age and I hope you will see it through.
> Be like Isaiah of old [and] walk the streets barefooted until the
> waters of hate roll back to the ocean of eternity.[18]

At Crozer, he had laughed as ML compared himself to fiery Old
Testament prophets like Isaiah. Now Wood was the one making the
comparisons:

> I know you are preaching like mad now. You have thrown Crozer
> aside and you have found the real God and you can tell the world
> now that he is a God who moves in a mysterious way. That he will be
> your battle ax in the time of war and preserve you from your enemy.[19]

Wood bore witness as his young friend became an almost mythic
figure, but no matter how much King's legend grew, Wood would never
forget that nineteen-year-old kid who had entered Crozer with big ambitions but no real idea how to accomplish them. "We never thought,
except from what King kept telling us," he said decades later, "that he
was going to become immortal."[20]

In 2011, when the Martin Luther King, Jr. Memorial was unveiled
on the National Mall in Washington, DC, Wood was asked to comment on the dramatic pose chosen for King's statue. Although Wood
had compared ML to ancient prophets and listened to ML's gargantuan
hopes and dreams, he still felt torn that the statue failed to capture his
friend as a normal human being. "I looked at the picture, and I'm trying to decide whether or not it was the best one they could have used
to represent the King that I knew who started out just a young boy."[21]

Rev. Marcus Garvey Wood in 2017. *Courtesy of Rev. Marcus G. Wood, Co-pastor, Providence Baptist Church, Baltimore, MD*

Wood also pondered what direction King's activism might have taken had he not been murdered. He credited his friend with transforming American attitudes about race, and argued that twenty-first century Americans were facing a different form of discrimination. "We changed from segregation by color to segregation by economics," said Wood. "And if King had lived, he would have had to tackle the economic side."[22]

———————

For seven years of ML's life, it was **Walter Raleigh McCall** who helped push him out of his comfort zone—yet history has been unkind to Mac, and his influence on ML has largely been forgotten. In almost all of the stories shared by former Crozer students and teachers, no other man—not even ML—was remembered as vividly as he was, but these same acquaintances almost unanimously derided his character. To those who didn't know him well, he could come off as aggressive, unforgiving, and downright confrontational.

But for those who pushed through his abrasive attitude, Mac became a friend for life. One man who came to know Mac very well was Snuffy Smith, who recalled with great clarity a moment in the early 1960s, after Smith placed McCall on the Crozer alumni board. When they saw each other again, Smith recalled Mac coming toward him with a cigar in his mouth and wide grin. "Doc! You old honkie! I'm gonna punch you in the eye!" Smith replied, "If you do, you nigger, I'm gonna kick you."[23] Mac then picked Smith up and gave him a kiss on both cheeks.

After graduation, Mac's and ML's paths separated. According to McCall, "We remained friends throughout, but were not as close in terms of being able to share in each other's experiences as much." He remembered a moment he had with ML in March 1968, three weeks before King was shot on a second-floor motel balcony in Memphis, Tennessee. At the time, McCall was director of the School of Religion at Morehouse College, and he was walking down a street in Atlanta near where King's Southern Christian Leadership Conference was based. From a distance, he saw ML approaching:

> He was walking down the street coming up to his office, and I noticed that he was coming alone. We greeted each other the way that we normally would. He said, "Mac, where are you going?" I said, "Don't ask me where am I going but where am I coming from." [Then] I said, "First of all, you've got no business being out here by yourself. Here you're walking down the street with not a single person with you." I said, "Fool, don't you know that you could get your darn head blown off?" And he laughed and we laughed. He said, "Shucks, man, even if I'm with somebody I could get my head blown off." He said, "Well, you don't worry about that." He passed it off lightly.[24]

The two men, now full-grown adults, wondered at this chance meeting, memories of the past flooding back. "It was at that time," McCall continued, "that he said, 'Man, we've got to get together. We haven't been together in a long time.' I said, 'OK, let's get together. Let's be in touch.'"

The two best friends went in opposite directions down the sidewalk. "That was the last time I saw him."

There was one other promise that ML had extracted from Mac, and it involved pool. Both men remembered so many nights in the catacombs of Old Main, playing pool and smoking cigarettes until three in the morning. "As a matter of fact," Mac said. "I was supposed to build

ML, now Dr. King, showing off the pool skills he developed in the catacombs of Crozer's Old Main during an "anti-slum" campaign in Chicago in February 1966. © Bettmann / Getty Images

him a pool table. . . . Of course, he died before I got a chance to build it for him."[25]

McCall passed away ten years later, in 1978.

After serving as ML's romantic rival, adviser, and debate partner, **Kenneth L. "Snuffy" Smith** became a lifelong public advocate of King's work. Snuffy remained at Crozer for the next four decades, even after the seminary relocated to Rochester, New York.

When it came to Betty, there were no hard feelings between the two men. By the end of 1953, Snuffy too had married someone else. He and his wife, Esther, shared a commitment to the cause of social justice. "We were both invited to marches during the '60s," she recalls.[26] In 1964, Snuffy decided to run for a seat in the Pennsylvania state legislature, competing as a Democrat against an opponent who had publicly rejected the idea of passing the Civil Rights Act. Snuffy was something of political unknown, so to bolster his chances, he contacted ML and asked if he could use a picture of him on one of his promotional flyers. ML agreed, and Smith passed them out around town. Unfortunately, he lost narrowly; according to Smith's recollection, he earned 102,500 votes to his opponent's 107,500, a margin of 49 percent to 51 percent.[27]

After King was assassinated, Professor Smith devoted himself to writing a book about the aspect of ML's life he knew best. *Search for the Beloved Community: The Thinking of Martin Luther King Jr.*, coauthored by Ira Zepp, was published in 1974. It still stands, decades later, as one of the deepest explorations of ML's theological influences.

But as committed as Smith was to documenting the philosophical underpinnings of King's work, he shared J. Pius Barbour and Marcus Wood's belief that history ought not lose sight of the man behind the message. While working on this book, I found myself returning to comments Smith made to that effect during a lecture in Rochester, New York, in the mid-1980s.

Kenneth Smith in June 1983.
Courtesy of Colgate Rochester Crozer Divinity School, Rochester, NY

At the time, Dr. King's legacy appeared to be in good shape. On November 2, 1983, President Ronald Reagan had signed a law designating Martin Luther King Day a federal holiday, which would first be celebrated on January 20, 1986. As he did so, Reagan praised Dr. King to the moon and back, saying of King's 1963 "I Have a Dream" speech in front of the Lincoln Memorial, "If American history grows from two centuries to twenty, his words that day will never be forgotten."[28]

Around the time Reagan made these remarks, Kenneth Smith was resting at home, on sabbatical from Colgate Rochester Crozer. Smith had listened to the Senate hearings regarding the Martin Luther King Day bill, bristling at the "asinine comments" by Senator Jesse Helms, who'd filibustered against the idea of honoring King with a holiday. Smith was also unmoved by Reagan's soaring words of praise—perhaps because Reagan had been reluctant to support the holiday as well, fretting about its tax implications all the way up to the day before he signed the bill.[29]

But what bothered him more about the lofty words commemorating the new holiday was that ML, his *friend* ("I would have trusted him with my life without thinking about it for a second"),[30] was being pushed into a two-dimensional form of immortality. Had ML's humanity already been forgotten, in less than two decades?

On January 15, 1986, Smith addressed a room full of King enthusiasts in Colgate Rochester Crozer's Bexley Hall. In five days, the first

Martin Luther King Day would be observed. Many in the audience were excited, but Rev. Smith had again been brooding. A few minutes into his talk, titled "The Radicalization of Martin Luther King Jr: The Last Five Years," he laid out his anxiety as plainly as a Baptist preacher could:

> Will the holiday be viewed as symbolic of the fact that King represented the brightest and the best of the American tradition of dissent in his struggle for social justice and peace, thus encouraging us to continue that struggle? Or will it assume simply a symbolic significance transcending its actual effect, thus turning King into just another irrelevant plastic hero, like Superman, perhaps to be sold at Christmastime, along with Rambo and Rocky. . . . I hope not, but I fear it will.[31]

You can hear the heaviness, the resignation, in Smith's voice when he says the words *I fear it will*. He could see the future, and he knew there was little he could do to avert it.

But he could speak out. As he continued, his southern drawl started to gain steam, and he told the crowd in front of him what would become of the young man with whom he'd once shot pool and smoked in the catacombs of Old Main:

> The King who will be eulogized will be the King of the March on Washington. . . . It is true that the "I Have a Dream" Speech was a rhetorical miracle, but it was not substantive. Nevertheless, this is the King who will be eulogized, because we [as a nation] have frozen Martin's feet to the steps of the Lincoln Memorial in 1963.[32]

Perhaps it was inevitable that King's legacy would lose its edges. Father Time gets us all—even those immortalized by history. But life resists being snuffed out without a fight. In this book, I've tried to push back against the deification, and offer as nuanced a view as possible of the young man King once was. "My brother," wrote Christine King, "was no saint, ordained as such at birth. Instead, he was an average and ordinary man, called by a God, in whom he had deep and abiding faith, to perform extraordinary deeds . . . for freedom, peace and justice. That, after all, is the best way each of us can celebrate Martin's life."[33]

The commemorative plaque currently on display outside Old Main on the former Crozer campus. This state marker, unveiled on July 27, 1992, was placed thanks in large part to the efforts of Chester resident Steven Evans.
Photo by the author

Appendix A
Crozer Incoming Class of 1948

Full Name	City	Previous Education	Notes
1. Edwin Alonzo Brooks	Alexandria, VA	BA Bucknell University 1948	Graduated with King in May 1951
2. Percy C. Carter	Spartanburg, SC	BA Benedict College 1948	Dropped out after year 2
3. Eugene Hildreth Drew	Rensselaer, NY	BA Alderson-Broaddus 1948	Graduated with King in May 1951
4. James Joseph Greene	Portsmouth, VA	BA University of Richmond 1949	Admitted conditionally; ended up graduating with King in 1951.
5. Lucius Z. Hall Jr.	Hartsville, SC	BA Mercer University 1948	Dropped out after year 1
6. Robert E. Hopkins	Scranton, PA	BA Alderson-Broaddus 1948	Dropped out after year 2

Full Name	City	Previous Education	Notes
7. Dupree Jordan	Atlanta, GA	BA Mercer University 1947	Dropped out after year 1
8. Martin Luther King	Atlanta, GA	BA Morehouse College 1948	Graduated May 1951
9. Joseph Timothy Kirkland	Philadelphia, PA	BA Virginia Union University 1948	Graduated with King May 1951
10. Wendall Atlas Maloch	Emerson, AR	BA Hillsdale College 1948	Graduated with King May 1951
11. Walter Raleigh McCall	Marion, SC	BA Morehouse College 1948	Graduated with King May 1951
12. Pierre S. Morgan	Philadelphia, PA	BA Virginia Union University 1948	Dropped out after year 1
13. Cyril George Pyle	Canal Zone, Panama	BA Virginia Union 1948	Graduated with King May 1951
* Nolton Woodrow Turner	Beach, VA	BA University of Richmond 1949	Joined class in year 2; withdrew temporarily in year 3; graduated May 1952
14. George T. Walton	St. Louis, MO	BA Shurtleff College 1948	Dropped out after year 2
15. Horace Edward Whitaker	Seaview, VA	BA Virginia Union 1948	Graduated with King May 1951
16. Marcus Garvey Wood	Charles Town, WV	BA Storer College 1948	Graduated with King May 1951

Appendix B
Events from ML's Student Body Presidency

Not much has been left behind regarding ML's work as Crozer's student body president. We know that he addressed the student body on several occasions and made sure the graduates of his class were given scarlet hoods. The most comprehensive information we have is for the two events below, which served as bookends to ML's year at the head of student government.[1]

Crozer Orientation Schedule

September 7, 8 & 9, 1950

Thursday, September 7	Friday, September 8	Saturday, September 9
Late Morning: Luncheon *Faculty and families welcome new students to the Crozer campus*	**9 AM:** Main Address *Dr. George W. Davis; topic: "Our Local Environment"*	**9:30 AM:** Devotions *Conducted by Dr. Raymond J. Bean.*
Early Afternoon: Addresses *Dean Charles E. Batten; Martin L. King, President of the Student Government Association*	**9:45 AM:** Information Session *Dr. Morton Scott Enslin; topic: "Responsibility for Academic Work"*	**9:45 AM:** Main Address *Professor Robert Keighton; topic: "The Crozer Heritage"*
4 PM: Psychological Tests	**10:30 AM:** Library Info *Edward Starr, librarian, explains the academic materials available on campus*	**10:30 AM:** Discussion *Moderated by Dean Charles E. Batten; topic: "As I See Crozer"*
6:30 PM: Dinner *Faculty and students, on campus*	**11:30 AM:** Devotions *Conducted by Dr. Raymond J. Bean*	**12:30 PM:** Luncheon
Around 7:30: Main Speaker *Rev. David MacQueen '44; topic: "What Crozer Has Meant to Me"*	**12:30 PM:** Luncheon *Following lunch, students are taken on a tour of Philadelphia*	**1:30 PM:** Tour of Valley Forge *"The entire student body of 60 men and women, representing 17 states and four foreign countries (Egypt, China, Japan and the Panama Canal Zone), will be taken on a tour and picnic at Valley Forge in charge of librarian Edward Starr"*

83rd Annual Commencement Exercises

May 6–8, 1951

Sunday, May 6	Monday, May 7	Tuesday, May 8
3:30 PM: In first-floor chapel of Old Main, Rev. Dr. Sankey L. Blanton delivers the baccalaureate speech *Theme: "The Cure for All Souls"* **4:30 PM:** Reception for the seniors. Located in the reception room of Old Main	**10:15 AM:** Annual Conference of Baptist Ministers of Philadelphia and Vicinity opens in the chapel *Main speaker: Dr. George D. Heaton, pastor from Charlotte, NC* **3:30 PM:** Alumni meet for a reunion. The Crozer classes 1901, '06, '11, '16, '21, '26, '31, '36, '41, and '46 are welcome **4 PM:** Sports and games **6 PM:** Alumni dinner. *Rev. R. Carrington Paulette, pastor from Mount Airy, NC; topic: "The Privileges of Sons"*	**10:30 AM:** Commencement Exercises begin inside Commencement Hall *Main speaker: Dr. Vernon B. Richardson, pastor of Baltimore's University Baptist Church; topic: "The Preacher's Heritage"* **12 PM:** Luncheon *Served in Old Main after formally leaving Commencement Hall*

Appendix C
A Brief History of the Crozers and Old Main

"I feel much of the vanity and deceit of riches. . . . To feel the utter worthlessness of riches and yet all the time to be making haste to be rich, is a strange feature in human nature, or, at least, in mine."

—John P. Crozer[1]

Samuel A. Crozer sat in his mother's parlor with his three brothers. It was November 2, 1866, and the topic of the day was how to best honor their father. John P. Crozer had passed away eight months ago, and before his death he'd requested his children turn the building on a hill he bequeathed to them into something of "benevolent use."[2] But the Crozer sons sat somewhat flummoxed as to how best to proceed.

Money wasn't an issue. Thanks to their father's entrepreneurial spirit, the family controlled a local cotton and textile empire, so they had enough resources and influence to turn any reasonable dream into a reality. The question was what dream to pursue: "What will be the best purpose to which the property can be applied?"[3] The cause of education had been on their minds, but if they did found a school, they wanted it to reflect the specific pursuits that defined their father's life.

Inevitably, the discussion turned toward religion. The sons were vividly aware of how invested their father had been in the Baptist faith. John P. Crozer's religious life started when he was baptized by a minister "in the Schuylkill River, near the Spruce Street wharf" at age fourteen in 1807.[4] The Schuylkill emptied out into the Delaware River, with which every resident of Chester was familiar. Throughout his life, Mr. Crozer reaffirmed his religious commitment by frequenting the First Baptist Church of Philadelphia, then attending Marcus Hook Baptist Church, and then, at this point a wealthy man, starting his own Upland Baptist Church, where he served as deacon.

As Crozer's sons conversed, it became clear that the best way to honor their father was to pay tribute to the faith he held so dear. "How can we make it tell most for the cause of Christ?"[5] They returned to an idea they'd first considered back in June, three months after their father passed: to found a theological seminary.

It would not be the first "benevolent use" to which John P. Crozer's building on a hill was dedicated. Situated on twenty-three acres, the structure that would eventually be called Old Main was erected in 1857 as one of many contributions Mr. Crozer made to the local community. Initially it functioned as a "normal school," where high school graduates

Postcard image of Old Main. *Courtesy of Kate Stier*

trained to become teachers. Unfortunately, the school was forced to close after three and a half years, due partially to a lack of enrollment but more because of a "succession of epidemics—small pox and scarlet fever."[6]

By the time the school closed, the United States was on the brink of the Civil War, and around 1861 the federal government made a deal with Mr. Crozer to turn the normal school and the surrounding area into a hospital for the military. Future Philadelphia City Hall architect John McArthur was hired to renovate and expand the building. McArthur's plan was for the hospital to have the ability to care for 945 patients. Its capacity was tested in early July 1863, however, when the Battle of Gettysburg claimed the lives of fifty thousand soldiers and injured tens of thousands more. Hospitals throughout the state were called on to care for the wounded, and Old Main found itself filled to the brim with seventeen hundred soldiers. So came the future ghosts of Old Main, who would be remembered through holes cut into dorm room doors and signatures scrawled on the walls of John McArthur's fourth-floor cupola.

A few of the hundreds of Civil War signatures scrawled across the cupola of the Old Main building. *Courtesy of Kate Stier*

By the time the war ended in 1865, Old Main was occupied by "two families and about one hundred students" enrolled at the Pennsylvania Military Academy.[7] But within a year, John P. Crozer had passed away, and in his memory the Crozer family was poised to sweep aside Old Main's connections to years of violent conflict and replace them with an institution emphasizing the teachings of peace.

By the end of that meeting in November 1866, the sons of John P. Crozer, led by Samuel, had firmly settled on establishing the Crozer Theological Seminary. They had also determined how to raise the funds to launch this ambitious venture. Among the four of them, with the help of their sister Margaret Knowles Crozer, they pooled their financial resources and made the following donations:

Buildings and grounds	$80,000
Cash for the erection of three houses for professors	$30,000
Cash for [lecture] endowment	$140,000
For library, by William Bucknell, Esq	$25,000
Total	$275,000[8]

The library had been Margaret's idea, and William Bucknell was her husband. Unfortunately, Margaret came down with tuberculosis right around the time of the founding. She passed away in 1870, at the age of forty-two. Her husband named the library building Pearl Hall in her honor, the name *Margaret* deriving from the Latin word for *pearl*.

Meanwhile, the Crozer family appointed Dr. Henry G. Weston as the seminary's first president and professor of pastoral duties. Dr. G. D. B. Pepper would accept the position of professor of Christian theology. Working together, these men and the Crozer family crafted a charter— a long and winding sentence that Martin Luther King Jr. would have frequently seen on the bulletins placed in his mailbox:

It is proposed to establish a Theological Seminary at Upland, Delaware County, Pennsylvania, under the auspices of the Baptist denomination, for the preparation of candidates for the sacred ministry, by providing them with thorough instruction in biblical, theological and other religious learning, by cultivating moral and religious affections and habits, and by training them in the practice of the various duties which devolve upon them as preachers, pastors and missionaries.[9]

In addition, they established a framework for the academic curriculum, dividing it into four categories: interpretation of the Bible, Christian theology, church history, and preaching and pastoral duties.

It's remarkable how true Crozer Theological Seminary remained to their charter and original curriculum. Even eighty years after the charter was written, when the Crozer sons who'd sat dreaming in their mother's parlor had long passed, Martin Luther King Jr. entered Crozer surrounded mainly by students with a Baptist background. Over time (to keep enrollment consistent) the school had come to welcome students from all Protestant denominations, but Crozer's heart was still immersed in the Baptist faith, just as John P. Crozer was immersed in the Schuylkill River, a fourteen-year-old just beginning to believe in something greater than himself.

Another connection between the Crozer of King's time and its foundational years was Samuel A. Crozer III, great-grandson of John P. Crozer, who served on the seminary's board of trustees for forty years. A fellow board member shared the following anecdote about him, which cannot be confirmed but is certainly plausible:

> In 1948, [Samuel Crozer] was making a routine visit to the Seminary when someone told him about an "unusual" student who had just enrolled. Sam inquired as to where the young man was staying, and after getting the information went to meet him. A few moments after knocking on the door, it was opened by a shy, husky man of about nineteen years of age. Mr. Crozer offered his hand and said, "My name is Crozer—what is yours?" The man responded, "My name is Martin Luther King."[10]

Samuel Crozer's position meant that he would also have shaken Martin Luther King Jr.'s hand when he graduated from the seminary in May 1951—no longer a timid, young man, but a confident leader of a class of seminarians, on a path toward righteousness.

Dr. James Beshai, or "Jimmy from Egypt," standing next to the Old Main sign inside the Crozer-Keystone Medical Center, sixty-five years after graduating from Crozer Theological Seminary. *Photo by the author*

Acknowledgments

The journey of this book started on the third floor of the Bellevue Public Library in Bellevue, Washington, in December 2012. I'd been working on a project about the lives of historical figures in their early twenties. I'd selected forty people, and when I started researching Martin Luther King Jr., I was surprised to find that even though there had been hundreds of books about Dr. King's life, not one focused primarily on his young adult life prior to the Montgomery bus boycott. Realizing I didn't have enough information to complete an in-depth portrait, I started digging into the endnotes of books such as *Bearing the Cross* and *Parting the Waters*. I checked archive centers and started to search for people still with us who knew King as a young man. After a year or so, I became hooked, and started to feel a sense of responsibility to provide a reliable picture of King before the bus boycott made him famous.

A massive thank-you to Yuval Taylor and Devon Freeny at Lawrence Hill Books / Chicago Review Press, who believed in this book and weren't afraid to take it on. Their feedback, patience, and considerate nature has made this a far better book than at first submission.

Dr. James "Jimmy" Beshai was not startled in the least when I called him in May 2015. His memory, at ninety, inspires me to no end, and his insights and recollections helped me to understand the culture of Crozer during ML's time there. The trip Dr. Beshai and I took to Old Main in Chester was revelatory as well. What's more, Jimmy is an incredibly intelligent and gracious human being.

Another big thank-you to Betty Moitz, who through our various forms of correspondence and interview gave me a clear understanding of her relationship with King. We wouldn't have been able to meet had it not been for the miraculous help of Erin Fletcher and Rev. Brewster Hastings.

I'd also like to thank Rev. Samuel McKinney, who allowed me to come to his home in December 2014 and talk about King's life at Morehouse and how he changed at Crozer.

Deacon Myrtha Allen of Providence Baptist Church was an immense help when it came to restoring the Crozer graduation photo—possibly the only one still in existence. In addition, it was a pleasure talking with Rev. Marcus Garvey Wood over the phone.

Other people I had the good fortune of talking with—Joe Thomasberger, Esther Smith, Jack Bullard, June Dobbs Butts, Dorothy Tasker (wife of Crozer seminarian Bill Tasker), Charles V. Willie, and Horace Whitaker Jr.—all helped to bring the world of Crozer back to life.

If you look through the endnotes, you'll see immediately the amount I owe to past historians. Taylor Branch's interview notes held at UNC–Chapel Hill were helpful in fleshing out many of King's former classmates. David Garrow's audio interviews were vital to my writing process, because the moment I began *hearing* the former classmates of King was when I decided to commit fully to the "Crozer project." For Garrow's kind and generous spirit, I cannot thank him enough.

I'm also grateful for the financial support of Artist Trust, a Washington State–based nonprofit arts organization that very generously awarded me a fellowship in May 2014, which I promptly used for travel expenses around the Chester/Philadelphia area. Their support was crucial in allowing me to pursue the Crozer research that is now in this book. Bottom line: Artist Trust saved the project.

Researcher and civil rights activist Patrick Duff was an incredible help with the "Summer of 1950" interlude. He has done great work regarding the home at 753 Walnut Street. Also, I want to thank Zilan Taymour, for her help in providing access to hard copies of the Crozer catalogs.

Thanks to my wonderful, stupendously intelligent, and hilarious uncle, Rev. Michael Frank, pastor of Brodway Christian Church in Cleveland, Ohio, for forty-one years. Rev. Frank read an early draft of this book and offered page-by-page commentary, making sure I described the classes of a seminarian correctly. His feedback, especially on the class discussions, was extremely helpful.

Thank you to my mother, for allowing me to borrow the car and drive across Pennsylvania in pursuit of people to interview. And my brother, Sean, for allowing me to crash in Manchester while rummaging through archives at Boston U. And my father, for helping me to dream up projects this large.

A big thank-you to Kate Stier, for allowing a strange, nomadic writer to tour Old Main in late August 2014, and again in January 2016. Also thanks to Rev. Bayard Taylor of Calvary Baptist Church, for providing me with insight (and lunch!) during my visit to Chester.

Special thanks to Tenisha Armstrong, David Lai, and Clayborne Carson at the King Papers Project at Stanford University, for helping to track down an interview, information about photographs, and other archival material. In addition, thanks to Sean Noel and Ryan Hendrickson at Boston University's Howard Gotlieb Archival Research Center and Tim Hogdon at the Louis Round Wilson Library at UNC–Chapel Hill for helping me to navigate their archives.

Colin Ainsworth at the *Delaware County Daily Times* helped provide clear pictures of King and his professors. Margaret Johnson of the Delaware County Historical Society helped track down photos as well. Thanks to both of you.

A bowing thank you to the King Center in Atlanta, for providing me with the Walter McCall transcript. In addition, the King Center Digital Archives were extremely helpful when I couldn't manage, due to either time, finances, or both, to visit the King Center in person. Tim Horning at the University of Pennsylvania Archives was the archivist every writer dreams of working with, and helped with King's grad-level classes at UPenn.

Wayne Watson's wonderful pencil sketches of King provided me with even more inspiration to finish the manuscript. His talents deserve their own book.

To Allan Harley and Mark Marino, two of the greatest friends anyone could ask for. Thank you for helping me fight back against the yawning darkness.

During the research and writing of this book, I was a member of the faculty at the University of Washington–Seattle, and also the USC International Academy. Their campus libraries and ILL departments helped with tracking down hard-to-find documents and recordings.

The following people deserve far more than this paragraph for their friendship and support over these past few years: Jennifer Bardi, Aaron Bidelspach, Nate Brown, Rob Dougherty, Michael Garnett, Hirofumi Goto, Noriyoshi Goto, Bernardo Gonzalez, Kyle Hogan, W. H. Horner, Mary Jo Jennings, John Katunich, Michael Laib, Avi Lidgi, Phil Lynch, Marina Rakhlin, Ben Stubbings, Jessica Warman, Carl Withers, and others dancing in the ether. *Thank you.*

Finally, I would like to thank my wife, Yuka, for her never-ending love and support, and our endless conversations. You are my light. *Alla belliſſima & leggiadra Madonna.*

Notes

Foreword by David J. Garrow

1. Garrow, *Bearing the Cross*, 638n26.
2. Ibid., 40–41.

Note to the Reader

1. Garrow, *Bearing the Cross*, 20.

Prologue: On a Bus in Georgia

1. King, interview by Haley.
2. Ibid.
3. Title of ML's speech confirmed by both King, *Papers*, 1:109; and Garrow, *Bearing the Cross*, 35. Hiram Kendall's involvement from "Savannah Girl Is Winner of Elks Oratorical Meet," *Atlanta Daily World*, April 22, 1944; Sarah Grace Bradley's from Reddick, *Crusader Without Violence*. See also "Contest Winner," *Atlanta Daily World*, April 16, 1944, which is the source of the photo reprinted in the text.
4. "Savannah Girl," *Atlanta Daily World*.
5. The first three chapters of Reddick, *Crusader Without Violence*, helped with roles of ML's parents, as did other biographies such as Lewis, *King*; and Garrow, *Bearing the Cross*; and early reports from New York Post journalist Ted Poston.
6. The official timekeeper, whose name was H. H. Dudley, was mentioned in "Savannah Girl," *Atlanta Daily World*.

7. King's speech was later published in Booker T. Washington High School's annual publication *The Cornellian*, May 1944.

8. Ibid.

9. Ibid.

10. Results officially reported in "Savannah Girl," *Atlanta Daily World*.

11. Quotes from King, interview by Haley.

12. Cannon, "Martin Luther King, Jr.," 211.

13. Ibid.

14. ML's quote is reprinted in Garrow, *Bearing the Cross*, 637. It's originally from Peters, "Our Weapon Is Love," 72.

15. Daddy King's self-description is from King Sr., *Daddy King*, 9.

16. ML's Simsbury letters, five in total, are collected in King, *Papers*, 1:111–117.

17. ML's quote is in ibid. The choir director's memories were reported in Swift, "King's Summers in State."

18. Pickens quote is from Wood, "Blacks Recall Connecticut Tobacco Farms." This 1989 *Journal Inquirer* article was the first in a major newspaper to discuss ML's experience in Simsbury, while Mike Swift's 1991 *Hartford Courant* article, cited previously, was the second. ML's quote is from King, *Papers*, 1:117.

19. King, *Papers*, 1:112. A handwritten copy of the letter appears in the volume as well.

20. Swift, "King's Summers in State."

21. This schedule is based on Wood, "Blacks Recall Connecticut Tobacco Farms," and Swift, "King's Summers in State," as well as an excellent documentary, *Summers of Freedom: The Story of Martin Luther King, Jr. in Connecticut* (January 2011), produced by students at Simsbury High School.

22. Swift, "King's Summers in State."

23. Ibid.

24. Farris, *Through It All*, 38.

25. King Sr., *Daddy King*, 128.

26. "Bitter feeling" is from Ted Poston, "Fighting Pastor: Martin Luther King," *New York Post*, April 10, 1957, quoted in King, *Papers*, 1:117. "Curtain had dropped" is as remembered in Coretta Scott King, *My Life*, 85.

27. Ted Poston, "Martin Luther King Jr. Didn't Want to be a Preacher!," *New York Post*, reprinted in *Baltimore Afro-American*, June 22, 1957.

28. For information on the murder of Maceo Snipes, see "Maceo Snipes," Georgia Civil Rights Cold Cases Project, August 15, 2014, https://scholarblogs.emory.edu/emorycoldcases/maceo-snipes/. For more on the Moore's Ford Bridge lynching, see Peter C. Baker, "A Lynching in Georgia," *Guardian*, November 2, 2016.

29. ML's full "Kick Up Dust" letter can be found in King, *Papers*, 1:121.

30. The Simsbury Historical Society verified ML's return trip to the tobacco farms in 1947, but there are no known letters written by ML during that summer.

31. "Laziest workers" from Emmett Proctor, notes from taped interview, April 15, 1970, Taylor Branch Papers, Southern Historical Collection, Louis Round Wilson Library, University of North Carolina, Chapel Hill, NC. ML's prank, called "the hot foot," in Wood, "Blacks Recall Connecticut Tobacco Farms."

32. Wood, "Blacks Recall Connecticut Tobacco Farms."

33. Ibid.

34. ML wrote these words for an article titled "The Purpose of Education" in the *Maroon Tiger*, Morehouse's campus newspaper, in January–February 1947. The full text appears in King, *Papers*, 1:123–124.

35. Ibid., 125.

36. Barbour's 1936 graduation from Crozer was first mentioned in Among Our Colored Citizens, *Chester Times*, May 21, 1936. According to a short article in the *Times* on November 13, 1945, Barbour also visited the Morehouse campus to talk with undergraduates during the fall of ML's second year.

37. ML's entire Crozer application can be found in King, *Papers*, 1:142–145.

38. King, *Stride Toward Freedom*, 91.

Year I: Genesis

1. Young and Alone: Term 1, September 14–November 24, 1948

1. King, "Loving Your Enemies" (sermon, Dexter Avenue Baptist Church, November 17, 1957), collected in *Papers*, 4:318.

2. ML's room number was confirmed by the National Register of Historic Places Inventory. Description of the dorm room was taken from Crozer, *Annual Catalogue* 41, no. 1 (January 1949).

3. Proctor, *The Substance of Things Hoped For*, 46–47.

4. Peters, "Our Weapon Is Love," 41–42, 72–73.

5. Student places of origin found in Crozer, *Annual Catalogue* 41, no. 1 (January 1949).

6. Enrollment count in ibid. The count includes "unclassified" students (those who had not yet finished their four-year degree) and international students participating in the school's "Oriental certificate" program.

7. Wood, notes from interview by Branch.

8. An excellent description of this "white transformation" can be found in Wood, *And Grace Will Lead Me Home*, 43.

9. Hall's hometown was confirmed in Crozer, *Annual Catalogue* 41, no. 1 (January 1949).

10. Hall's service as an infantry lieutenant is from Stewart, notes from interview by Branch. "Just couldn't take a joke" is from Stewart, interview by Garrow.

11. Stewart, interview by Garrow.

12. Whitaker, interview by Garrow. The nickname "Whit" appears in letters written between Whitaker and King, a few of which appear in full in King, *Papers*, 2:86, 100. (Volume 2 of the *Papers* contains the post-Crozer correspondence between King and Whitaker, Rev. Barbour, and Walter McCall, among others.)

13. Pyle, interview by Garrow.

14. "Three flights of stairs" was determined after I visited the Old Main building in late August 2014. Earliest recorded mention of the "catacombs" nickname is in Kenneth Smith, remarks at Martin Luther King Day celebration (Bexley Hall, Colgate Rochester Crozer Divinity School, Rochester, NY, 1979), cassette. Smith also declared the basement "the dungeon."

15. The detail of Hall's furniture being placed outside the building came from Moitz, correspondence with the author, September 2014–February 2016.

16. ML's allowance is confirmed in a letter from ML to his mother, Alberta: "So far I have gotten the money (5 dollars) every week." King, *Papers*, 1:161.

17. Many of the details regarding the Hall incident were found in Wood, *And Grace Will Lead Me Home*; and Wood, interview by Garrow.

18. Wood, *And Grace Will Lead Me Home*. Hall's one-year enrollment indicated by his inclusion in Crozer, *Annual Catalogue* 41, no. 1 (January 1949), and not the subsequent volumes.

19. All three letters of recommendation can all be found in their entirety in King, *Papers*, 1:151–155.

20. ML's daily class schedule was reconstructed by collating his transcript (available at the King Center Digital Archive, www.thekingcenter.org/archive/document/mlks-transcript-crozer-theological-seminary) with the course titles and schedules listed in Crozer, *Annual Catalogue* 40, no. 1 (January 1948). His GPA was computed using current academic calculation methods (e.g., B = 3.0), weighted by credit hours. For those interested in additional scheduling details, on September 18, 1948, the *Chester Times* published the following list of the term's vespers speakers. September 23: Robert L. Schock, Army and Air Force Chaplain in the Carlisle Barracks, Carlisle, PA. September 30: Dr. Rittenhouse Neisser, Professor Emeritus, Crozer. October 7: Dr. Maynard L. Cassady, Applied Christianity Professor, Crozer. October 14: Dr. Albert C. Outler, Theology Professor, Yale Seminary. October 21: Dr. Patrick M. Malin, Economics Professor, Swarthmore College. October 28: Dr. James B. Pritchard, Old Testament Professor, Crozer. November 4: Observance of the Isaac Watts Bicentennial (Watts, an English poet and hymn writer, wrote "Joy to the World" and "When I

Survey the Wondrous Cross"). November 11: Dr. Herbert Haslam, Religious Administrator, Fellowship House, Philadelphia. November 18: Dr. Morton S. Enslin. New
Testament Professor, Crozer.

21. Background information from Pritchard's obituary, *New York Times*, January 19,
1997, www.nytimes.com/1997/01/19/us/james-pritchard-87-a-biblical-archeologist
.html.

22. Thomasberger, interview by the author.

23. Pritchard, notes from interview by Branch, June 25, 1984. Not all of Pritchard's black
students entered Crozer with fundamentalist views; Rev. Samuel D. Proctor, who
graduated from Crozer several years before ML, clearly understood what the Crozer
faculty was trying to accomplish: "In the hands of the fundamentalists, Christianity
had become an embarrassment to Jesus." Proctor, *The Substance of Things Hoped
For*, 48.

24. Pritchard, notes from interview by Branch, June 25, 1984.

25. "O.T." abbreviation mentioned in, among others, J. Pius Barbour, letter to King,
December 21, 1954, in King, *Papers*, 2:322: "No man in 'O.T.' yet." Daddy King's
Make it plain dictum was mentioned in Coretta Scott King, *My Life*, 8.

26. King, *Papers*, 1:161.

27. Pritchard, notes from interview by Branch, June 25, 1984.

28. Grades found in folder 703, p. 109, Taylor Branch Papers, Southern Historical Collection, Louis Round Wilson Library, University of North Carolina, Chapel Hill, NC.
The quote is from Pritchard, notes from interview by Branch, June 29, 1984.

29. See Thelen, ed., *Journal of American History* 78, for a roundtable discussion about
King's plagiarism.

30. King, *Papers*, 1:181–195

31. James B. Pritchard to Coretta Scott King, February 22, 1987, quoted in King, *Papers*,
1:162. See also Pritchard, notes from interview by Branch, June 25, 1984: "We knew
[King] best as a babysitter. We paid 35 cents an hour to babysit with our girls."

32. I mapped out King's campus options during my August 2014 and January 2016 visits
to Old Main, with help from Crozer, *Annual Catalogue* 40, no. 1 (January 1948). "He
was a normal human being" is from Whitaker, interview by Garrow.

33. E. E. Aubrey, "Junior Orientation Outline," folder 33, box 2, Edwin E. Aubrey Papers,
courtesy of University Archives & Records Center, University of Pennsylvania,
Philadelphia.

34. "Stern and unyielding" in Whitaker, interview by Garrow. "Stern" again and "Dumbest class" in Wood, *And Grace Will Lead Me Home*, 45. Wood added, "Dr. Aubrey
informed us that we would certainly have to study more, if we hoped to graduate. He
kept pointing out that Crozer was a 'high-class' school, and that he intended to keep
it that way . . . an attitude that seemed to be contradicted, only two months later,

when he resigned his post and took a position at the University of Pennsylvania." Ibid., 45–46.

35. Pritchard, notes from interview by Branch, June 25, 1984.

36. Aubrey, "Junior Orientation Outline."

37. Date of Cassady's death reported in Crozer, *Annual Catalogue* 41, no. 1 (January 1949). A front-page obituary in the *Chester Times*, October 25, 1948, mentioned Cassady's illness, which had lasted several months. In it, Aubrey called Cassady "one of the most outstanding men in his field in the country." The test was penciled in on Aubrey's "Junior Orientation Outline."

38. ML's grade can be found on his Crozer transcript, available at the King Center Digital Archive, www.thekingcenter.org/archive/document/mlks-transcript -crozer-theological-seminary.

39. Proctor, *The Substance of Things Hoped For*, 51.

40. Ibid.

41. First published by the *Crozer Quarterly* in 1948, then later included in Keighton, *The Man Who Would Preach*, 121–126.

42. Lawrence, notes from interview by Branch. Rev. George Lawrence was a student of Keighton's, a year behind King. Keighton told Lawrence directly that professors chided him about knowing Shakespeare better than the Bible.

43. Smith, notes from interview by Branch. It's clear Kenneth Smith disliked Keighton; he said the professor's courses wouldn't have helped King because they didn't help him.

44. This is the impression left by Keighton's *The Man Who Would Preach*, in which he consistently urges ministers to improve their status and find ways of increasing dignity.

45. Beshai, correspondence with the author, January 17, 2016.

46. "Product of his environment" is from Warren, *King Came Preaching*, 31. "Little evidence" is from Frank Galey and Jack Hopkins, "'He Had Very Definite Feeling About Rights,'" *Delaware County Daily Times*, April 5, 1968.

47. King, *Papers*, 6:72.

48. Wood, *And Grace Will Lead Me Home*, 47.

49. Exact location of the chapel confirmed on my August 2014 visit to Old Main.

50. Lischer, *The Preacher King*, 26, does an excellent job describing the life of MLK as a "PK," or preacher's kid.

51. Hoopes, correspondence with the author.

52. "Crozer Seminary Holds Candlelight Service Tuesday," *Chester Times*, December 19, 1949.

53. Hoopes, correspondence with the author. "Text painting" could also be used to describe the way a preacher modulates his or her voice. When attempting to uplift or energize an audience, his or her vocal pitch will scale upward. When attempting to discuss death and sadness, his or her voice will soften and scale down.

54. Reddick, *Crusader Without Violence*, 3, indicates that King "did quite a bit of walking during seminary."

55. Barbour, "A Defense of the Negro Preacher," in Reid, *The Negro Baptist Ministry*, 13–14.

56. Whitaker, interview by Garrow.

57. "One of my sons" is in Galey and Hopkins, "'He Had Very Definite Feeling.'" "He could eat more" is from Lewis, *King*, 28. "Full of fun" is included in King, *Papers*, 1:161–162.

58. Lischer, *The Preacher King*, 67–71, does a great job describing King's relationship with Barbour. It is also where the term "Barbour University" (coined by Crozer students) first appears in print.

59. Glen Justice, "Chester Remembers a Minister's Minister," *Philadelphia Inquirer*, August 7, 1994.

60. Galey and Hopkins, "'He Had Very Definite Feeling.'"

61. Whitaker, interview by Garrow. Whitaker also mentions how King would come over to his place to talk.

62. Gandhi discussions mentioned both by Horace Whitaker and Marcus Wood in their interviews by Garrow.

63. The *a matter of arithmetic* sentiment was conveyed by Barbour in the *National Baptist Voice*, March 1956, and is quoted in King, *Papers*, 3:16–17.

64. *Pennsylvania Remembers Dr. King* (video, Commonwealth Media Services, 1991), available online via Pennsylvania Historical and Museum Commission, YouTube, January 19, 2016, www.youtube.com/watch?v=nLQiJNBI_6Q. This twenty-minute video spotlights Professor Kenneth L. "Snuffy" Smith and the Barbour family, among others.

65. One example of his commentary in the *Chester Times* was a letter to the editor from July 31, 1948, in which he spoke out in favor of economic justice: "The truth of the matter is that we have reached a state in our economy where our old ideas of laissez-faire and the law of supply and demand are entirely outmoded." Barbour's salary is mentioned in Lischer, *The Preacher King*, 68.

66. *Pennsylvania Remembers Dr. King* (video).

67. ML's letter to his mother is from October 1948, and is collected in King, *Papers*, 1:161.

68. Peters, "Our Weapon Is Love," 72

69. "Charles Turney Remembers Martin Luther King" *Dispatch*, January 16, 1991. Turney would end up becoming a professor at Catawba College in Salisbury, NC.

2. Breaking Free: Term 2, November 30, 1948–February 16, 1949

1. McCall, transcript of interview by Holmes.

2. Ted Poston, "He Never Liked to Fight!," *New York Post*, reprinted in *Baltimore Afro-American*, June 15, 1957.

3. Quotes in this paragraph and background in the opening paragraphs in McCall, transcript of interview by Holmes.

4. Ibid.

5. Daddy King's reputation was also mentioned by Marcus Wood, in interviews and his book *And Grace Will Lead Me Home*.

6. In both Whitaker's and Wood's interviews by Garrow, the men recounted very clearly the constant life struggles of Walter McCall, the man who just couldn't seem to catch a break. *In spite of my ailments* is a McCall quote recalled in Wood, notes from interview by Branch.

7. Whitaker, notes from interview by Branch.

8. McCall, transcript of interview by Holmes. Mac quotes the song's lyrics during the interview.

9. Dr. Lloyd Burrus, "The King's Daughter," *New York Amsterdam News*, July 13, 1974. The article was released a week after ML's mother was shot to death while playing the organ at Ebenezer.

10. Moitz, correspondence with the author, September 2014–February 2016, and interview by the author, January 4, 2016. Information on Eddystone High School was confirmed via "95 Awarded Diplomas at Eddystone Graduation," *Chester Times*, June 7, 1946.

11. Moitz, e-mail correspondence with the author, November 2, 2014.

12. Moitz, e-mail correspondence with the author, October 3, 2014.

13. Wood, interview by Garrow.

14. ML's daily class schedule was reconstructed by collating his transcript (available at the King Center Digital Archive, www.thekingcenter.org/archive/document/mlks-transcript-crozer-theological-seminary) with the course titles and schedules listed in Crozer, *Annual Catalogue* 40, no. 1 (January 1948). His GPA was computed using current academic calculation methods (e.g., B = 3.0), weighted by credit hours.

15. Warren, *King Came Preaching*, 31. Warren interviewed Enslin on March 7, 1966.

16. Thomasberger, interview by the author. Joe Thomasberger entered Crozer the fall after King graduated and had the pleasure of learning from Pritchard and Enslin back to back. In interviews Pritchard and Enslin are often spoken of in the same sentence.

17. Lawrence, notes from interview by Branch.

18. Pritchard, notes from interview by Branch, June 25, 1984. Trustee quote is from Tasker, interview by the author. Dorothy Tasker was married to William Robert "Bill" Tasker, a former classmate of King's, two years behind. Dorothy Tasker served as the president and a member of the Crozer board of trustees.

19. Pritchard, notes from interview by Branch, June 25, 1984; Tasker, interview by the author.

20. Beshai, correspondence with the author, September 10, 2016.

21. Beshai, interview with the author.

22. King, *Papers*, 1:195–209.

23. Reddick, *Crusader Without Violence*, 79.

24. Wood, notes from interview by Branch.

25. King, *Papers*, 6:84

26. Taylor Branch laid out a variety of sermon styles in Branch, *Parting the Waters*, 76–77.

27. Assembled from material in King, *Papers*, 6:80–85.

28. Glen Justice, "Chester Remembers a Minister's Minister," *Philadelphia Inquirer*, August 7, 1994.

29. Dan Hardy, "Recalling Their Friend, Dr. King," *Philadelphia Inquirer*, January 14, 1990. Biographical background on Barbour is from Betty Hibbert, "J. Pius Barbour Has Preached at Church 31 Years," *Delaware County Daily Times*, February 22, 1964.

30. King, *Papers*, 6:80.

31. Wood, *And Grace Will Lead Me Home.*

32. Lischer, *The Preacher King*, 69. Lischer found the quoted text in the Boston University archives "on the inside cover of one of his class notebooks." Lischer suggests that ML should have been focusing on Aquinas and Augustine when he scribbled his note, which probably means it was written during Davis's Great Theologians class.

33. Reddick, *Crusader Without Violence*, 15.

34. King, *Papers*, 6:103.

35. Smith, notes from interview by Branch, November 3, 1983.

36. Reddick, *Crusader Without Violence*, 79.

37. "Most beautiful spot in Chester" was related most directly in Tasker, interview by the author. Chevy "Power Glide" is from Whitaker, notes from interview by Branch.

38. Garrow, *Bearing the Cross*, 41.

39. Dupree Jordan, "Pride Worse Foe Than Reds, Theologian Says," *Chester Times*, December 13, 1948.

40. Garrow, *Bearing the Cross*, 40.

41. Ibid.

42. Jordan, "Pride Worse Foe Than Reds."

43. Farris, *Through It All*, 46

44. Ibid., 45, 48.

45. Ibid., 49

46. Mac's recollections, like most of Mac's words in this book, came from McCall, transcript of interview by Holmes. "Eating is my great sin" can be found in Reddick, *Crusader Without Violence*, 3.

47. Farris, *Through It All*, 49.

48. Stone, notes from interview by Branch.

49. Wood, interview by Garrow.

50. Moitz, interview by the author, January 3, 2016, and e-mail correspondence with the author, October 3, 2014.

3. Finding a Voice: Term 3, February 22–May 6, 1949

1. Untitled article, *Chester Times*, February 26, 1949.

2. A version of this sermon is included in King, *Papers*, 6:88–90. The book speculates that King delivered it on March 3, pointing to a reference in the text to boxer Joe Louis retiring "two nights ago," but this was likely a preliminary reference based on the date when King was *writing* that part of the sermon. My assumption that he gave the sermon on March 9 is based on a newspaper account (Helen Hunt Reports, *Chester Times*, March 9, 1949) that names "Rev. Martin L. King" as the speaker at a Calvary event that day.

3. Farris, *Through It All*, 45.

4. Maya Angelou, *I Know Why the Caged Bird Sings* (New York: Random House, 2015; orig. publ. 1969), 32.

5. King, *Papers*, 6:88–90.

6. *Pennsylvania Remembers Dr. King* (video, Commonwealth Media Services, 1991), available online via Pennsylvania Historical and Museum Commission, YouTube, January 19, 2016, www.youtube.com/watch?v=nLQiJNBI_6Q.

7. Linn Washington, "Dr. Martin L. King's Battles Against Racial Discrimination Began in Philadelphia Region," *Philadelphia Tribune*, January 17, 1997. Washington wrote some wonderful annual tributes to Dr. King throughout the 1990s.

8. *Pennsylvania Remembers Dr. King* (video).

9. ML's daily class schedule was reconstructed by collating his transcript (available at the King Center Digital Archive, www.thekingcenter.org/archive/document/mlks -transcript-crozer-theological-seminary) with the course titles and schedules listed

in Crozer, *Annual Catalogue* 40, no. 1 (January 1948). His GPA was computed using current academic calculation methods (e.g., B = 3.0), weighted by credit hours.

10. Keighton, *The Man Who Would Preach*, 13

11. Pritchard, notes from interview by Branch, June 25, 1984.

12. *Pennsylvania Remembers Dr. King* (video).

13. Enslin, *Christian Beginnings*, 373–388.

14. Ibid.

15. Ibid.

16. Enslin, recommendation letter for ML, collected in King, *Papers*, 1:382.

17. Toyohiko Kagawa, *Kagawa in Lincoln's Land*, edited by Emerson O. Bradshaw, Charles E. Shike, and Helen F. Topping (New York: National Kagawa Co-ordinating Committee, 1936), https://archive.org/stream/kagawainlincolns00kaga.

18. Ibid.

19. R. Schildgen, "How Race Mattered: Kagawa Toyohiko in the United States," *Journal of American–East Asian Relations* 5, no. 3/4 (Fall–Winter 1996): 227–253, via JSTOR, www.jstor.org/stable/23612675.

20. Keighton, *The Man Who Would Preach*, 50.

21. Ibid., 46.

22. Crozer's *Annual Catalogue* editions for 1948–1951 (vols. 40–43) detail the amenities of Old Main, such as the tennis court. Many seminarians mentioned their pool, Ping-Pong, and shuffleboard games during interviews.

23. King, *Papers*, 6:594

24. Ibid., 105–106

25. Ibid.

26. Ibid.

Year II: Exodus

4. A New Devotion: Term 1, September 13–November 23, 1949

1. King, *Papers*, 2:322.

2. McKinney, interview by the author.

3. Barbour, "A Defense of the Negro Preacher," in Reid, *The Negro Baptist Ministry*, 13–14.

4. All of the sermons in this section can be found in King, *Papers*, 6:90, 94, and 97.

5. Stewart, interview by Garrow.

6. Smith's quote is from "Dr. H. W. Smith Appointed Interim President at Crozer," *Chester Times*, May 10, 1949. The description of Smith comes from Wood, *And Grace Will Lead Me Home*; and Wood, notes from interview by Branch.

7. The descriptions of Sakurabayashi and En-Chin Lin are from Stewart, notes from interview by Branch. Lin's educational info comes from the University of Pennsylvania commencement catalogs for June 1949 and February 1955, courtesy of the University of Pennsylvania Archives. En-Chin Lin ended up earning his doctorate from UPenn in 1955, with a dissertation titled "Educational Changes in China Since the Establishment of the People's Republic and Some Steps Leading to Them." Most of Crozer's previous international students had also come from China, including three Chinese students who completed their Oriental certificates in May 1949: Dorothy Lei Hsu (Foochow), Yu-En Hsu (Foochow), and Matthew Pek-Lok Wai (Shanghai). Crozer, *Annual Catalogue* 42, no. 1 (January 1950): 40, 43.

8. Stark, interview by Garrow.

9. Ibid.

10. Stewart, interview by Garrow.

11. The program can be found at the King Center Digital Archive, www.thekingcenter .org/archive/document/crozer-theological-seminary-student-chapel-order-service . King was listed as the Devotions Committee Chairman in Crozer, *Annual Catalogue* 42, no. 1 (January 1950).

12. King, *Papers*, 6:106.

13. Davis, *Existentialism and Theology*, 80–81.

14. Whitaker, notes from interview by Branch; see also Whitaker, interview by Garrow.

15. Horace Whitaker mentioned that Mac and Davis crushed apples in the fall. Whitaker, notes from interview by Branch.

16. ML's daily class schedule was reconstructed by collating his transcript (available at the King Center Digital Archive, www.thekingcenter.org/archive/document /mlks-transcript-crozer-theological-seminary) with the course titles and schedules listed in Crozer, *Annual Catalogue* 41, no. 1 (January 1949). His GPA was computed using current academic calculation methods (e.g., B = 3.0), weighted by credit hours. For those interested in additional scheduling details, on September 12, 1949, the *Chester Times* published the following list of vespers speakers. September 15: Charles E. Batten, Dean of Students, Crozer. September 22: Dr. Frederick K. Stamm, Congregational Minister and Host of NBC Radio's *Highlights of the Bible*. September 29: Dr. E. Felix Kloman, Minister, Christ Church, Philadelphia. October 6: Dr. Morton S. Enslin, New Testament Professor, Crozer. October 13: Rev. Mervin A. Heller, Executive Secretary, Reading Council of Churches, Reading, PA. October 20: Dr. George W. Davis, Christian Theology Professor, Crozer. October 27: Rev. Thomas E. Ellis, Minister, Grace Baptist Church, Belleville, NJ. November 3: Dr. Reuben E. E. Harkness, Church History Professor, Crozer. November 10: Rev. R. Stuart Grizzard,

Minister, Orange Baptist Church, Orange, VA. Nov. 17: Edward C. Starr, Curator, American Baptist Historical Society, Crozer. December 8: Dr. James B. Pritchard, Old Testament Professor, Crozer.

17. "Pleas for Deeper Theology Made at Crozer Session," *Chester Times*, September 13, 1950. Davis also discussed Christian theology in this manner with new students during the 1949 September orientation.

18. King, *Papers*, 1:232.

19. Keighton, *The Man Who Would Preach*, 81.

20. Barbour, "A Defense of the Negro Preacher," in Reid, *The Negro Baptist Ministry*, 13–14.

21. Helen Hunt Reports, *Chester Times*, October 22, 1949. The service took place the next day, October 23.

22. Barbour, "A Defense of the Negro Preacher," in Reid, *The Negro Baptist Ministry*, 13–14.

23. Crozer, *Annual Catalogue* 42, no. 1 (January 1950).

24. King, *Papers*, 1:211–224.

25. Quoted in ibid., 211.

26. From a paper for George Davis, collected in King, *Papers*, 1:234.

27. William Moitz's death was reported in an obituary in the *Chester Times*, May 9, 1949.

28. Moitz, correspondence with the author, September 2014–February 2016, and interview by the author, January 3, 2016.

29. The poll can be found on Gallup's website, www.gallup.com/poll/117328/marriage.aspx. The book *Interracialism*, a collection of essays edited by Werner Sollors (Oxford University Press, 2000), helped with the history.

30. Pyle, interview by Garrow.

31. Moitz, correspondence with the author, and interview by the author.

32. Ibid. ML also shared his torment with Horace Whitaker, as indicated in Whitaker, interview by Garrow, and notes from interview by Branch.

33. Stark, interview by Garrow. The quote comes from Walter Stark's wife, who joined her husband's interview.

34. Pyle, interview by Garrow.

5. Mordecai's Fire: Term 2, November 29, 1949–February 15, 1950

1. King, *Papers*, 1:272.

2. Ibid., 4:475.

3. "Truman, Pope Appeal for World Peace," *Chester Times*, December 23, 1949.

4. Beshai, correspondence with the author, February 21, 2016.

5. King, *Papers*, 6:104.

6. Ibid.

7. King, *Stride Toward Freedom*, 92.

8. Barbour made these comments in a September 1968 interview with biographer David L. Lewis, and they were placed in the endnotes of Garrow, *The FBI and Martin Luther King Jr.*, 304.

9. Dr. Elizabeth Flower, "Experience with Martin Luther King," essay in the Elizabeth F. Flower Papers, University Archives & Records Center, University of Pennsylvania, Philadelphia. Special thanks to UPenn archivist Tim Horning for helping with King's UPenn professors.

10. ML's daily class schedule was reconstructed by collating his transcript (available at the King Center Digital Archive, www.thekingcenter.org/archive/document/mlks -transcript-crozer-theological-seminary) with the course titles and schedules listed in Crozer, *Annual Catalogue* 41, no. 1 (January 1949). His GPA was computed using current academic calculation methods (e.g., B = 3.0), weighted by credit hours.

11. Flower, "Experience."

12. One longtime Chester resident recalled Confederate soldiers "being buried along the fence" at what would later be known as Chester Rural Cemetery. "Oldest Spanish American War Veteran Misses 1st May 30 Parade in 65 Years," *Chester Times*, May 29, 1951.

13. Flower, "Experience."

14. Ibid.

15. Ibid.

16. Ibid.

17. "African Americans at Penn," University Archives & Records Center website, accessed October 19, 2017, www.archives.upenn.edu/histy/features/aframer/gallery.html.

18. Keighton, *The Man Who Would Preach*, 14

19. King, *Papers*, 6:106–107.

20. The minister is, full disclosure, my uncle Rev. Michael Frank. He graduated from Bethany Seminary and went on to become minister of Broadway Christian Church in Cleveland, Ohio, for forty-one years. His quotes are from e-mail correspondence, March 26, 2016.

21. Keighton, *The Man Who Would Preach*, 16.

22. Seward Hiltner, "How Far Can the Pastor Go in Counseling?," *Crozer Quarterly*, April 1948, 100.

23. Barbour, letter to King, December 21, 1954, collected in King, *Papers*, 6:322–323. The examples of Longfellow, Plato, and Ovid were taken from sermons that ML preached over the summer of 1949, which can also be found in volume 6 of *Papers*.

24. Example taken from Hiltner, "How Far Can the Pastor Go," 97–108.

25. Ibid. Speaking of the minister as a "spanker," King mentioned to L. D. Reddick in *Crusader Without Violence* that Daddy King had spanked ML until he was fifteen years old.

26. Obituary for Seward Hiltner, *Princeton Seminary Bulletin*, 1986, 76–78, http://journals. ptsem.edu/id/PSB1986071/dmd012.

27. Hiltner, "How Far Can the Pastor Go," 97–108.

28. "His style of thinking" is from Thomasberger, interview by the author. "The atmosphere" is from King, letter to George W. Davis, December 1, 1953, collected in *Papers* 2:223.

29. Slapping incident related in Reddick, *Crusader Without Violence*, 60. L. D. Reddick's book also does a good job of describing the Atlanta of ML's childhood.

30. King, *Papers*, 1:281.

31. George W. Davis, "Liberalism and a Theology of Depth," *Crozer Quarterly* 28 (January 1951): 195.

32. Davis, *Existentialism and Theology*, 82.

33. King, *Papers*, 1:295.

34. Helen Hunt Reports, *Chester Times*, January 14, 1950. The precise setting of the youth event would be the Grace Community United Methodist Church at 1213 Central Avenue in Chester, since the article refers to "Central av. above Concord rd."

35. Though King delivered this speech often, it has been reported most frequently that he gave it on October 26, 1967, to students at Barratt Junior High School in Philadelphia. Video of his Barratt appearance is available online via the King Center, "MLK: What Is Your Life's Blueprint?," YouTube, July 6, 2015, www.youtube.com /watch?v=kmsAxX84cjQ.

36. Ibid.

37. "Howard U. Prexy at Confab in India," *Pittsburgh Courier*, December 17, 1949.

38. Quoted in McKinney, *Mordecai, the Man and His Message*, 327. Johnson was speaking in front of "650 dignitaries from the fourteen nations composing the North Atlantic Treaty Organization (NATO)" in London, June 6, 1959.

39. "Cowardice Hurts White Southerners," *Pittsburgh Courier*, October 15, 1949.

40. "Fisk Prexy Attends Conference in India," *Pittsburgh Courier*, December 17, 1949; "Tartt Bell, in India, Tells of World Pacifist Sessions," *Anniston (AL) Star*, December 22, 1949; "Dr. Mordecai Johnson on Indian Tour," *Journal and Guide* (Norfolk, VA), December 10, 1949.

41. Quoted in James L. Hicks, "World's Political Fate Rests with Dark Races," *Baltimore Afro-American*, March 18, 1950. Johnson was speaking at the Essex House in New York to "200 members of the Howard Alumni Club of New York City."

42. The precise date is unknown; ML stated that Dr. Johnson had "just returned" from India (King, *Stride Toward Freedom*, 96), so the event would probably have fallen somewhere between January and March 1950.

43. Peter C. Mohr, "Journey Out of Egypt: The Development of Negro Leadership in Alabama from Booker T. Washington to Martin Luther King," thesis, quoted in Garrow, *Bearing the Cross*, 638.

44. A. M. Rivera Jr., "Dr. Johnson Says World Will Feed All," *Pittsburgh Courier*, August 13, 1949.

45. Ibid. The article compared the atmosphere of the Raleigh convention to that of "an old-fashioned camp meeting." For Dr. Johnson's experience delivering newspapers, see "Recipe for Success," *Baltimore Afro-American*, March 10, 1951. Johnson recalled distributing papers "house to house in an entire section in my town, which is known as 'West Paris.'"

46. King, *Stride Toward Freedom*, 83–84.

47. Christine King Farris, Martin Luther King, Jr. Leadership Lecture (Boston University, April 3, 2009), http://hgar-srv3.bu.edu/videos/video?id=360354. The quote occurs around the forty-eight-minute mark.

48. Unattributed "Quotes" feature, *Portsmouth (NH) Herald*, May 28, 1949. The original source or setting for Dr. Johnson's quote is unknown.

6. Chosen to Lead: Term 3, February 21–May 5, 1950

1. Moitz, e-mail correspondence with the author, October 4, 2014.

2. Ibid., October 5, 2014.

3. Moitz, interview by the author, January 3, 2016.

4. Wood, *And Grace Will Lead Me Home*, 50.

5. Whitaker, interview by Garrow.

6. Anecdote in Moitz, e-mail correspondence with the author, October 4, 2014, and interview by the author, January 3, 2016.

7. Betty's Moore College of Art graduation is in Moitz, e-mail correspondence with the author, November 2, 2014.

8. R. E. E. Harkness, "The Scientific Spirit in Religion," *Religious Education*, January 1, 1928.

9. ML's daily class schedule was reconstructed by collating his transcript (available at the King Center Digital Archive, www.thekingcenter.org/archive/document/mlks

-transcript-crozer-theological-seminary) with the course titles and schedules listed in Crozer, *Annual Catalogue* 41, no. 1 (January 1949). His GPA was computed using current academic calculation methods (e.g., B = 3.0), weighted by credit hours.

10. See, for instance, R. E. E. Harkness, "Roger Williams—Prophet of Tomorrow," *Journal of Religion* 15, no. 4 (October 1935): 400–425.

11. Smith, notes from interview by Branch, November 3, 1983.

12. R. E. E. Harkness, "The Development of Democracy in the English Reformation," *Church History* 8, no. 1 (March 1939): 3–29.

13. King, *Papers*, 1:313–327.

14. Martin Luther King Jr., *A Call to Conscience: The Landmark Speeches of Dr. Martin Luther King Jr.*, edited by Clayborne Carson (New York: Warner Books, 2001), 161.

15. "Martin King Heads Crozer Student Body," *Chester Times*, April 24, 1950. According to the article, voting had concluded a week before.

16. "Not all that big" is from Whitaker, interview by Garrow. "Indeed an honor" is in Marcus Wood, "Reflecting: My Life with the Late Martin Luther King," typed report, May 5, 1986, found in folder 703, p. 1, Taylor Branch Papers, Southern Historical Collection, Louis Round Wilson Library, University of North Carolina, Chapel Hill, NC. The fourteen seminarians in ML's middle-year class were Edwin Brooks, Percy Carter, Eugene Drew, James Greene, Robert Hopkins, Martin Luther King Jr., Joseph Kirkland, Wendall Maloch, Walter McCall, Cyril Pyle, Nolton Turner, George Walton, Horace Whitaker, and Marcus Wood. The black students were Carter, King, Kirkland, McCall, Pyle, Whitaker, and Wood.

17. Stewart, interview by Garrow.

18. Stark, interview by Garrow.

19. Helen Hunt Reports, *Chester Times*, March 4, 1950.

20. Wood, *And Grace Will Lead Me Home*, 48–49.

21. "NAACP to Meet" in "Lodge to Hold Open House," *News Journal* (Wilmington, DE), May 4, 1950.

22. *Picture in Your Mind*, directed by Philip Stapp (1948).

23. "Lodge to Hold Open House," *News Journal*.

Interlude: The Summer of 1950

1. McCall, transcript of interview by Holmes.

2. In case you're wondering, the "Three Levels of Fellowship" were based on the concepts of sensuality, economics, and love. Further details can be found in King, *Papers*, 6:107. Recollections from ML's childhood friend are in Williams, notes from interview by Branch.

3. Dobbs Butts, interview by the author.

4. King Sr., *Daddy King*, 128.

5. Ibid.

6. Ibid.

7. "Statement of Pearl E. Smith (colored)," interview by Chief Clifford D. Cain, County Detectives Office (Mount Holly, NJ, August 28, 1950). As for Ernest Nichols, according to Linn Washington, "The Dream Started Here," *Philadelphia Inquirer*, February 5, 1989, Nichols was "born in Germany," and "entered his country's armed forces when he was 16 and served in World War I, first as a gunner on a submarine and later in the German army." Once the war concluded, he "immigrated to the United States."

8. Blue-collar clientele and other details come from two primary sources: Judge W. Thomas McGann, "Dr. Martin Luther King's Passage Through the County," *Burlington County Times*, February 9, 1986; and Lawlor and Washington, "Beginnings."

9. The official statement by Nichols's attorney W. Thomas McGann is collected King, *Papers*, 1:327–329. It provides a more favorable explanation for why Mr. Nichols acted the way he did, claiming it was well known that Mr. Nichols had served "colored patrons" before.

10. "Statement of Pearl E. Smith (colored)."

11. See, for instance, Oates, *Let the Trumpet Sound*, 27–28.

12. "Statement of Pearl E. Smith (colored)." See also *Papers*, 1:329 for the official complaint document signed by Pearl, ML, and Mac (but not Doris Wilson). Pearl's and ML's names are crossed out—perhaps because, as explained later in the interlude, they eventually withdrew their participation.

13. Lawlor and Washington, "Beginnings."

14. Ted Poston, "He Never Liked to Fight!," *New York Post*, reprinted in *Baltimore Afro-American*, June 15, 1957.

15. Quote from the Maple Shade solicitor, George Barbour (not related to Rev. Barbour), is from Washington, "Before Montgomery." Other details in the case were in "N.J. Inn Keeper Held After Four Charge Refusal," *Philadelphia Tribune*, June 20, 1950. (A massive thank-you to Maple Shade activist and researcher Patrick Duff for digging up gems such as this.) Mac's thank-you is from McCall, transcript of interview by Holmes.

16. Farris, *Through It All*, 71.

17. Ibid.

18. Christine's quote is in ibid., 72. Title of ML's sermon is from King, *Papers*, 6:46.

19. Washington, "Before Montgomery."

20. Mac's quote is in McCall, transcript of interview by Holmes. Almanina's is in Washington, "Before Montgomery."

21. The attorney's quote is in McGann, "Dr. Martin Luther King's Passage." He recalls McCall's involvement in Lawlor and Washington, "Beginnings."

22. McCall, transcript of interview by Holmes.

23. Carrie Harper, Atlanta News, *Pittsburgh Courier*, July 15, 1950.

24. Poston, "He Never Liked to Fight!"

25. "Rev. King Lauds City on Strides to Integration," *Philadelphia Tribune*, October 28, 1961. ML's commentary is noteworthy not only for describing the incident as a "sit-in" (which contemporary reports and the accounts of Pearl Smith and Walter McCall make clear was not literally true) but also for claiming that the Reverend Ray Ware was with him during the incident at Mary's Café. Nowhere could I find evidence that Ray Ware was involved.

26. Sermon dates are from King, *Papers*, 6:46. Information on "Propagandizing Christianity" is from a later version delivered in ML's early days at Dexter Avenue Baptist Church (September 12, 1954) and published in King, *Papers*, 184–185.

Year III: Revelation

7. Forbidden Love: Term 1, September 12–November 22, 1950

1. Proctor, *The Substance of Things Hoped For*, 71

2. Wood, *And Grace Will Lead Me Home*, 46. According to Wood, the men had to wait to take them again "the following spring."

3. The date of the exams appears in Crozer, *Annual Catalogue* 43, no. 1 (January 1951): 3. The comprehensive examination guidelines are available at the King Center Digital Archive, www.thekingcenter.org/archive/document/crozer-theological-seminary-comprehensive-examinations.

4. "Women's division" is per Whitaker, notes from interview by Branch.

5. Joel King, notes from interview by Branch. Uncle Joel also said of his older brother's role as a disciplinarian, "Brother was old school. You got in the house."

6. Whitaker, notes from interview by Branch.

7. Ibid.; Joel King, notes from interview by Branch.

8. NBC report quoted in Religious News Service, The Week in Religion, *Courier-Journal* (Louisville, KY), September 23, 1950. The number of attendees and the governor's plea come from "Gov. Duff Urges Equal Opportunity for All," *Lebanon Daily News*, September 7, 1950.

9. Comprehensive examination guidelines, King Center Digital Archive, www.thekingcenter.org/archive/document/crozer-theological-seminary-comprehensive-examinations.

10. King, *Papers*, 1:390–391.

11. Bullard, interview by the author.

12. First-year seminarian Charles Harlow, from McMinnville, Oregon, remembered coming off the bus with three suitcases and a large box. Facing an arduous trek up the hill to Crozer's Old Main, he saw a young man coming through the maple trees who said, "You look like you need a hand. I'm Martin Luther King." Charles E. Harlow, "My Time with Martin Luther King Jr.," interview by Clovice Lewis Jr., January 20, 2013, via Carol Cole-Lewis, YouTube, February 1, 2013, www.youtube.com /watch?v=rqKyPbCqaj4.

13. Thomasberger, interview by the author.

14. Bullard, interview by the author.

15. Ibid.

16. Beshai, correspondence with the author, May 14, 2015.

17. Beshai, correspondence with the author, May 7, 2015.

18. Ibid.

19. Beshai, correspondence with the author, May 9, 2015.

20. Esther Smith, interview by the author.

21. Moitz, letter correspondence with the author, fall 2014.

22. Beshai, correspondence with the author, May 14, 2015.

23. "We dropped our g's" is from Lawlor and Washington, "Beginnings." Smith's first impressions of ML and Mac are in *Pennsylvania Remembers Dr. King* (video, Commonwealth Media Services, 1991), available online via Pennsylvania Historical and Museum Commission, YouTube, January 19, 2016, www.youtube.com /watch?v=nLQiJNBI_6Q.

24. Betty's quote from Moitz, letter correspondence with the author, fall 2014. Bologna anecdote from Stark, interview by Garrow.

25. Moitz, letter correspondence with the author, fall 2014.

26. Wood, *And Grace Will Lead Me Home*, 50.

27. Whitaker, interview by Garrow.

28. From "Paul's Letter to American Christians" (sermon, June 3, 1958), collected in King, *Papers*, 6:342–343.

29. Lawlor and Washington, "Beginnings."

30. Moitz, interview by the author, January 3, 2016.

31. Wood, *And Grace Will Lead Me Home*, 50.

32. Whitaker, interview by Garrow.

33. J. Pius Barbour, interview by David L. Lewis, quoted in Garrow, *Bearing the Cross*, 41.

34. Moitz, letter correspondence with the author, fall 2014.

35. "St. Paul's Aux Hears Rev. Batten," *Chester Times*, April 27, 1954.

36. Numerous articles in the *Chester Times* between 1948 and 1954 track Dean Batten's involvement with the local community.

37. ML's daily class schedule was reconstructed by collating his transcript (available at the King Center Digital Archive, www.thekingcenter.org/archive/document /mlks-transcript-crozer-theological-seminary) with the course titles and schedules listed in Crozer, *Annual Catalogue* 42, no. 1 (January 1950). His GPA was computed using current academic calculation methods (e.g., B = 3.0), weighted by credit hours. The Problems of Esthetics course description was created based on ML's notes in the class (available at the King Center Digital Archive www.thekingcenter.org/archive /document/problems-esthetics). For those interested in additional scheduling details, on September 27, 1950, the *Chester Times* published the following list of the term's vespers speakers. October 5: Edward C. Starr, Librarian, Crozer. October 12: Rev. Francis Lee Albert, Chaplain, Fourth Naval District. October 19: Rev. Dr. J. Pius Barbour, Editor, *National Baptist Voice*. October 26: Robert C. Middleton, Pastor, Haddonfield, NJ Baptist Church. The fact that Rev. Barbour was invited to speak suggests that President Blanton may have been taking cues from his senior class, the majority of whom were African American.

38. Beshai, correspondence with the author, January 17, 2016.

39. Bullard, interview by the author.

40. Ibid.

41. The full text of ML's essay, as well as the original handwritten paper, can be found in King, *Papers*, 1:359–379.

42. Ibid. On the other hand, one of ML's teachers at Morehouse, English professor Gladstone Lewis Chandler, believed it was seminary that awakened ML: "I give Crozer a lot of credit for the fruition that he experienced." Gladstone Lewis Chandler, interview by Donald H. Smith, December 4, 1963, transcribed in Taylor Branch Papers, Southern Historical Collection, Louis Round Wilson Library, University of North Carolina, Chapel Hill, NC.

43. King, review of *Personality: Its Study and Hygiene* by Winifred V. Richmond, collected in *Papers*, 1:357.

44. King, review of *A Functional Approach to Religious Education* by Ernest J. Chave, collected in ibid., 356. ML's work for this class largely absolves Batten of any blame for failing to address ML's plagiarism habit. Not only is it *almost* entirely absent of cribbing, but at the end of the Chave review (which didn't receive a letter grade), Batten at least addresses ML's insufficient sourcing in a general comment: "For your future use, you should give complete bibliographical details in listing date, author, etc."

45. "Live wire" is from Thomasberger, interview by the author. Joe Thomasberger entered Crozer one year after ML left. "Very open-minded" is from Beshai, correspondence with the author, January 17, 2016.

46. Raymond J. Bean, "The Influence of William Miller in the History of American Christianity" (PhD dissertation, Boston University, 1949), lii.

47. King, *Papers*, 1:335.

48. Ibid., 340.

49. Ibid., 340–341.

50. Perhaps the one professor who did the most to advise ML regarding his citations was Walter R. Chivers, ML's Morehouse College sociology professor. In his comments on a paper of ML's titled "Ritual," Chivers emphasizes the need to "document." This essay can be found in King, *Papers*, 1:127–141. I've used the term "voice merging" out of agreement with Keith Miller's literary assessment of King in his excellent book *Voice of Deliverance: The Language of Martin Luther King Jr. and Its Sources.*

51. Details of the Crozer radio project come from Fred Echelmeyer, "FM Radio Station at Crozer Seminary to Be Memorial to Wife of Dr. Nathan Plafker," *Chester Times*, February 26, 1949.

52. ML's class notes were previously available through the King Center Digital Archive, www.thekingcenter.org/archive/. According to King, *Papers*, 6:626, they are permanently collected in folder 162, King Papers Project Archives, Stanford University, Stanford, CA.

53. Echelmeyer, "FM Radio Station at Crozer."

54. John Stokes Adams Jr., "Esthetic of Music and The Rational Ideal," in *Philosophical Essays in Honor of Edgar Arthur Singer, Jr.*, edited by F. P. Clarke and M. C. Nahm (University of Pennsylvania Press, 1942), 223.

55. John Stokes Adams Jr., "Contemporary Philosophy and Philosophy of Science," *Philosophy of Science* 18, no. 3 (July 1951): 218–222.

56. "Finest amateur pianist" comes from a letter of recommendation written by UPenn Psychology Professor Francis W. Irwin, August 27, 1959. Adams's "sensitivity" was mentioned not just by Irwin but also University of Texas Professor R. M. Martin in a recommendation letter dated September 27, 1959. Both letters are courtesy of the University of Pennsylvania Archives.

57. Fourteen pages of ML's class notes are available at the King Center Digital Archive, www.thekingcenter.org/archive/document/problems-esthetics.

58. Ibid.

59. King, *Papers*, 1:333, 390, 391.

60. Bullard, interview by the author.

61. "Stress Personal Evangelism at Crozer Conclave," *Chester Times*, November 4, 1950.

62. Whitaker, interview by Garrow. Keith Miller's excellent book *Voice of Deliverance* was very helpful in understanding just how much influence Daddy King still had on ML, no matter how far north he went.

63. Committee chairmen are listed in Crozer, *Annual Catalogue* 43, no. 1 (January 1951).

64. Beshai, correspondence with the author, May 12, 2015.

65. Smith, "Martin Luther King Jr.: Reflections of a Former Teacher."

66. Beshai, correspondence with the author, May 14, 2015.

67. "Like cats and dogs" is from Whitaker, notes from interview by Branch. Professor Smith himself recalled the "bull sessions" several times, including in Smith, notes from interview by Branch, October 12 and November 3, 1983.

68. Front page stories, *Chester Times*, November 27, 1950. The damage to the silver maples reported in "Crozer Loses Some Stately Landmarks," *Chester Times*, April 17, 1951.

69. McCall, transcript of interview by Holmes.

70. Ibid.

71. The encounter between Kirkland and King was mentioned by Kirkland's wife in Lydia Kirkland, notes from interview by Branch.

8. The Recommended Plagiarist: Term 2, November 28, 1950–February 13, 1951

1. King, *Papers*, 1:380–381.

2. Ibid.

3. Whitaker, notes from interview by Branch.

4. Beshai, correspondence with the author, September 10, 2016.

5. King, *Papers*, 1:390.

6. Andrew Burgess, correspondence with the author via Michael Frank.

7. Beshai, correspondence with the author, May 12, 2015.

8. King, *Papers*, 1:390.

9. Proctor, *The Substance of Things Hoped For*, 59–60.

10. King, *Papers*, 1:407.

11. Beshai, correspondence with the author, May 12, 2015.

12. ML's daily class schedule was reconstructed by collating his class list (King, *Papers*, 1:48) with the course titles and schedules listed in Crozer, *Annual Catalogue* 42, no. 1 (January 1950). His GPA was computed using current academic calculation methods (e.g., B = 3.0), weighted by credit hours.

13. King, *Papers*, 1:392–406. For more information, consult the Dr. Martin Luther King, Jr. Archive, Howard Gotlieb Archival Research Center, Boston University, which has seventy-six additional pages of class notes related to King's Philosophy of Religion class, as well as examination answers.

14. "Crozer Installs Dr. Blanton as 5th President," *Chester Times*, May 8, 1950.

15. Ibid.

16. "Reaction of War Motivated Crozer Head to Join Ministry," *Chester Times*, February 20, 1951.

17. Bullard, interview by the author.

18. Crozer, *Annual Catalogue* 43, no. 1 (January 1951).

19. Blanton's emphatic recommendation is in King, 2:164. "As often as you can" is in Sankey Blanton, letter to Martin Luther King Jr., October 3, 1951, available at the King Center Digital Archive, www.thekingcenter.org/archive/document /letter-sankey-blanton-mlk.

20. Adelaide Kerr, "Cultured French to Return Home," *Bee* (Danville, VA), July 6, 1945.

21. Ibid.; "Dr. Paul Schrecker Feels State Capitol Out of Keeping with Agricultural State," *Lincoln (NE) Evening Journal*, August 1, 1944. Schrecker made the Lincoln, Nebraska, news because of his odd critique of the city: "Why must they have a state capitol that would fit into a bazaar civilization rather than into an agricultural one?"

22. Immanuel Kant, *The Metaphysical Elements of Justice*, part 1 of *The Metaphysics of Morals*, translated by John Ladd, (Indianapolis: Bobbs-Merrill, 1965), 86.

23. Immanuel Kant, *Groundwork for the Metaphysics of Morals*, edited by Lara Denis, translated by Thomas K. Abbott (Toronto: Broadview, 2005), 87.

24. A typewritten draft of the letter is available at the website of the Martin Luther King, Jr. Research and Education Institute, Stanford University, https://kinginstitute.stanford .edu/king-papers/documents/letter-birmingham-jail.

25. Ibid.

26. An interesting read on this topic is William P. Deveaux, "Immanuel Kant, Social Justice and Martin Luther King Jr.," *Journal of Religious Thought* 37, no. 2 (Fall–Winter 1981).

27. Smith, notes from interview by Branch, October 12, 1983.

28. Ted Poston, "He Never Liked to Fight!," *New York Post*, reprinted in *Baltimore Afro-American*, June 15, 1957.

29. "Eastern Baptist Laces Crozer Seminary Five," *Chester Times*, January 12, 1951; see also "Court Victor by 104-41," *Philadelphia Inquirer*, January 12, 1951.

30. The full names of the Crozer players, in the order of the box score: Jesse H. Brown, Raymond Joseph Dietrich, Benjamin Albert Friend, Reese Arthur Mahoney, Lawrence James Seyler, Billy Clifton Reardon ("Redden" is most likely a misspelling), Martin Luther King Jr., Curtis Leroy Hoffman, Calixto Oliveira Marques (it should be noted that Marques did not have three field goals but three free throws; sorry, Calixto—great name, though), and George Edward Fagons. The full names come from Crozer, *Annual Catalogue* 43, no. 1 (January 1951).

31. Zion Baptist service mentioned in Sunday Services in South Jersey Churches, *Courier-Post*, January 13, 1951. (A special thanks to Patrick Duff of Camden, NJ, for discovering the article.) Temple Baptist service mentioned in Helen Hunt Reports, *Chester Times*, January 27, 1951.

32. "Rev. McCall Says the Younger Generation Needs Discipline," *Chester Times*, January 22, 1951.

33. Whitaker, notes from interview by Branch.

34. "Waynesboro Man Hurt on Baltimore Pike," *Staunton News-Leader*, February 15, 1951. Nolton Turner ended up graduating from Crozer in May 1952. William Coleman struggled to recover from his severe injuries, and took his own life the morning of January 15, 1952. He was thirty-five years old, with a wife and two sons. "Mr. Coleman to Be Buried Today," *Staunton News-Leader*, January 16, 1952.

35. Beshai, correspondence with the author, October 7, 2017.

9. A Divine Cause: Term 3, February 20–May 4, 1951

1. Galja Barish Votaw, "'Consecrated Intelligence' Keynote of Crozer Study," *Chester Times*, February 22, 1951.

2. Ibid.

3. "Crozer Ministry Conference Draws Pupils from 11 States," *Chester Times*, February 24, 1951.

4. Proctor, *The Substance of Things Hoped For*, 71.

5. Helen Hunt Reports, *Chester Times*, February 24, 1951, and April 14, 1951.

6. King, *Papers* 6:113–119.

7. Wood, *And Grace Will Lead Me Home*, 89. Many other seminarians must have heard ML's Amos recitations. Julian O. Grayson, who graduated from Crozer in 1950, wired a seven-word message to King on February 4, 1956, after his home was bombed: "Fight On Amos God Is With You." King, *Papers*, 3:126.

8. Wood, *And Grace Will Lead Me Home*, 48.

9. Linn Washington, "City of Brotherly Love Profoundly Impacted King," *Philadelphia Tribune*, January 17, 1997.

10. Lawlor and Washington, "Beginnings."

11. Dobbs Butts, interview by the author.

12. Stone, notes from interview by Branch.

13. "Crozer Loses Some Stately Landmarks," *Chester Times*, April 17, 1951.

14. Ibid.

15. ML's daily class schedule was reconstructed by collating his class list (King, *Papers*, 1:48) with the course titles and schedules listed in Crozer, *Annual Catalogue* 42, no. 1 (January 1950). His GPA was computed using current academic calculation methods (e.g., B = 3.0), weighted by credit hours.

16. *Pennsylvania Remembers Dr. King* (video, Commonwealth Media Services, 1991), available online via Pennsylvania Historical and Museum Commission, YouTube, January 19, 2016, www.youtube.com/watch?v=nLQiJNBI_6Q.

17. Reddick, *Crusader Without Violence*, 79. Snuffy Smith cited this quote in his own article: Smith, "Martin Luther King Jr.: Reflections of a Former Teacher."

18. *Pennsylvania Remembers Dr. King* (video).

19. Smith, "Martin Luther King Jr.: Reflections of a Former Teacher."

20. ML's oral report is collected in King, *Papers*, 1:436–439. The names of the seminarians in the class are listed in ibid., 462–463. Details regarding his classmate George W. Lawrence are in Lawrence, notes from interview by Branch.

21. King, *Papers*, 1:436–439.

22. Smith, "Martin Luther King Jr.: Reflections of a Former Teacher."

23. A good introduction to Rauschenbusch is Christopher H. Evans, *The Kingdom Is Always but Coming: A Life of Walter Rauschenbusch* (Grand Rapids, MI: Wm. B. Eerdmans, 2004; paperback publ. Baylor University Press, 2010).

24. Smith, "Martin Luther King Jr.: Reflections of a Former Teacher."

25. Quoted in Jeffrey Hart, These Days, *Daily Notes*, August 1972.

26. Walter Rauschenbusch, *Christianity and the Social Crisis* (Eugene, OR: Wipf and Stock, 2003; orig. publ. 1907), 368.

27. "A pity" comes from Beshai, correspondence with the author, May 14, 2015. "Tremendous capacity" is in Reddick, *Crusader Without Violence*.

28. Smith and Zepp, *Search for the Beloved Community*, 26.

29. The outline was compiled using three sources: Smith and Zepp, "Personalism," in *Search for the Beloved Community* (Valley Forge, PA: Judson, 1974), 99–118; and two works by Edgar S. Brightman, *Philosophy of Religion* and *The Finding of God*. Both of Brightman's books are cited in essays by King, collected in *Papers*, 1:232, 433.

30. King, *Where Do We Go from Here* (Boston: Beacon Press, 2010; orig. publ. 1967), 105.

31. King, *Papers*, 1:432.

32. Beshai, correspondence with the author, May 12, 2015.

33. "Crozer Begins Commencement," *Chester Times*, May 5, 1951.

34. "Awards Made at Seminary Exercises," *Chester Times*, May 8, 1951.

35. Marcus Wood, "Reflecting: My Life with the Late Martin Luther King," typed report, May 5, 1986, found in folder 703, p. 1, Taylor Branch Papers, Southern Historical Collection, Louis Round Wilson Library, University of North Carolina, Chapel Hill, NC.

36. Ibid.

37. "Degrees Awarded to Ten at Crozer Commencement" and "Awards Made at Seminary Exercises," *Chester Times*, May 8, 1951.

38. "Awards Made," *Chester Times*.

39. King, *Papers*, 3:294. After leaving Crozer, Batten went on to coauthor a short 1960 book titled *Fit To Be Tied: An Approach to Sex Education and Christian Marriage*.

40. King, letter to Francis Stewart, July 26, 1954, collected in *Papers*, 2:280.

41. King Sr., *Daddy King*, 130.

42. Crozer, *Annual Catalogue* 42, no. 1 (January 1950).

43. "Awards Made," *Chester Times*.

44. Sakurabayashi's original letter can be found in Dr. Martin Luther King, Jr. Archive, Howard Gotlieb Archival Research Center, Boston University. The letter was also published in Patrick Parr, "A Note of Concern to Wounded MLK from a Friend in Japan," *Japan Times*, January 14, 2015.

45. King, "A Conception and Impression of Religion Drawn from Dr. Brightman's Book Entitled *A Philosophy of Religion*," collected in *Papers*, 1:416. This quote was also included in Clayborne Carson, with Peter Holloran et al., "Martin Luther King, Jr., as Scholar: A Reexamination of His Theological Writings," *Journal of American History* 78 (June 1991): 99.

Epilogue: Beyond Crozer

1. "Dr. King's Notes on Ministry," King Center Digital Archive, www.thekingcenter.org/archive/document/dr-kings-notes-ministry.

2. King, *Papers*, 2:158–159.

3. Information on ML's Niagara visit comes primarily from Whitaker, notes from interview by Branch.

4. Ibid. According to King, *Papers*, 6:159, "Going Forward by Going Backward" was also known as "Rediscovering Lost Values." Under the latter title, King was recorded delivering a version of this sermon in Detroit on February 28, 1954. It is the earliest known recording of a King speech.

5. The original typed copy of this letter, dated March 22, 1962, is available at the King Center Digital Archive, www.thekingcenter.org/archive/document/letter-pastor-h-edward-whitaker-mlk.

6. Moitz, interview by the author, January 3, 2016.

7. King, *Papers*, 5:571.

8. The Moitz Christmas card was in the Dr. Martin Luther King, Jr. Archive, Howard Gotlieb Archival Research Center, Boston University. Reprinted with permission.

9. Bennett, *What Manner of Man*, 40.

10. Martin Luther King Jr., address at the Southern Baptist Theological Seminary, April 19, 1961, typed transcript, 6, available at the King Center Digital Archive: www .thekingcenter.org/archive/document/address-mlk-southern-baptist-theological -seminary

11. Moitz, interview by the author, January 3, 2016.

12. *Martin Luther King Jr.: The Man and the Dream* (A&E Biography, January 19, 1998). The film misidentifies Betty as "Betty Moatz." (It also has an ominous, foreboding score throughout, which struck me a bit odd.)

13. King, *Papers*, 4:463–464.

14. Ibid., 2:323

15. Ibid., 4:463.

16. Barbour, "A Defense of the Negro Preacher," in Reid, *The Negro Baptist Ministry*, 13–14.

17. Frank Galey and Jack Hopkins, "'He Had Very Definite Feeling About Rights,'" *Delaware County Daily Times*, April 5, 1968.

18. King, *Papers*, 3:129–130.

19. Ibid.

20. Pat Warren, "Dr. Martin Luther King Colleague Remembers His Legacy," CBS Baltimore, August 22, 2011, http://baltimore.cbslocal.com/2011/08/22 /dr-martin-luther-king-colleague-remembers-his-legacy/.

21. Ibid.

22. Ibid.

23. Smith, notes from interview by Branch, October 12 and November 3, 1983. It's clear from Branch's notes that Mac and Snuffy shared great friendship and respect; in the November interview, Smith referred to his friend as the "salt of the earth."

24. McCall, transcript of interview by Holmes.

25. Ibid. According to Snuffy Smith, the pool table ML used while at Crozer was, as of 1983, in the possession of a professor named Ted Wheaton. Smith, notes from interview by Branch, November 3, 1983.

26. Esther Smith, interview by the author.

27. Smith, notes from interview by Branch, October 12, 1983, revealed the margin of votes Snuffy lost by.

28. Reagan's full remarks are available at the American Presidency Project, www.presidency
.ucsb.edu/ws/?pid=40708.

29. Kenneth Smith, "The Radicalization of Martin Luther King Jr.: The Last Five
Years" (speech, Bexley Hall, Colgate Rochester Crozer Divinity School, Rochester, NY, January 15, 1986). The quote is from around three to four minutes into
the lecture.

30. Kenneth Smith, remarks at Martin Luther King Day celebration (Colgate Rochester
Crozer Divinity School, Bexley Hall, Rochester, NY, 1979), cassette.

31. Smith, "The Radicalization of Martin Luther King Jr." The quote is from around three
to four minutes into the lecture.

32. Ibid.

33. Farris, "The Young Martin."

Appendix B: Events from ML's Student Body Presidency

1. Orientation schedule adapted from "Crozer Seminary Orientation Program Is
Launched Today," *Chester Times*, September 7, 1950. Commencement schedule from
"Crozer Begins Commencement," *Chester Times*, May 5, 1951.

Appendix C: A Brief History of the Crozers and Old Main

1. MacQueen, *Crozers of Upland*, 20. In addition, pp. 20–32 were used for reference
throughout.

2. "The Crozer Theological Seminary," *Evening Telegraph* (Philadelphia, PA), November 5, 1867.

3. Ibid.

4. MacQueen, *Crozers of Upland*, 21.

5. "Crozer Theological Seminary," *Evening Telegraph*.

6. MacQueen, *Crozers of Upland*, 20.

7. "Crozer Theological Seminary," *Evening Telegraph*.

8. Ibid.

9. See, for instance, Crozer, *Annual Catalogue* 42, no. 1 (January 1950).

10. Anecdote told by Norman Baumm and reported in MacQueen, *Crozers of Upland*,
107.

Selected Bibliography

Books

Bennett, Lerone. *What Manner of Man: A Biography of Martin Luther King, Jr.* Chicago: Johnson, 1964.

Branch, Taylor. *Parting the Waters: America in the King Years, 1954–63.* New York: Simon and Schuster, 1988.

Brewster, Gurdon. *No Turning Back: My Summer with Daddy King.* Maryknoll, NY: Orbis, 2007.

Burrow, Rufus, Jr. *God and Human Dignity: The Personalism, Theology and Ethics of Martin Luther King Jr.* Notre Dame, IN: University of Notre Dame Press, 2006.

Cone, James H. *Martin & Malcolm & America: A Dream or a Nightmare.* Maryknoll, NY. Orbis, 1991.

Davis, George Washington. *Existentialism and Theology: An Investigation of the Contribution of Rudolf Bultmann to Theological Thought.* New York: Philosophical Library, 1957.

Diedrich, Maria. *Love Across Color Lines.* New York. Hill and Wang, 1999.

Enslin, Morton Scott. *Christian Beginnings.* New York: Harper & Brothers, 1938.

Farris, Christine King. *Through It All: Reflections on My Life, My Family, and My Faith.* New York: Atria Books, 2009.

Garrow, David J. *Bearing the Cross: Martin Luther King, Jr., and the Southern Christian Leadership Conference.* New York: Morrow, 1986.

————. *The FBI and Martin Luther King Jr.* New York: W. W. Norton, 1981.

————. *Protest at Selma: Martin Luther King Jr., and the Voting Rights Act of 1965.* New Haven, CT: Yale University Press, 1978.

Keighton, Robert E. *The Man Who Would Preach.* New York: Abingdon Press, 1956.

King, Coretta Scott. *My Life with Martin Luther King, Jr.* New York: Holt, Rinehart and Winston, 1969.

King, Martin Luther, Jr. *The Autobiography of Martin Luther King, Jr.* Edited by Clayborne Carson. New York: Warner Books, 1998. NOTE: *This is not actually a formal autobiography written by Dr. King but a curated collection of material meant to demonstrate the arc of King's life.*

————. *The Papers of Martin Luther King, Jr.* Edited by Clayborne Carson. Vols. 1–6. Berkeley: University of California Press, 1992–2007. *Vols. 1 and 6 were especially helpful with the material in this book.*

————. *Stride Toward Freedom: The Montgomery Story.* New York: Harper & Row, 1958.

King, Martin Luther, Sr., with Clayton Riley. *Daddy King: An Autobiography.* New York: Morrow, 1980.

Lewis, David L. *King: A Critical Biography.* University of Illinois Press, 1970; Illini, 1978.

Lischer, Richard. *The Preacher King: Martin Luther King, Jr. and the Word That Moved America.* New York: Oxford University Press, 1995; paperback ed. 1997.

MacQueen, David A. *The Crozers of Upland, 1723–1926.* Wilmington, DE: Serendipity Press, 1982.

Marable, Manning. *Malcolm X: A Life of Reinvention.* New York: Viking, 2011.

McKinney, Richard I. *Mordecai, the Man and His Message: The Story of Mordecai Wyatt Johnson.* Washington, DC: Howard University Press, 1997.

Miller, Keith D. *Voice of Deliverance: The Language of Martin Luther King, Jr., and Its Sources.* New York: Free Press, 1992.

Miller, William Robert. *Martin Luther King, Jr.: His Life, Martyrdom, and Meaning for the World.* New York: Weybright and Talley, 1968.

Oates, Stephen B. *Let the Trumpet Sound: The Life of Martin Luther King, Jr.* New York: Mentor, 1982.

Proctor, Samuel D. *The Substance of Things Hoped For: A Memoir of African-American Faith.* Valley Forge, PA: Judson Press, 1999.

Reddick, Lawrence Dunbar. *Crusader Without Violence: A Biography of Martin Luther King, Jr.* New York: Harper, 1959.

Reid, Ira De Augustine. *The Negro Baptist Ministry: An Analysis of Its Profession, Preparation and Practices*. Philadelphia, PA: H&L Advertising Co., 1951. *Moorland-Spingarn Research Center at Howard University provided me with a copy of Reid's survey.*

Smith, Kenneth L., and Ira G. Zepp. *Search for the Beloved Community: The Thinking of Martin Luther King Jr.* Valley Forge: Judson Press, 1974.

Tawney, R. H. *Religion and the Rise of Capitalism: A Historical Study*. New York: Harcourt, Brace, 1926.

Warren, Mervyn. *King Came Preaching: The Pulpit Power of Dr. Martin Luther King Jr.* Downer's Grove, IL: InterVarsity Press, 2001.

Wood, Marcus Garvey. *And Grace Will Lead Me Home: The Ministry of Rev. Marcus Garvey Wood; Covering Fifty Years, 1945–1995*. Baltimore: Gateway Press, 1998.

X, Malcolm, with Alex Haley. *The Autobiography of Malcolm X*. New York: Ballantine Books, 1992; orig. publ. 1965.

Interviews by David J. Garrow

Unless otherwise indicated, interviews are on cassette in the DJG Papers.

Carter, Harold. Baltimore, MD, January 27, 1986.

Pyle, Cyril. Philadelphia, PA, January 28, 1986.

Smith, Kenneth. Rochester, NY, January 31, 1986.

Stark, Walter. Philadelphia, PA, January 28, 1986.

Stewart, Francis. Atlanta, GA, March 29, 1984.

Whitaker, Horace. Boston, MA, December 3, 1985. King Papers Project Archives, Stanford University, Stanford, CA.

Wood, Marcus G. Baltimore, MD, January 27, 1986.

Interviews by Taylor Branch

Quotes from Branch are taken from interview notes collected in folders 701 and 703, Taylor Branch Papers, Southern Historical Collection, Louis Round Wilson Library, University of North Carolina, Chapel Hill, NC.

King, Joel. January 9, 1984.

Kirkland, Lydia. December 9, 1983.

Lawrence, George. Phone interview. February 24, 1984.

Pritchard, James. Phone interviews. June 25 and 29, 1984.

Smith, Kenneth. October 12 and November 3, 1983.

Stewart, Francis. December 23, 1983.
Stone, Juanita Sellers. March 6, 1984.
Whitaker, Horace. July 31, 1984
Williams, Larry. December 27, 1983.
Wood, Marcus Garvey. October 4, 1983.

Interviews by the Author

Beshai, Dr. James. E-mail correspondence, May 2015–October 2017.
———. Interview, Media, PA, January 4, 2016.
Bullard, Jack. Phone interview, February 20, 2016.
Burgess, Peter. E-mail correspondence via Michael Frank, June 17, 2016.
Dobbs Butts, June. Phone interview, April 20, 2016. *Ms. Dobbs also mailed various helpful materials related to King.*
Frank, Michael. E-mail correspondence, January 2014–July 2016.
Hoopes, Roberta "Bobbie." Letter and e-mail correspondence, September 27, 2015.
McKinney, Rev. Samuel. Interview, Renton, WA, December 12, 2014. *A shortened version of this interview was published in Seattle Magazine, January 15, 2015, www.seattlemag.com/article/reverend-samuel-mckinney-remembers-his-friend -dr-king.*
Moitz, Betty. Interview, private location, January 3, 2016.
———. Letter and e-mail correspondence, September 2014–February 2016.
Sakurabayashi, Makoto. Correspondence, January 2016.
Smith, Esther. Phone interview, February 21, 2016.
Tasker, Dorothy. Interview, Media, PA, January 4, 2016.
Thomasberger, Joseph. Phone interview, March 19, 2016.
Whitaker, Horace Edward., Jr. Phone interview, July 3, 2017.
Willie, Charles Vert. Phone interview, April 27, 2016.
Wood, Marcus Garvey. Phone interview, September 4, 2016.

Other Interviews

King, Martin Luther, Jr. Interview by Alex Haley. *Playboy*, January 1965.
McCall, Walter. Transcript of interview by Herbert Holmes, Atlanta, GA, March 31, 1970. Provided by the King Center, Atlanta, GA.

Articles and Essays

Cannon, Poppy. "Martin Luther King, Jr." In *Heroes for Our Times*, edited by Will Yolen and Kenneth Seeman Giniger. Harrisburg, PA: Stackpole Books, 1968.

Cone, James H. "Martin Luther King, Jr., Black Theology—Black Church." *Theology Today* 41 (January 1984): 409–420.

Farris, Christine King. "The Young Martin: From Childhood Through College." *Ebony*, January 1986, 56–58.

Garrow, David J. "The Intellectual Development of Martin Luther King Jr.: Influences and Commentaries." *Union Seminary Quarterly Review* 40 (January 1986): 5–20

Lawlor, Julia, and Linn Washington. "Beginnings: From Hill to Mountain." *Philadelphia Daily News*, January 16, 1986.

Niebuhr, Reinhold. "Walter Rauschenbusch in Historical Perspective." *Religion in Life* 27 (Autumn 1958): 527–536.

Peters, William. "Our Weapon Is Love," *Redbook*, August 1956, 41–42, 72–73.

Smith, Kenneth. "Martin Luther King Jr.: Reflections of a Former Teacher." *Bulletin of Crozer Theological Seminary* 57, no. 2 (April 1965): 2–3.

Swift, Mike. "King's Summers in State Fostered Famous Dream of Freedom. *Hartford Courant*, January 21, 1991.

Thelen, David, ed. *Journal of American History* 78 (June 1991). *The entire volume is devoted to the plagiarism discovered in MLK's course work, and is essential reading for anyone looking to learn more about the issue.*

Washington, Linn. "Before Montgomery, There Was Philadelphia: Dr. Martin Luther King's Theories Started in Area." *Philadelphia Tribune*, January 14, 1994.

Wood, Alex. "Blacks Recall Connecticut Tobacco Farms." *Journal Inquirer*, July 17, 1989.

Index

Italicized page references denote illustrations